SPATIAL CYCLES

This book is one of a series of studies in Spatial Economic Analysis stimulated by theoretical and applied research conducted within the Netherlands Economic Institute, Rotterdam, and published by Gower. Titles in the series are:

J.H.P. Paelinck (ed.), *La Structure Urbaine en Europe Occidentale/ Urban Structure in Western Europe*

J.H.P. Paelinck and P. Nijkamp, *Operational Theory and Method in Regional Economics*

L.H. Klaassen, J.H.P. Paelinck and Sj. Wagenaar, *Spatial Systems: A General Introduction*

J.H.P. Paelinck and L.H. Klaassen (with J.P. Ancot, A.C.P. Verster and Sj. Wagenaar), *Spatial Econometrics*

W. Molle (with B. van Holst and H. Smit), *Regional Disparity and Economic Development in the European Community*

N. Vanhove and L.H. Klaassen, *Regional Policy: A European Approach*

L.H. Klaassen, J. Bourdrez and J. Volmuller, *Transport and Re-urbanisation*

L.H. Klaassen, W. Molle and J.H.P. Paelinck (eds), *Dynamics of Urban Development*

J.H.P. Paelinck (with J-P. Ancot and H. Kuiper), *Formal Spatial Economic Analysis*

W. Molle and L.H. Klaassen (eds), *Industrial Mobility and Migration in the European Community*

W. Molle, *Industrial Location and Regional Development in the European Community: the FLEUR model*

W. Molle and E. Wever, *Oil Refineries and Petrochemical Industries in Western Europe*

J.H.P. Paelinck (ed.), *Human Behaviour in Geographical Space*

Leo van den Berg, *Urban Systems in a Dynamic Society*

Leo van den Berg, Leland S. Burns and Leo H. Klaassen (eds), *Spatial Cycles*

Spatial Cycles

mo

Edited by
LEO VAN DEN BERG
LELAND S. BURNS
and
LEO H. KLAASSEN

Gower

Published by
Gower Publishing Company Limited
Gower House, Croft Road
Aldershot, Hants GU11 3HR
England

Gower Publishing Company
Old Post Road
Brookfield, Vermont 05036
USA

British Library Cataloguing in Publication Data

Spatial cycles. — (Studies in spatial analysis)
    1. Cities and towns — Mathematical models
    I. Berg, Leo van den   II. Burns, Leland S.
    III. Klaassen, Leo H.   IV. Series
    307.7'6   GF125

Library of Congress Cataloging-in-Publication Data

Spatial cycles. (Studies in spatial analysis)
    Includes index.
    1. Regional planning.   2. City planning.
    3. Regional economics. 4. Urban economics.
    5. Urban policy.
    I. Berg, Leo van den.   II. Burns, Leland Smith.
    III. Klaassen, Leo H. (Leo Hendrik)
    IV. Series
    HT 391. S645   1986   307.76   86-4730

Printed in Great Britain by
Blackmore Press, Longmead, Shaftesbury, Dorset

ISBN 0 566 05063 3

Contents

List of tables ix

List of figures xii

List of contributors xiv

Foreword and acknowledgements xvi

1   Introduction: cities and regions; trends and cycles, 1
    Leo van den Berg, Leland S. Burns and Leo H. Klaassen

    The setting 1
    Cycles and the urban–rural dichotomy 4

2   Overview, *Leland S. Burns* 9

    Spatial dynamics at urban scale 9
    Spatial dynamics at regional scale 18

3   Change and non-change in the urban realm; some 23
    trends, constants, and emerging forms in urban
    structure, *Michael A. Goldberg*

    Trends and issues in urban structure 23
    Summing up and sketching a research and
        policy agenda 35

4   Analysis of episodes in urban event histories,   43
     Börje Johansson and Peter Nijkamp

     Events and episodes in urban dynamics   43
     Urban dynamics as an event history   45
     Statistical analysis of event histories   49
     Interaction between industrial and infrastructural
       episodes   53
     Urban episodes illustrated by a simple model   58
     A space—time core—periphery model   62
     Final comments   63

5   Urban change: a changing process, *Rolf H. Funck*   67
     and Ulrich C.H. Blum

     The urban system and the process of urban change   69
     A dynamic model of urban development   72
     Empirical evidence   80

6   The contagiousness of urban decline, *Leo van den Berg* 84
     and Leo H. Klaassen

     A general theory of urban development   85
     Statistical evidence in Western Europe   89
     Future trends in urban development   91
     The problems of dynamic urban systems   96
     Conclusion   98

7   Is disurbanisation foreseeable in Japan? — a comparison 100
     between US and Japanese urbanisation processes,
     Tatsuhiko Kawashima

     Disurbanisation in the United States   101
     Relative disurbanisation in Japan   112
     Conclusion   124

8   Urban revival? *Leo van den Berg, Leo H. Klaassen and*   127
     Jan van der Meer

     Introduction: some theoretical considerations   127
     Urban development, 1950—74   129
     The development of the agglomerations since 1970   132
     The future   142

     Appendix   145

9   **Regional dynamics,** *Leo H. Klaassen*   146

     Introduction: a quadripartition of regions   146
     Regional cycles   151
     Policy implications   153

10   **Urban and regional income development in The**   158
     Netherlands: an integrative approach, *Leo van den Berg,*
     Leo H. Klaassen and Jan van der Meer

     Urban income and spatial economic development   159
     Changes in urban income, 1950—78   162
     Urban income and regional economic development   166
     Urban development stages related to regional income
       dynamics   172
     Conclusions   172

11   **Cyclical patterns in US regional development,**   175
     Leland S. Burns

     Data and regions   177
     The analytical framework   181
     Empirical testing   184
     Cycle components   194
     The determinants of instability   197
     Interpretation and conclusions for policy   202

     Appendix: Formulas for calculating concentration,
       amplitude and volatility   205

12   **The fiscal costs of city decline: a case study of**   209
     education, *Gordon C. Cameron and Stephen Bailey*

     The nature of fiscal costs   212
     The objectives of the study and the methodology
       of measurement   215
     Primary and secondary education scenarios   218
     Assessing the fiscal costs of decline, 1950/51—
       1979/80.   223
     Costing future decline: methodological and other
       problems   233
     Costing future decline: the data   236
     The relationship between future costs and form
       of rationalisation   246
     Conclusions   248

     Appendix: Manchester and Newcastle   249

13 Urban growth and decline as a force in regional   253
    development: issues and a research agenda,
    Leland S. Burns

        Demographic shifts   254
        Migration   256
        Central cities   256
        Suburbs and new towns   258
        Fiscal impacts   259
        Capital investment projects   260
        Summary: a research agenda   263

Index   267

Tables

6.1	The phases of urban development	88
6.2	Urban development in Western Europe	89
6.3	Growth and decline of West European agglomerations	90
6.4	Agglomeration size and urbanisation phase, 1975	90
7.1	Spatial cycle hypothesis	101
7.2	Population changes in the US, 1940–1980, 30 largest SMSAs and their central cities	102
7.3	Categorisation matrix for large metropolitan areas	105
7.4	Three categories and nine groups of US SMSAs	110
7.5	Population of Functional Urban Cores, Japan, 1960–1980	114
7.6	Population growth rates of the 30 largest Functional Urban Cores (FUCs) and their central cities (1960–1980)	118
7.7	Three categories and nine groups of FUCs	120
7.8	ROXY index (type II) for urbanisation in Japan	122
7.9	ROXY index (type II) for urbanisation in the US	122
8.1	The sample of Dutch agglomerations	130
8.2	Annual growth rate of the 24 selected Dutch agglomerations in percentages of the total agglomeration population, 1950–1982	133
8.3	Annual population growth of cores, rings, and total agglomerations, by size classes, The Netherlands, 1970–1982	134

8.4	Annual population growth by components of natural increase and migration, in percentages of total population, by size classes, The Netherlands, 1970—1982	136
8.5	Gross migration flows, central cities of the four largest agglomerations, in percentages of their total population, The Netherlands, 1970—1982	138
8.6	Agglomerations classified by urbanisation stage and size class, The Netherlands, 1970—1982	140
A8.1	Demographic development in the agglomerations, by size class, 1970 and 1982	145
9.1	Schematic division of regions	148
9.2	Relative income position, Dutch regions, 1950—1960	149
9.3	Relative income position, Dutch regions, 1960—1975	149
9.4	Relative labour-reserve position, Dutch regions, 1960—1965	150
9.5	Relative labour-reserve position, Dutch regions, 1965—1975	150
9.6	Shift in position of regions, by income, 1950—1975	152
9.7	Shift in position of regions, by labour reserve, 1960—1975	152
A9.1	Shares of population per regional type, relative to national total, The Netherlands, 1950—1978	155
A9.2	Shares of income by regional type, relative to national total and to population shares, The Netherlands, 1950—1975	156
A9.3	Shares of the registered labour reserve by regional type, relative to national total and to population shares, The Netherlands, 1950—1975	157
10.1	Income per head of population and per income earner, The Netherlands, 1978	163
10.2	Summary of Dutch regions by development stage, income per capita, 1950—1960 and 1960—1975	168
10.3	Comparing urban development and income development	169
11.1	Five-year per capita income growth rates, ratio of nine regions to US, 1950—1955 to 1973—1978	178
11.2	Correspondence between Dutch and US frameworks	183
11.3	Schematic division of development stages	183
11.4	Rankings of states on volatility, amplitude and independent variables	198
11.5	Correlation matrix	200
11.6	Regressions on volatility and amplitude, US regions and states	202

12.1   Shares of population and block grant per head by
        type of area, England and Wales, 1974/75 and
        1981/82   211
12.2   School age population (5—15 years), seven local
        authorities, England and Wales, and Scotland,
        UK, 1951—1971   220
12.3   School age population, seven local authorities,
        England and Wales, and Scotland, UK, 1971—1981   221
12.4   Primary education revenue expenditure, seven local
        authorities and total, UK, 1950/51 to 1973/74   224
12.5   Per capita expenditure on primary education relative
        to England and Wales, six local authorities, UK,
        1950/51 to 1979/80   226
12.6   Total real expenditure (1963) per pupil on primary
        and secondary education, seven local authorities
        and total, UK, 1950/51 to 1973/74   228
12.7   Pupil—teacher ratios, seven local authorities and total,
        UK, 1950/51 to 1973/74   229
12.8   Total real expenditure (1963) per pupil on primary
        and secondary education, five local authorities
        and total, UK, 1974/75 to 1979/80   230
12.9   Pupil—teacher ratios, six local authorities and total,
        UK, 1974/75 to 1979/80   231
12.10   Per capita expenditure on secondary education relative
        to England and Wales, six local authorities, UK,
        1950/51 to 1979/80   232
12.11   Peaks and troughs in pupil numbers, seven cities,
        England and Wales, and Scotland, UK   237
12.12   Ages of schools and type of accommodation, six cities,
        England and Wales, and Scotland, UK, 1978   238
12.13   Potentially surplus accommodation at pupil troughs,
        seven cities, England and Wales, and Scotland, UK   239
12.14   Implications of projected rolls for school accom-
        modations at pupil troughs, seven local authorities,
        UK   240
12.15   Implications of projected rolls for school teachers,
        seven local authorities, UK   241
12.16   Potential annual cost reduction in years of pupil
        troughs, seven local authorities, UK   242
12.17   Potential annual cost reduction in years of pupil
        troughs, Manchester and Newcastle, UK   245

Figures

4.1	A representation of urban episodes	51
4.2	Illustration of events and episodes	52
4.3	Episodes in a challenge—response view of urban history	55
4.4	Introduction of a new activity and phasing out an old	57
4.5	Urban agglomeration with a ring and a core	61
4.6	A system of cities	62
5.1	The city as a system	69
5.2	Outline of a model of urban development	70
5.3	Distribution of endogenous parameters as determined by degree of urban agglomeration and congestion	76
5.4	Development of urban population	81
5.5	Development of urban income	82
5.6	Development of the urban budget	83
6.1	Extension of the interdependent urban system	95
7.1	Three types of spatial cycle schemes	107
7.2	Main spatial cycles of type-β scheme, its sub-stages, and relationships between sub-stages and cells of categorisation matrix	108
8.1	Urban development stages	130
8.2	The sample of Dutch agglomerations	131
8.3	Urban change by phase, The Netherlands, 1950—74	132

8.4	Urban change by phase, The Netherlands, 1950–60 to 1978–82, by region	139
8.5	Urban change by phase, The Netherlands, 1950–60 to 1978–82, by size class	139
9.1	Regional division of The Netherlands	147
9.2	Regional development stages	153
10.1	Income per earner; by agglomerations, cores, rings and rest of The Netherlands, 1950–78	163
10.2	Income per earner; agglomerations by size class, The Netherlands, 1950–78	165
10.3	Income per earner; agglomerations by region, The Netherlands, 1950–78	165
10.4	Income per earner; cores and rings by size class, The Netherlands, 1950–78	166
10.5	Income per earner; cores and rings by region, The Netherlands, 1950–78	167
11.1	US states and regions	179
11.2	Income level, growth, and change during prosperity and depression	182
11.3	Cycles in the growth of relative per capita income, US regions and states	186
11.4	Differences in volatility	194
11.5	Volatility, US states	195
11.6	Differences in amplitude	196
11.7	Amplitude, US states	197
12.1	Effects of population and economic decline	217
12.2	Unit costs and pupil numbers	222

Contributors

Stephen Bailey, Lecturer, Glasgow College of Technology, Glasgow, Scotland.

Leo van den Berg, Lecturer, Department of Urban and Regional Economic Research, Faculty of Economics, Erasmus University, Rotterdam, The Netherlands.

Ulrich C.H. Blum, Research Assistant, Faculty of Economics and Institute for Economic Research and Policy, University of Karlsruhe, Karlsruhe, West Germany.

Leland S. Burns, Professor, Graduate School of Architecture and Urban Planning, University of California, Los Angeles, California, USA.

Gordon C. Cameron, Professor, Department of Land Economy, University of Cambridge, Cambridge, England.

Rolf H. Funck, Professor, Faculty of Economics and Institute for Economic Research and Policy, University of Karlsruhe, Karlsruhe, West Germany.

Michael A. Goldberg, Herbert R. Fullerton Professor of Urban Land Policy, Faculty of Commerce and Business and Business Administration, University of British Columbia, Vancouver, B.C., Canada.

Börje Johansson, Centre for Regional and Urban Research, University of Umea, Umea, Sweden.

Tatsuhiko Kawashima, Professor, Faculty of Economics, Gakushuin University, Toshima-Ku, Tokyo, Japan.

Leo H. Klaassen, Professor, Department of Urban and Regional Economic Research, Faculty of Economics, Erasmus University; and Past President, Netherlands Economic Institute, Rotterdam, The Netherlands.

Jan van der Meer, Lecturer, Department of Urban and Regional Economic Research, Faculty of Economics, Erasmus University, Rotterdam, The Netherlands.

Peter Nijkamp, Professor, Faculty of Economics, Free University, Amsterdam, The Netherlands.

Foreword and acknowledgements

The underlying theme of this book has its genesis in a major study of European urban growth and decline[1] sponsored by the Vienna Centre, and in a conference paper[2] published here in revised form as Chapter 9. The book itself owes its origin to a meeting, 'Long Swings in Regional Development', graciously hosted in 1983 by the Department of Land Economy at the University of Cambridge.

The meeting's participants agreed that the earlier work deserved expansion both in depth and in geographical coverage. Moreover, the several empirical researches that would comprise the eventual collection should be carried out in a framework that would permit making international comparisons, as was done in the Vienna Centre project.

The lack of complete data published by the government statistical bureaux of the several countries chosen for the sample, together with the researchers' idiosyncratic research styles, however, made achieving the latter goal impossible. For this reason, the glue that holds the essays together is not an internationally standard research framework but, rather, the common theme of a cyclical interpretation of metropolitan and regional development, and the authors' shared concern

1   L. van den Berg, R. Drewett, L.H. Klaassen, A. Rossi and C.H.T. Vijverberg (1982), *Urban Europe: A Study of Growth and Decline*, Pergamon, Oxford.
2   L.H. Klaassen, 'Regional Dynamics' (1982), paper presented at the meetings of the Regional Science Association, Surfers' Paradise, Australia.

for explaining aspects of that interpretation whether in terms of the international transmission of staged development or otherwise.

In retrospect, the shortcoming seems an advantage, for valid international comparisons can still be drawn, albeit with more caution and from a somewhat more limited sample than was originally envisioned and, perhaps more importantly, the variety of viewpoints presented surely offers a wider range of material to capture the reader's interest.

Most of the essays were prepared expressly for this volume; none are reprints of previously published work. Many have been presented in preliminary form at conferences — and particularly the Second International Congress of Arts and Sciences sponsored by the World University and held in 1984 at Erasmus University in Rotterdam, and meetings of the Regional Science Association — and have been improved following discussions at those meetings. As they appear in this volume, the essays have been revised and edited in an effort to highlight their commonalities and to unify their style.

The editors are grateful to the contributors for their willingness to interrupt their routine, and often to postpone other research, in order to meet editing and publication deadlines and, even more importantly, to produce research on topics that may not have been at the centre of their current interests. The editors also thank those who have contributed their clerical skills to the production of this volume, particularly to Ets Otomo who typed many versions of the papers.

Leo van den Berg
Leland S. Burns
Leo H. Klaassen

Rotterdam and Los Angeles
November 1985

1 Introduction: cities and regions; trends and cycles

LEO VAN DEN BERG, LELAND S. BURNS AND LEO H.
KLAASSEN

The setting

Much of the history of urbanisation and of regional development has
been written in terms of secular trends that are presumed to have
maintained themselves over long periods and will persist tenaciously
into the future. For example, the world has urbanised and will
continue urbanising. Cities have expanded and many will do so in the
future. Regional and urban economies have grown and their futures
promise more of the same. Increasing environmental pollution, traffic
congestion and crime have degraded the quality of life. And so on.

People tend to think about urban development in much the same
way that the subject is described in the literature. The man in the
street speaks of life in the city being better (or worse) today than it
was 20 years ago. He fails to note that 1968, perhaps, was a
particularly good (or bad) year as a farmer might have, or that the
1970–73 period was dismal, as an economic planner might. It is the
long haul over the past as well as into the future that seems to count
when urban matters occupy the centre of discussion, and events
occurring during the years separating 'now' from 'then' seem to be lost
in the straight-line interpolation along the continuum of events
between them.

The contrast between the evidence of the 1950s and 1960s, when
suburbs burgeoned at the expense of the central cities, and the population data for the 1970s, which indicated that the metropolitan

system in many an industrialised nation was shrinking relative to the rural sector, was regarded as a turning point between urban growth and decline. Whether termed 'a sharp break' with the past or as the onset of 'counterurbanisation', the reversal was greeted not only as an occurrence as unique as it was surprising, but one that simply initiated a new long-term trend in a different direction. The 'new' future of central cities and of entire urban systems would be characterised by persistent decline after many decades of growth and expansion — unless, of course, another sharp break again reversed the trend.

Relentlessly monotonic trends, or rarely broken trends, are two ways of describing urban and regional development. A third view, and perhaps a more realistic one, is that such processes are cyclical in nature. Vulnerable subnational units swing from phases of population growth to decline and back again to growth, and from economic prosperity to depression with an eventual return to prosperity. That, somewhat oversimplified, is the central message or thesis of this book. Graphically, wiggles, rather than straight or kinked lines more accurately describe the reality of development. On *a priori* grounds, there is good reason for believing in the superior power of cycles, rather than of linear or kinked trends, as the basis for describing past urban and regional development, and for assessing its future course. It is more than drawing biological analogies with plant and animal life that move through their life cycles running from birth, through growth and decline, and ending in death, for those kingdoms' cycles are singular rather than continuous and iterative; and they are finitely bounded by life expectancies that are mere fractions of the lifetimes of cities and regions.

While the analogy between developmental cycles of cities and regions and those of living things is tenuous, there is a strong conceptual similarity between time and space as organisers of activities. But the similarity leads to an irony. Regional and urban analysis has little difficulty explaining and prescribing for variations among subnational units arrayed along a spatial continuum, perhaps measured as a distance or set of distances from some focal point such as a major activity concentration. In fact, analyses of this sort are at the very heart of the field and provoke policy makers' actions to even out (or in rare cases to distort) the differences. Time has obvious similarities to space for both are continua for ordering actions. Just as the activity that occurs at a point in space is reciprocally related to the activities taking place at surrounding points, activity at a moment of time influences, and is influenced by, what happens during the preceding and following moments. Almost in disregard for time—space similarities, regional and urban analysts have preferred to examine differences among spatial units in static cross-sections rather than in

2

patterns of differences over a time continuum of spatial units. As a consequence, the subtle time differences in spatial development have received less than warranted attention.

There is a more pragmatic explanation of why regional and urban development is cyclical in nature. Local, provincial and regional areas may be seen as mini-national economies sharing many of the same characteristics with the larger national entities. Like nations, regions react to exogenous shocks, and their economies are influenced by multipliers and accelerators just as national economies are. Their growth trajectories are subject to shifts in world markets, trade cycles, relative price changes, and competition from outside. Why then shouldn't their economies behave cyclically, as do the economies of their parent units? Moreover, any local economy is an amalgam of industries, each with its own cycle. Thus economies of areas highly dependent on automobile production, such as Detroit, Michigan, or Wolfsburg, Germany, should follow cycles of approximately five-year duration, as does the car industry. Except for localities blessed by highly diversified employment mixes, subnational economies would be expected to fluctuate in tandem with the cycles experienced by their major producers.

Even more realistically, there is the evidence provided by examples showing how regional and metropolitan change, and particularly 'breaks' that interrupt change (or reverse the direction of change), emerge as cyclical in nature when development is traced carefully and over reasonably long periods:

— Bavaria ranked with Northern Italy, Holland and Belgium as one of the wealthiest regions in the seventeenth century but, during the industrial revolution, declined rapidly compared to the Rhine—Ruhr area; today, however, the amenities of Southern Bavaria, as part of the Alps region, have made the region one of the most favoured locations for new activities.

— Appalachia boomed in the heyday of mining but lost its economic base with the substitution of petroleum for coal, and declined drastically; with the energy crisis of the early 1970s and the shift in relative energy prices, however, parts of the most distressed area in the US returned to life.

— After decades of uninterrupted growth, Pittsburgh became the first major US metropolitan area of the postwar era to lose population in absolute numbers; after restructuring, population and the economic activities that support it, it is returning and the region once again thrives as a favoured site for new industry.

— New England, the cradle of the US, prospered into the inter-war period but, with the loss of the textile industry to the Deep South, started a decline that continued for many decades; today, the growth of research and information technology has spurred the region's revival.

All these cases furnish examples not only of interrupted growth trends, but of development encompassing a whole, or nearly whole, cycle. The cases also illustrate how the cyclical interpretation provides both comfort and hope for some areas but provokes distress and fear in others. If cycles accurately describe urban and regional development, prosperous areas should be concerned that they can maintain their status while distressed areas are offered the hope of happier days.

Cycles and the urban—rural dichotomy

Implicit in these arguments is the belief that spatial units are distinct from each other. This may hold true in a physical sense but not functionally. In fact, vestiges of functional independence of regions appears to be rapidly disappearing as the world 'shrinks' and spatial units become more and more integrated. This change too lends itself to cyclical interpretation, with the relations between urban and rural developments varying through time. During the earliest stages of urbanisation, labour was drawn from the countryside to concentrated industrial growth poles. So enticing were the employment opportunities and income prospects offered that the rapidly industrialising centres soon extended their influence across vast distances, shaping the social and economic destinies of even the most remote areas. The current counterparts of industrialisation operate at world scale, with attraction extending well beyond national frontiers and embracing most of the factors of production, including of course labour. Many industrialised nations that have traditionally depended on the developing countries only for raw materials supplies, now rely on them for their work forces as well. In Northern Europe, *Gastarbeiter* from the Mediterranean and North African nations work at tasks once performed by the indigenous labour force. Other industrialised nations, such as Canada and the US, 'import' labour by shipping unfinished goods to lower-wage regions such as Southeast Asia for assembly into finished products and re-export. Development has led to the internationalisation of capital with financial resources flowing from nation to nation in the quest for higher and more stable rates of return.

Returning to the national scale, as prosperity increases the relation between urban and rural development gradually changes in sign and character. This holds true no less for areas within agglomerations, as between central cities and suburbs. Urbanisation stimulates a flight to the suburbs by those who seek increased amenities but continue to work in the central districts. Functional bonds are strengthened as suburban populations continue to depend on centres not only for jobs but for the high-level, specialised services and facilities that they offer. With increasing integration of functions, what once was an urban growth pole becomes a functional urban region or an agglomeration, where urban growth continues at expanded spatial scale. As employment grows, the regions grow, and migration continues unabated so long as better opportunities are not found elsewhere. Much of this is history, for we know that, both in economic and demographic terms, the growth of many large industrial areas of North America and Western Europe has come to an end. Areas that traditionally grew from migration have lost their relative attractiveness as places for carrying on life's essential activities, and are increasingly becoming expulsion areas. The expulsion process tends to spread, as happened before with the development of growth poles and attraction areas. Once more, local influences tend to spread across regional boundaries and beyond.

Given these changes and the increasingly blurred distinctions between city and countryside, it makes little sense to study separately *regional*, as distinct from *urban*, developmental processes. There is even less reason for studying the prospects for future spatial development in frameworks as arbitrarily distinguished as these. The signs are that intra- and inter-regional and urban developments will more and more entangle themselves in linked webs as international economies become increasingly and mutually dependent. Western industries — and particularly those concentrated in large urban areas — have increasingly been pulled toward the developing countries of the Third World. In the industrialised nations, the quaternary, or information-intensive, sector has grown in tandem with declines in agriculture and manufacturing, and other primary and secondary sectors. The new activities are footloose with respect to their manpower needs. High skills are required and that kind of manpower shows a growing preference for choosing to live where the quality of life is high. These are the areas endowed with abundant amenities including excellent housing, neighbourhoods, environments, public services, and safety. Areas unable to satisfy such formidable requirements will lose qualified professionals to those that can, and firms supplying the information-intensive services will follow suit. Employment and industry thus shift from the traditional regional—economic points of gravity.

The changed relative attractiveness of cities and regions entails a different, spatially decentralised distribution of population, investment, employment, purchasing power, housing, facilities, pollution, transport infrastructure, etc. The more activities that decentralise, the greater become the opportunities for spatial interaction which, in turn, will undoubtedly stimulate the integration of inter- and intra-regional and urban developments.

Many other tendencies will also influence future spatial evolution. Among them are demographic factors. Large elderly components of the population are emerging in many nations as a consequence of increased longevity and decreased mortality and morbidity. Those of retirement age who are no longer tied to employment concentrations for their jobs, are free to move elsewhere. Their locational preferences, like those of the emergent quaternary industries, tend to be footloose. Many of them will settle in communities that are safer and cleaner than the cities where they worked, and cheaper into the bargain.

The migration behaviour of the aged may be reinforced as accelerated automation, robotisation, and computerisation continue to make obsolete present ways of doing work, and as schemes are introduced to redistribute the remaining work among those left in the labour force. One such scheme will be the time-honoured one of shortening the work week. In the Netherlands, average hours of work have dropped to half what they were 80 years ago — from about 3,600 to 1,600 hours a year — and the process does not seem to have abated. The response, however, has changed. Formerly, an increase in labour productivity was accompanied by improved rewards for work. That possibility was exploited in negotiations both for higher wages and for more leisure time. Although rising incomes used to go hand-in-hand with contracting worktime, in the present political situation shorter hours are feasible only if earnings received for less time on the job are reduced as well. That situation may well be temporary, however, and future worktime reductions may once again be negotiated on the same conditions as before. Be that as it may, working hours will almost certainly continue to shrink, whether by cutting the length of the work day or the number of days worked per week, or by earlier pensioning.

Each alternative has different spatial consequences. By freeing time for commuting, shorter work days or work weeks provide additional stimulus for the further decentralisation of agglomerations toward more remote residential communities. Earlier retirement, on the other hand, increases the propensity of moving to places with a preferred residential climate. In the former case there will be dispersion of commuters and, in the latter, dispersion of people making permanent moves. Both bear importantly on the spatial distribution of the population but the consequences of each differ.

Another factor in that connection is the speed with which society adopts technological innovation, such as computers and robots. High rates of acceptance stimulate the growth of the information sector and accelerate the pace of spatial dynamics and, with it, the need for more carefully guiding the course of regional and urban change.

The first step in designing effective guidance mechanisms is understanding the processes of spatial development and identifying their dynamic properties. In particular, it should be admitted that today's traditional growth centre may become tomorrow's problem area. In short, the currently favoured growth nuclei may be in jeopardy.

It follows from the foregoing that it is erroneous to regard the separate elements of the 'settlement system' as static units that maintain their current stage of development. Subnational elements are subject to internal changes and their structural shifts, though on a smaller scale, are comparable to those occurring at the national level. As we have seen, urban conurbations have decentralised from core to suburbs, usually led by population and followed by industry, but with time lags that lead to adjustment problems. The time lag is a major cause of the traffic problems confronting larger cities, for example. One-way flows, making a heavy claim on transport capacity during peak hours, are one particularly unpleasant consequence of the lop-sided development of the urban spatial pattern. Cities must confront other problems of imbalance as well. At the moment, the exodus from the larger European cities seems to have come to a standstill and the populations of some agglomerations have begun to grow once again. The phenomenon may be cyclical, however. During the current era of reduced economic growth and uncertain income prospects, potential movers are less willing to commit themselves to suburban moves and hesitate to take on long-term obligations such as a house purchase, with all that decision entails as to financing and higher commuting costs. Perhaps with the return of favourable expectations about the economic climate and their impact on personal finances, the number leaving centres may once more exceed the number of new settlers (who lately have been mostly foreign workers).

There will be other considerations as well. Central city governments have not been inactive even during the trying times of recent years. They have worked to improve the quality of urban life by restricting traffic, upgrading landscaping, laying out pedestrian zones, and providing other amenities that foster reurbanisation. While the central cities have been made more attractive as places for living, working and shopping, it is doubtful whether these often cosmetic measures will be effective in retaining current populations or attracting new residents as economic growth returns, especially in view of rapid environmental degradation.

Indeed, the problems of noise, crime and pollution tend to make purely economic discussions about cities appear rather naive. Cities form part of society just as their development reflects the development of society. Highly involved, complex societal relations are by no means built on economic variables alone. Relying solely on economic phenomena to explain social change betrays an enormous over-estimation of the economy as a determining factor in societal evolution.

In spite of the shifts noted above, the settlement systems of different countries tend to develop along very similar lines. Patterns of evolution are essentially the same with metropolitan areas moving through the stages of urbanisation, suburbanisation, and disurbanisation, in roughly that order. Time lags explain most apparent differences between metropolitan development patterns in the economically less developed and the more developed nations. For example, ten years ago the Eastern European settlement system had not yet reached that stage when large agglomerations lose population. Yet disurbanisation, then current in Western Europe, has recently overtaken Budapest, East Europe's most advanced metropolis and, in the future, is likely to spread to other agglomerations.

If the successive stages of development occur in all countries, with leads and lags explained by differences in level of development, the less developed nations can learn much from the experiences gained by those in the lead. With time on their side, they can discover for themselves not only what policy responses have worked but also what mistakes have been made in responding to change. If they learn well, once their countries reach that stage, they can avoid repeating those same mistakes.

That thought seems applicable to Eastern and Western Europe but can it be generalised to the developing countries? There is unquestioned need for gaining better insight into Third World development and for providing answers to such questions as to whether and how various cultures generate different patterns of urban development, whether modern technologies should be introduced to developing countries at earlier stages than they were in Europe and the United States, and finally whether these countries will insist on making their own mistakes rather than profiting from lessons learned elsewhere.

2 Overview

LELAND S. BURNS

The essays written for this volume take the arguments presented in the previous chapter to their next stage. They fall into roughly two categories. The first set, Chapters 3 to 8, deals chiefly with demographic changes and cyclical processes of growth and decline at the level of cities and suburbs, metropolitan areas and agglomerations. The second set, Chapters 9 to 13, has a primary focus on economic changes that involve a cyclical movement between prosperity and depression at the regional level.

The nine research papers that follow this introductory chapter are anchored at their beginning and end by more speculative essays, Chapters 3 and 13, that are intended as provocative discussions of the current issues and problems at, respectively, the urban and regional level. Each of these two essays finishes with a set of topics that their authors conclude are unresolved at this juncture and significant enough to require illumination by new research.

Spatial dynamics at urban scale

The first of the speculative essays, 'Change and non-change in the urban realm' (Chapter 3), assesses the dynamic factors that promote, reflect, or are the consequence of urban development against a backdrop of more static factors that change reluctantly, or perhaps not at all. Demographic and economic changes offer the starting point for examining the influence of change and 'non-change' on the evolution of urban areas as they progress through their development stages. Among the long list of change factors that interact to shape cities and settlement systems are increases in mobility, car ownership, rising household incomes, and demographic characteristics such as fertility, household formation and composition, ageing, and migration. The interactions among and between change and non-change factors influence the cyclical behaviour of central cities, suburban rings, and outlying peripheries through phases of growth, decline, and regeneration.

Not only are change and non-change factors to be reckoned with, but there is also the juxtaposition of countervailing forces that, through their combined effect, neutralise in part the dominant forces. Consider, for example, the tension between trends that have centrifugal consequences such as population decentralisation and the advantages that central cities retain as sites for, particularly, industrial and commercial activities. As another example, while rising incomes increase rates of car ownership and stimulate demands for road networks that in turn foster dispersal, there are centripetal counterforces, such as agglomeration or urbanisation economies and centralisation policies, that either encourage new development in central cities or help to contain existing activities.

The chapter emphasises the impact of changing demographic characteristics and raised incomes on residential location during past decades, and on other land use patterns. On balance, these shifts have encouraged decentralisation by lessening the importance of the 'friction of distance'. Yet, account must be taken of the multitude of advantages still offered by central cities as activity sites. Among these are the externalities that are particularly favourable to the development of new small-scale industry plus the availability of land and underutilised industrial structures.

Assessing future outcomes is more difficult, though perhaps more realistic, given the realisation that cycles, rather than trends, more accurately describe urban spatial development. Just as revised expectations can mark the end of a period of sustained growth or decline, changing optimism about an area's potential can alter the pattern and quality of spatial development. The 'domino effect' initiated by a negative signal explains disinvestment that leads eventually to central city decline. Positive signals can generate renewed optimism that sparks the beginning of new rounds of investment. The author of the chapter, Michael Goldberg, puts it well when he asserts that 'the spatial pattern of investments therefore is tied to spatial variations in expectations and perceptions of risk and return. As this spatial pattern of expectations and investments changes, so does the structure of the city region.' Expectations play a major, and often decisive, role in the dynamic land use drama of where and when investments are placed and, as a consequence, in the quality and spatial patterns of urban development.

Technological advance — a topic that, like Banquo's ghost, appears and reappears throughout this volume — further threatens established urban forms. By providing opportunities for footloose development, encouraging the replacement of labour with capital, displacing the workplace from traditional concentrations to the home (perhaps akin to Toffler's 'Electronic cottage'), and supporting the growth of information-intensive activities, the revolution in technology encourages scattered development and the broad-scale dispersal of activities. If this is the urban future, can the city maintain itself as a defined unit of settlement, retaining its *raison d'être* as a centre for propinquity and sociability, in the face of the technological challenge? Moreover, what role will (or should) be played by government, as another countervailing force, in mediating change? Again, the contrary forces promoting centralisation and dispersion stand opposed and only the net balance of both will determine the final outcomes. Of one thing we can be sure: the countervailing forces will shift in magnitude and in cyclical fashion with the consequences played out on the urban landscape.

Just as later chapters juxtapose city centres with suburbs and metropolitan with rural systems, for example, Goldberg confronts change with non-change plus the variety of other conflicting factors that alter urban spatial patterns in cyclical ways. Among the factors slow to change are the standing stock of structures that usually outlive their occupants by many decades. There is also discovery and rediscovery that introduces the cyclical element. Much that passes for innovation, or new ways of doing things, really involves rediscovery of old devices forgotten in the grand sweep of history. Mixed use zoning is little different from non-zoning, for example. The rediscovery of traditional architectural forms, either through emulation of historical styles and their incorporation into new structures, as for example in the post-modern movement, or the realisation that existing structures built in a past era have considerable aesthetic merit — and the potential for rehabilitation or for recycling into new uses — is another case in point. And perhaps at the basis of it all is 'a constancy in the human spirit that likes propinquity and satisfies deep-seated social needs'. Keeping in mind the seeming permanence of certain factors, as contrasted with the transience of others, helps in our understanding of urban dynamics. Sobering is the realisation that, of the many urban dimensions, so little *does* change. For example, each year's additions to the US housing stock represent an increase in the inventory of only about 2 per cent, a statistic worth keeping in mind by the futurists who foresee radical differences between the city of tomorrow and the city of today, or those who claim that increasing energy prices — if indeed they *do* increase — will, in the twinkling of an eye, destine a return to the compact city of an earlier age.

Chapter 4, 'Analysis of episodes in urban event histories', pursues the change versus non-change dichotomy theoretically and expands the theme that fluctuating growth paths describe metropolitan development. Börje Johansson and Peter Nijkamp, the authors, portray urban history as a series of events, each of which alters a given state of affairs. Formally, an episode is a 'change pattern that is distinctive and separate from previous patterns, although part of a larger series of episodes in urban history'. An event, on the other hand, marks the 'transition from one episode to another'. Examples would be switches (events) from rapid growth (an episode) to stagnation (another episode) over a time interval or, in urban finance, from solvency to bankruptcy, or shifts in regional employment from dependency on manufacturing activity to services. The evolution of an urban area or a region can thus be divided into a series of episodes joined by events that mark the change between episodes. A formal methodological framework embodying both events and episodes as a means of studying urban evolutionary patterns and variations in those patterns seems appropriate given the unsteady path of urban evolution.

A scenario, modelled with the formality of product cycle theory, illustrates the cyclical process from initial growth signals to stagnation and eventual downturn. An event such as a newly established productive activity founded on new knowledge, or on an innovation, or on inherited knowledge, starts the process. Output, productivity, and efficiency increase, but with eventual modifications that take into account external competition as a strategy for increasing market shares. The specialisation that breeds efficiency also stimulates the growth of a host of linked activities. Decreasing marginal returns to scale accompany increased output, however, and, as a consequence of specialisation, eventual stagnation and a loss in flexibility follow. In this way, an event — the inauguration of a new production process — initiates an episode of industrial development. Throughout, progress is marked by a series of events distinguishing one episode from the next.

Steady progress is in large part governed by success in overcoming three types of constraints. First, a regional economy moving from one episode to the next must pass a threshold that requires a minimum endowment of private and public facilities, human resources, and scientific knowledge. Second, bottlenecks created by agglomeration diseconomies such as congestion or a deteriorating infrastructure, or

12

by obsolete plant and equipment, threaten continued growth. Third, there must be a synergistic balance between public overhead capital and private productive capital, including R & D resources. Transition from episode to episode thus becomes a matter of challenge and response, with constraints and exogenous market factors presenting the challenge for response by private and public policy decisions.

Episodes are modelled under a set of varying conditions (as various forms of subsystem interaction, for example), in differing contexts (such as core—periphery configurations), and with alternative assumptions (for instance, about the degree of closure of an urban or regional economy) in order to 'shed light on non-linear change processes in interacting (spatial) subsystems'.

Chapter 5, 'Urban change: a changing process', offers yet another model of urban growth and fluctuations but, in contrast to the emphasis given in the previous chapter to modelling urban change within the grand sweep of history, this effort more intimately concerns itself with urban structure and the various effects its elements have on future growth patterns. Rolf H. Funck and Ulrich C.H. Blum see the city as a metasystem consisting of human resources (or population), financial resources (consisting of private and public capital assets), and natural resources. Interrelations between the three subsystems and the metasystem are termed processes that, in turn, have economic, social and cultural, and political and administrative dimensions. Taken together they describe the cyclical aspects of urban development.

The elements of urban development, and of spatial structuring that give urban areas their unique character, are shaped into an urban development model that describes the economic process, population or human resources, and capital assets including infrastructure (seen by Johansson and Nijkamp as a potential bottleneck). The nature of social and cultural factors is exemplified by changes during recent decades in West Germany, such as the ageing of the population, the shifting ethnic structure resulting from differences in birth rates of the German population and the 'guest workers' from abroad, and increasing spatial segregation between centre and suburb. The political and administrative process is seen as the mechanism for exploiting urban assets, for legitimising citizens' rights, for resolving conflicts, and for establishing the institutions and providing the guidelines that shape the urban future and give cities their power.

The factors and subsystems are structured into a multiplier—accelerator model that (most likely) generates cyclical outcomes. Finally, the model is empirically estimated for a West German city and, depending on the assumptions used, generates a set of scenarios portraying future population size, personal income level, and fiscal capacity.

13

Leo van den Berg and Leo H. Klaassen, in Chapter 6, pose the menacing question, is urban decline contagious? A staged model of urban development — but one quite different from those of either Johansson and Nijkamp or Funck and Blum — prefaces their empirical answer. During the first stage of the model by van den Berg and Klaassen, migrants from the rural periphery in search of urban employment act as the catalyst for the familiar process of urbanisation. The metropolitan area, or agglomeration, to which they move continues to grow with each new wave of arrivals, but eventually with an internal redistribution of population favouring suburban areas at the expense of central cities or cores. The first stage is past, and the second has made its appearance. As suburban land is developed to capacity, population begins to spill over into areas beyond the metropolitan borders, and the area moves into its third phase. Disurbanisation describes the stage when suburban growth fails to compensate for losses at the centre and, as a consequence, the population of the entire agglomeration starts to shrink in absolute numbers. Finally, when for various reasons the core either grows once again, or at least its decline is masked by the magnitude of suburban loss, the agglomeration has moved into the most advanced development stage, reurbanisation, and the cycle is renewed.

How well does the model approximate real world urban development? Analysis of data covering 30 years of European urban history provides the validation. With the passage of time, the number and proportion of West European metropolitan areas at urbanisation and suburbanisation stages has dropped. Suburbanisation peaked in West Europe in the 1960s. During the next decade, the proportion disurbanising grew sharply and, in the late 1970s, reurbanisation emerged.

Another cut at the population data shows how size affects staging. In 1975, for example, over half the small agglomerations were suburbanising, while the majority of their larger counterparts had entered the stage of disurbanisation.

The picture in Eastern Europe, though very different, was consistent with the hypothesis that staging is a function of the level of economic or industrial development. All those metropolitan areas, later to industrialise and economically less developed, continued to grow, while their more advanced Western European counterparts declined. Stage thus depends on level of development. The results suggest urbanisation waves related to space and time where the earlier the metropolitan region industrialised, the sooner it declined.

The prognosis for the future of agglomerations is a gloomy one. If quality of life considerations, including access to urban services, continue to assume increasing importance in the migration decisions of labour, and if there is a continued trend favouring footloose employment over site-specific jobs, then today's major population centres will lose their dominance as the nuclei of economic and social life.

To return once again to the main focus of their chapter, van den Berg and Klaassen predict that not only will established centres lose their agglomerative power, but the distributions of population towards outlying areas will quicken the speed with which those areas pass through their development cycles. Thus, decline infects surrounding areas with the same pathologies.

Tatsuhiko Kawashima's chapter, 'Is disurbanisation foreseeable in Japan?' (Chapter 7), expands on van den Berg and Klaassen's intriguing pair of concepts that, first, the staging of urban development is related to stage of economic development and, second, disurbanisation is contagious. Kawashima not only succeeds in answering the question posed in the title of his chapter, but addresses another that is at once more general and of no less importance. Does a nation's overall level of economic development determine the distribution of its metropolitan areas over stages of the urban cycle? The answer is provided by adding comparative analysis of two additional countries to the European set analysed in the previous chapter. To rephrase the argument, if the countries (or the metropolitan areas within a country) that industrialised first were also the first to disurbanise, then those later to be visited by industrialisation will disurbanise later, after moving through the preliminary stages of urbanisation and suburbanisation.

Employing a slightly modified methodology, the analysis draws on population data for US Standard Metropolitan Statistical Areas (SMSAs) and for Japan's rough equivalents, Functional Urban Cores (FUCs). The paper starts with the US, then moves on to Japan, a logical sequence since, if the hypothesis holds, the US would lead the way through the stages of the urbanisation spectrum and Japan would follow.

The analysis for the US traces the evolution of its metropolitan system through 30 years of recent history. The system was clearly in the expansionary phases of urbanisation and suburbanisation during the 1960s, with the decline of only a single central city hinting at subsequent declines of spatially more widespread magnitude. History has demonstrated that other SMSAs would later follow suit, with the nation's larger units moving squarely into the disurbanisation stage during the 1970s. A spatial disaggregation of the metropolitan data shows that the central cities were bellwethers for changes that would subsequently spread throughout most of the metropolitan system. For the typical case, roughly 20 years elapsed between the signal from the central city until decline of the total metropolitan region.

Not all SMSAs disurbanised, however. That fact, when considered with the spatial distribution of disurbanising and growing areas, yields tentative evidence further supporting the link between level of economic development and stage of urbanisation. Grouping SMSAs by stage and by region demonstrates that, of the 30 largest sampled, the ten disurbanising were all concentrated in either the Northeast or North Central regions, the North Central and the Southeast contained the nine verging on disurbanisation, and the remaining 13 growing SMSAs were located in the South or West. Thus the wave of disurbanisation 'is surging from the combined Northeast—North Central regions to the combined South—West regions, and travelling westward within the latter'.

What does this surprisingly regular evidence contribute to a better understanding of the linkage between development and urbanisation? The North Central and Northeast are not only the areas containing the majority of disurbanising metropolises, but also the first of the nation's regions to industrialise, and they remain even today as the centres of industrial activity. In that respect, the regions are similar to Western Europe (including the UK). SMSAs in the South and Western regions, analogous to the agglomerations of Eastern Europe that industrialised later, are still experiencing the earlier expansionary stages but, nonetheless, moving relentlessly in the direction of their forebears.

Returning to the US—Japanese comparison, Kawashima's impressive evidence shows that Japan's metropolitan system of FUCs, evaluated during the same period, has followed a similar path, but lagging the US system, as predicted. The early signs of decline appeared first in the biggest FUCs, just as they did in Europe's largest agglomerations and the US's major SMSAs. However, the international differences and lags within the system were important. Japan's urban system had not reached the disurbanisation stage by 1980 though it was moving steadily in that direction. Population tended to concentrate into the 86 FUCs comprising the urban set during the latter half of the 1970s, but at rates that have declined continuously since 1960. And it is likely that rates have turned negative in more recent years. Within the urban system, however, Kawashima predicts that, for the first time in postwar history, the smaller FUCs will begin to grow faster than the larger ones. To answer the threatening question posed at the outset: disurbanisation that characterised the development of the US metropolitan system in the 1970s can be expected to reach Japan in the 1980s as cities progress in orderly fashion through their development phases.

If the staging of urbanisation is linked to development and the time elapsing since the commencement of industrialisation, as the analyses of previous chapters strongly suggest, then the agglomerations of countries that were first to industrialise should also be the most advanced. Since Northwest Europe — including the UK, the Netherlands, Belgium, and Northern Germany — were the first to experience the industrial revolution, we should expect to find their largest metropolitan areas leading the cycling through development stages. That was, in fact, suggested in the comparisons between East and West Europe in Chapter 6, and the US—Japan comparison of Chapter 7. It also means that those areas earliest to industrialise should be leading the way into the fourth stage of the cycle, re-urbanisation.

The question of whether or not this holds true is the subject of Chapter 8. In asking 'Urban Revival?', Leo van den Berg, Leo H. Klaassen and Jan van der Meer pose a question with more positive overtones, at least for the metropolitan system, than Kawashima's. The chapter asks whether urban revival will characterise the future development of the Dutch agglomerations and, indeed, of the system of metropolitan areas and conurbations in other industrialised nations that have experienced relative and absolute losses of population and jobs for a decade or longer. The analysis offers more than a straight-forward answer to this deceptively simple question. Nor is the answer mere speculation about the course of urban events and episodes in the years ahead.

Since successful prediction relies on insight and knowledge of past events, much of the analysis is an attempt to provide a systematic, cyclical interpretation of urban growth and development in the Netherlands since 1950. As the theory predicts, and the empirical evidence demonstrates, the agglomerations passed sequentially through the well defined stages of urbanisation, sub-urbanisation, and disurbanisation. Moreover, the stage effect transferred downward through the size hierarchy. The largest and most urbanised agglomerations, such as Amsterdam, The Hague, and Rotterdam, were the innovators in the sense that they were the first to suburbanise at the expense of their cores. As the smaller agglomerations followed suit in subsequent periods, the largest began to disurbanise, that is, to lose population in the aggregate. By the early 1970s, the major agglomerations were squarely in the stage of disurbanisation while the system's smaller units were still urbanising. Towards the end of that decade, however, as the medium-sized and small agglomerations continued their move towards disurbanisation, there were strong hints that the largest agglomerations had begun to move back to the urbanisation phase. Hence the question posed in the chapter's title.

The answer to the question requires an examination of the factors causing the population shifts that have, in turn, pushed metropolitan areas through their development phases. These are the pillars that underlie the chapter's analysis. Rising incomes and relatively declining transport costs foster spatial decentralisation. Push factors such as the declining quality of life in central cities, the mismatch between the quality of the housing inventory in central cities and demographic characteristics, plus shifting consumer tastes and preferences, provide additional centrifugal impetus. But with a downturn in the business cycle — as the one precipitated by the oil crisis in the early 1970s — relative transport costs rise, real incomes stabilise or decline, and long-distance travel becomes an increasingly costly luxury. Moving further out from central job concentrations for those seeking the superior amenities of suburban and rural life becomes financially unfeasible. With tight labour markets, the option of changing jobs to higher-amenity locations offers a no more realistic option. In short, labour stays put during a downturn especially when expectations of a return to prosperity are uncertain.

The recession starting in the late 1970s and extending into the current decade has helped contain, and retain, metropolitan populations, thus slowing the spatial dynamics of the earlier, more prosperous era. Public policy implemented to 'reurbanise' the population by upgrading the quality of life in cities, and particularly in central cores, has played an uncertain role in stemming the outflow and an even more dubious part in attracting new migrants. It is likely that the policy impacts have been masked by the greater importance of the business cycle. Unless containment policies can be made more effective, the return of better times will probably herald a return to disurbanisation rather than revival.

Spatial dynamics at regional scale

Chapters 9, 10 and 11 should be read as a group, for each provides a variation on a common theme. Their Leitmotiv is that the economic development of regions and metropolitan areas follows a logical, predictable, sequential, cyclical process. By stressing economic development at the regional level, these chapters distinguish themselves from earlier ones that deal with demographic changes at the metropolitan level, and the cycles they follow.

Setting the stage in the first of these, 'regional dynamics', Leo H. Klaassen defines four types of regional development and proceeds to argue that, in most cases, regions evolve from type to type sequentially and iteratively. Over time, regions with high and growing employment and income lose their positions as prosperous areas, decline to the status of potential development areas, and eventually become actual development areas. The sequence continues with development areas, characterised by low and declining incomes and employment rates, becoming potentially prosperous areas, then — returning full circle — actual prosperous areas. And so on, as regional economies move cyclically through the several phases of development. Importantly, the process is neither linear nor single-valenced but a recursive one that regions repeatedly run through cyclically as they swing between periods of prosperity and depression.

The movements are traced for a set of Dutch regions distinguished between the intensively urbanised major conurbations such as the Randstad, their emanation zones, and the periphery. Empirical tests based on longitudinal income and employment data verify that, over time, the several regional types indeed shifted position in the predicted sequence.

The cycle hypothesis is explored further and in more detail in the next two chapters that focus on the time path of income as a generic measure of development level and quality of life. Chapter 10, 'Urban and regional income development in The Netherlands', traces the spatial implications of cyclical development since 1978. This chapter, by demonstrating how economic development diffuses in cyclical fashion through subnational hierarchies, complements the earlier chapters that traced the international spread of urban cycles through a hierarchy of nations ordered according to their level of development.

As with the studies based on population, this research on income levels shows that the very largest agglomerations, and particularly their central cities, were the first to decline. Within the metropolitan sphere and with the passage of time, decline spread downwards through the size hierarchy to the smaller agglomerations, then to those located in spillover areas, and finally to the periphery. As the largest agglomerations shifted from a period of suburbanisation in the 1950s to disurbanisation in the 1970s, their economic fortunes shifted in parallel from prosperity to recession. With decline of the entire metropolitan sphere, the non-urbanised remainder enjoyed rising prosperity.

Leland S. Burns's analysis of regional income development in the US (Chapter 11) differs slightly in concept but his major conclusion — that regional economies follow orderly cyclical paths in their development — conforms to the research on Dutch regions. Analysis of a time series for the 1950—80 period shows that per capita income moved iteratively through the four definable stages for the 50 states, plus the District of Columbia, just as it did for the regions of the Netherlands. Determinants for two measures of cyclical variation, volatility and amplitude, are identified and statistically estimated for the impact they have on instability. The research identifies primary employment in natural resource-based industry, such as agriculture, as a major contributor. Other significant influences are the diversification of the regional economy, as measured by the similarity of its employment structure to the nation's, and the pace of economic growth. The more diversified the structure, the more stable is the economy. Rapid growth is associated with large fluctuations indicating a trade-off between the policy goals of growth and stability.

'Aggregate reductions in the demand for urban labour, persistent and heavy underutilisation of the labour force, the withdrawal of private sector investment, the physical, social and economic decay of the inner city, and discrimination in housing and labour markets against the poor, and especially against ethnic minorities' are among the consequences of disurbanisation enumerated by Gordon C. Cameron and Stephen Bailey in introducing Chapter 12, 'The fiscal costs of city decline'. Their research addresses one of the least studied consequences, the threats to the maintenance of quality education. Population loss, and the uncertainties accompanying it, present particularly challenging problems to local authorities since resources cannot easily be withdrawn from a sector with long-run commitments to maintaining capital and labour. The high costs of accommodating ever larger service-dependent populations, and parallel decreases in local revenues, exacerbate the problem.

To determine whether fiscal squeeze has threatened the continued delivery of a critical service, the authors contrast the behaviour of per capita expenditure on primary and secondary education since 1950 in a sample of declining and non-declining British cities. The analysis of a 30-year time series of operating data leads to a surprising result. Contrary to expectations, increasing unit costs were not the result of a persistent drop in numbers of pupils. Rather, costs rose in disurbanising areas as local authorities attempted to raise the quality of service delivered, often to catch up to a national average of provision. Teacher—pupil ratios rose in periods of student growth; they rose too in the face of declining pupil numbers as authorities sought to upgrade the level of input per pupil. Thus, rising unit costs accompanied urban change, whether positive or negative. The case studies demonstrate, however, that the direction and magnitude of cost changes were conditioned by the nature of local response.

Earlier chapters have shown how spatial cycles spread geographically with the level of an area's economic development determining the staging of its cycle. Generally, too, the longer a region or nation has been industrialised, the more advanced its metropolitan system has become. For this reason, the most economically advanced nations — and, not coincidentally, those earliest to industrialise — are currently paying the costs of disurbanisation. The analysis of how the UK's national and local governments have dealt with service delivery during disurbanisation offers lessons for the industrialising nations that are likely to follow suit in the years ahead. After all, because the UK was the cradle of industrialisation and her cities were among the first to realise the consequences of large-scale disurbanisation, her experiences in coping with declining metropolitan population, shrinking fiscal capacity, and falling service demands, should be particularly instructive to other nations and areas that can expect to face similar problems.

The book concludes with a chapter by Burns (Chapter 13) that, like Goldberg's (Chapter 3), deals with issues and trends shaping past and current spatial development, casts an eye towards the future, and in the process identifies areas in need of further research.

While we can be sure that recent, and probably enduring, demographic and social shifts − particularly the ageing of the population, the changing size and composition of households, and the emerging economic and political role of women − have received considerable attention in the literature, research has yet to probe very deeply into their spatial consequences. The same applies to the internationalisation of the metropolis. The challenges to research are to make the spatial translation of these powerful form-giving forces.

Other factors also threaten to disrupt traditional patterns of spatial organisation. An era in which labour seeks locations offering amenities, rather than the economic incentives predicted by the neoclassical models, requires a new understanding of migration determinants. Rapid technological advance also poses a serious threat to familiar locational patterns, just as it jeopardises labour markets, ways of doing business, and indeed, the whole fabric of established living patterns.

If technological change, played out in the work place, displaces office employment from urban cores to suburbs, the current revival of economic life in the central city would become a cyclical aberration of very short duration. Research could productively address the long-term viability of central city investments and their possibility for 'sustaining robust labour markets, particularly in light of the threats of technological advance'. Suburbs, no less, are increasingly subject to accelerating physical, functional, and economic decline as metropolitan areas in the industrialised and post-industrial nations move relentlessly into the stage of disurbanisation.

Fewer subjects have more profound influences on time−space relationships than does capital budgeting, a field which also ranks as one of the most understudied in local public finance and as rarely examined in the annals of urban and regional research. The difficulties of valuing in economic terms intergenerational transfers of benefits are particularly acute when urban assets consist not only of the daily used infrastructure — roads, bridges, mass transit vehicles, water and sewer systems, parks and schools — but of irreplaceable treasures, such as structures with great historical merit or unique environmental features. In periods when public resources are particularly scarce, deferred maintenance (often synonymous with *no* maintenance) may seem rational given the fact that pay-back periods for such expenditures extend over decades, and possibly over generations. Yet a well maintained physical infrastructure may be a necessary ingredient in a well balanced recipe for revitalisation even though conventional investment criteria might accord it low priority. In addition to proposing a re-examination of the criteria, and the ways that they are applied, Burns proposes the 'urban capital agenda' as a novel device for ordering capital development priorities, specifying factor inputs, coordinating projects, and timing their implementation as stabilisation instruments.

Finally, we are just beginning to unravel the complexities of stagnant and declining economies, having devoted most of our research resources to investigating the causes and consequences of growth, and the appropriate policy responses for managing it. 'Understanding decline', writes Burns, 'is far more complicated than simply multiplying the equations of growth models through by minus one, assuming that a sort of Palladian symmetry governs dynamics regardless of direction.'

3 Change and non-change in the urban realm; some trends, constants, and emerging forms in urban structure

MICHAEL A. GOLDBERG

During the twentieth century, cities around the world have undergone extraordinary changes in scale and spatial structure. Despite these changes, there do appear to be some significant constants and some re-emerging urban forms. This chapter is intended to provide a broad framework against which specific urban structural issues and research can be displayed. Accordingly, the chapter sets out major issues facing both researchers and policy makers with respect to the structure and cyclical behaviour of urban areas. Major variables that are likely to affect the future course of urban spatial evolution will also be identified. Finally, a research agenda will be set out which spans a range of the more important questions likely to face both researchers and policy makers over the coming decade or so.

To accomplish these ends, we begin by briefly examining some of the major trends that have commanded policy and research attention over the past few decades. In view of the trends (and constants) we move on to examine some of the central issues and variables upon which these issues hinge. Our focus will be confined to urban Western Europe and North America, a broad enough context to jeopardise meaningful generalities without further widening the scope to include Third World cities as well. We close with a research and policy agenda.

Trends and issues in urban structure

Concern about urban structure accelerated greatly during the 1960s with the rapid expansion of suburbs and highways. A considerable literature on the subject developed. The structure of cities was examined historically (Passonneau, 1963; and Meadows, 1957) through a crystal ball (Wurster, 1963; and Webber, 1963). It was discussed conceptually and analytically (Foley, 1964; Hoch, 1969; and Schnore, 1963), and finally, its impacts on policy were explored (Alonso, 1964; and Guttenberg, 1964). More recently there have also been attempts to synthesise urban structural concepts across cultures (Korcelli, 1976), as well as between the growth and decline phases of cycles (van den Berg et al., 1982). Obviously, there has been no lack of interest in the subject. However, there have been a number of 'emergent realities' (to borrow from Bourne, 1982) that call for a review of the central issues likely to impact upon urban form over the decades ahead. The present effort addresses a pot-pourri of these issues.

Running in parallel with the dramatic increases in income and economic well-being experienced by the developed nations during the past quarter of a century, has been an equally dramatic increase in mobility with consequent impacts on urban growth patterns. Greater affluence has been accompanied by rising car ownership, increased road mileage, and the remarkable spatial expansion of urban areas. Both intra-urban and inter-urban mobility have been affected. Decentralisation has been one emergent and broadly based trend against which to explore urban structural change.

Against the backdrop of dispersal and its attendant centrifugal forces, we can discern at a more local level the coalescing of regional activity nodes, in essence a local centripetal tendency. These two trends, operating at quite different spatial scales, are not inconsistent, and in fact might well be complementary, providing advantages to both donor and recipient urban areas.

The generally decentralising urban population can enjoy increases in urban living standards through moving from overcrowded excessively large urban municipalities to relatively underpopulated suburban, ex-urban and non-metropolitan areas. By losing population the larger urban realms can improve their quality of life by realising fewer diseconomies of scale while still continuing to benefit from urban scale economies. For the receiving areas, growth can provide more varied services and the realisation of scale economies that their previous smaller size precluded.

Decentralisation at the urban and metropolitan scale has been occurring for the past half-century and has been widely documented (Hoyt, 1964; Morrill, 1970; Nelson, 1969; Thomlinson, 1969; and Weller, 1967), to name a scant few who have examined the issue empirically. Intra-urban decentralisation has been hailed by some as providing opportunities for new social, economic and individual development (Webber, 1963, 1964 and 1968) and condemned by others (Dantzig and Saaty, 1973; Mumford, 1961; and Jacobs, 1961).

At the more macro scale of national settlement systems a great deal of attention has recently focused on growth and decentralisation, particularly at the non-metropolitan level and particularly in the US. The shifts in human settlement systems both in developed and developing countries has been widely documented (Berry and Dahmann, 1977; Hansen, 1978; Korcelli, 1982; Tweeten and Brinkman, 1976; and Burns, 1982). There has also been disagreement, however, about both the generality of the process and the need to examine it much more closely (Berry, 1976 and 1978; Gertler, 1983; Bourne, 1982; Hooper, Simmons and Bourne, 1983; and Porell, 1982). The utility of such mobility and its consequences for existing urban regions has also been called into question (Morris, 1978; Norton, 1979; Solomon, 1980; and Sternlieb and Hughes, 1975). Finally, the relevance of these trends for European cities has recently begun to be explored and their generality questioned (Hall and Hay, 1980; and van den Berg et al., 1982).

While the long-term centrifugal trends seem fairly well established, growing evidence suggests increasing centripetal pressure around these dispersed nodes (Dunphy, 1982; Baerwald, 1982; Noguchi, 1982; and Solomon, 1980). Evidence also supports the notion that even within the declining older central cities, there is considerable regeneration and recentralisation (Solomon, 1980; Clay, 1979; Leven, 1978; and Laska and Spain, 1980); regeneration is posited by van den Berg et al., under the rubric of 'reurbanisation' (1982, pp. 40–5). (The topic is addressed in detail in later chapters of this volume.)

Thus the foregoing lends credence to the broad trends set out initially about decentralisation and centralisation as complementary and simultaneously occurring phenomena working jointly to shape cities and city systems. They serve as a starting point for the following discussion which builds on their findings and seeks to raise a number of issues about the trends, their generality, their continuance and their meaning for public policy.

What follows focuses on unknowns and critical variables whose future course will greatly affect the scale and structure of urban areas. Obviously, the specific circumstances surrounding each issue will vary from country to country, and from city to city. These specific manifestations, however, do not detract from the general importance of the following discussion, though national and local differences must be considered when relating the present argument to particular circumstances and settings.

(1) Demographic variables and behaviours. Several critical variables have major consequences for urban structure: fertility, household formation, ageing, and migration. Recent demographic trends such as the extraordinary growth of single and two-person households have had significant impacts on urban form. With the decline in fertility that has attended the formation of these smaller households has come a greater willingness and ability to live at higher densities. Moreover, with the advent of the dual-income household has come a preference for centrality which in turn is encouraged by low fertility rates and high household incomes. Household formation and fertility are both behaviourally based and combine to present formidable and variable forces in the shaping of the future city (Alonso, 1983). Changing age profiles in developed countries suggest major shifts in housing types and locations toward more central and smaller units in higher-amenity locations and implies both intra-urban and inter-urban population movements favouring considerably more compact and denser urban realms (Alonso, 1983; and Brown, 1983).

Migration behaviour ranks among the most important of all demographic phenomena. Despite an enormous literature on the subject, relatively little is yet understood about the causes of international and inter-regional population flows (Bourne, 1983). Because of the massiveness of potential migratory streams compared with the standing current population of recipient regions, migration can have major consequences for urban scale and structure. One has only to look at the effects of migration on the US 'sunbelt' during the past two decades and the parallel effects on the 'frostbelt'. These population movements are volatile, defy *ex post* analysis, and clearly elude any attempts at forecasting. The absence of a better understanding of migration behaviour pretty well dooms us to discuss urban structure without an appreciation of likely future urban scale, a frustrating and fruitless chore at best.

(2) Residential location behaviour. The demographic issues set out above provide an essential background for looking at residential location behaviour for the characteristics of the population shape residential location preferences. The age, size and fertility traits of the urban household influence the size of the required housing unit, the amount of desired land and the location within urban areas. Because many demographic characteristics are behavioural — particularly household formation and dissolution and fertility — and volatile, we can expect locational shifts as a consequence. Adding to this changes in tastes and perceptions of living quality, we can envisage quite

dramatic shifts in intra-urban location that underpin much of the change in urban structure that has occurred over the past several decades. The consequences for the central city, the surrounding suburbs and the outlying 'exurbs' are obvious. Equally obvious should be potential impacts on the residential neighbourhoods that make up the core city, its suburbs, and its exurbs. Changing intra-urban preferences and population movements have led both to problems of population loss and excessive growth within the same urban area and at times in adjoining governmental units.

Because residential land use typically accounts for two-thirds to three-quarters of an urban region's developed area, substantial impacts on spatial structure can be expected from changes in residential location preferences. Such preferences therefore are key shapers of urban form and need to be better identified, and the scope for variability in preferences and housing location patterns more fully appreciated.

(3) Industrial location patterns and forces. If we envision major changes in residential mobility, the shift in industrial location must be viewed as truly radical. During the past few decades industrial facilities have become increasingly footloose and freed from a host of technological and locational constraints that bound them to reasonably well defined regions and sites within regions (Hoover, 1975). The loosening of locational requirements has meant that, increasingly, firms are free to move to high-amenity areas. In an era of pipelines and coal slurries, jumbo jetfreighters, superhighways, and manmade ship channels, only in exceptional circumstances is an industrial facility tightly tied to a set of transportation or resource-based locational requirements. The explosion in US non-metropolitan and sunbelt employment is evidence of the growing footlooseness of these activities (Tweeten and Brinkman, 1976). There are still reasons, however, for locating industrial activities in central cities.

First, central cities still offer externally provided economies of scale, or 'agglomeration economies' (Moomaw, 1981). Small firms in particular take advantage of such external economies, making up in part for their lack of internal scale economies — the so-called incubator hypothesis (Struyk and James, 1975). This is likely to be of increasing importance in the future since we know that new and small firms account for virtually all private sector employment growth (Birch, 1979) and, given presently high rates of unemployment, there will undoubtedly be significant moves to create jobs. Because of externalities there should be a corresponding increase in central city jobs as new and young firms seek to take advantage of these externally provided economies and as governments push to create employment through enhancing the environment for new and small job-creating firms.

Second, the availability of large quantities of appropriately zoned and vacant industrial land, and of sound but frequently vacant industrial buildings, should also encourage industrial regeneration in central areas, particularly since the bulk of industrial jobs is likely to be in light as opposed to heavy industries. The large professional component of newer high technology firms should also interact with the demographic forces cited above to make the central city an attractive place for professional and technical employees in these newer kinds of manufacturing firms (Berry and Elster, 1983). Ample evidence, however, suggests that possibilities for central area industrial growth may well be limited (Sternlieb and Hughes, 1975; Evans and Eversley, 1980; and Bradbury, Downs and Small, 1982). The issue remains up in the air and therefore in need of resolution.

(4) Retail commercial locational forces and issues. The centrifugal forces noted at the outset of this chapter have perhaps nowhere been as much discussed as with respect to retail and commercial activities. Much of the US urban crisis has revolved around the declining retail base of larger and older frostbelt cities. Detroit is the most widely cited example with the closing of its major central city department store but the story is not dissimilar from other US cities. As people have left central cities so have the retail services that they require. Within the general pattern of retail and office dispersal, however, there is also the agglomerating centripetal force which is coalescing much office and retail development about well defined and increasingly tightly focused non-CBD nodes of activity (Baerwald, 1982; and Noguchi, 1982). In the Vancouver region this trend has become established regional development policy as the regional government has sought to focus development in the urban area around six suburban nodes called 'regional town centres', each of which will be serviced by transit and shaped by flexible multi-use zoning regulations (Kellas, 1983).

Closely related to retail and commercial coalescence has been the evolution of a new form of urban land use. Mixed Use Developments or 'MXD's (Witherspoon, et al., 1976; and McKeever, et al., 1980), typically combine office/retail and increasingly residential activities in one integrated and usually dense development. The innovation's success attests to its utility. The MXD has provided a vehicle for increasing the density of suburban centres and making them more urban in character. It has also been a key element in many recent central city developments and redevelopments, again providing new focus for otherwise dispersing activities.

Despite the growing focus and density of non-central nodes, however, there is still substantial outward movement of retail and office activity as customers and the labour force disperse. It is highly likely that the spread of offices and retailing out into the suburbs and beyond into the exurbs will continue. A critical issue is whether these activities will provide for more highly focused nodes or a more uniform distribution of activities over the urban region. The consequences for urban form of the tension between dispersion and coalescence is great indeed, but awaits additional study to assess the outcome.

(5) Investment behaviour: individuals, corporations and governments. In the end, cities and their surrounding areas take and change shape because investment decisions are made that give substance to the behaviours and trends previously discussed. Accordingly, the investment decision is the key decision to probe if we are to comprehend the nature of future urban spatial structures. A number of unknowns loom large because investment decisions are so subject to expectations about the actions of others in both private and public realms.

Expectations lie at the heart of investment behaviour, yet the role of governments and private investors in shaping expectations is at best imperfectly understood. At work is the classic 'prisoner's dilemma' where people have positive expectations when they see others also being positive and investing as a result. A large element of self-fulfilment also surrounds expectations and expectation-forming behaviour: if people believe an area is a good place to invest, they too will invest, helping to create the very environment they wanted. Disinvestment in US central cities bears sad witness to the reverse, where people with negative expectations place a high risk premium on central city investments and thus do not invest or reinvest, setting in motion a negative disinvestment/expectations cycle (Goetze, 1979; Mark and Goldberg, 1982; and Clay, 1979). Implicit in these notions is a theory of cyclical turning points that arise when expectations shift, on balance, from negative to positive and from positive to negative. Factors altering expectations span the gamut from actual changes in recent investment and location behaviour, to relative prices and attractiveness of competing neighbourhoods and urban regions, to mere anticipation of likely future changes in attractiveness. The spatial pattern of investments therefore is tied to spatial variations in expectations and perceptions of risk and return. As this spatial pattern of expectations and investments changes, so does the structure of the city region.

Of special importance is the role of government in providing the milieu within which expectations are formed and acted upon. Tax and subsidy policies and direct investments by government are clearly critical. Given the ephemeral nature of expectations, however, government must beware of the possibly unanticipated consequences from otherwise well intentioned policies. For example, urban renewal was designed to provide new built form and promote private investment. Unfortunately, bulldozing so destabilised target neighbourhoods that disinvestment actually occurred, longstanding trading and social patterns were disrupted, and further disinvestment occurred. Freeways had a similar undesirable effect on central city vitality by providing direct competition for scarce centrally located sites through opening up vast (and cheap) suburban lands, depreciating the value of centrality, promoting declines in demand for central city land and housing, thus initiating its own negative expectations/disinvestment spiral (deLeon and Enns, 1973). Rigid zoning by-laws that restrict investment and land use options can also have undesirable impacts on investment behaviour and hasten land use change and urban decline instead of protecting the zoned area from deleterious change (Mark and Goldberg, 1982).

In summary, investment behaviour and the expectations that determine it is central to shaping urban areas. The interactions between governments and individuals (both households and firms) are enormously important, not well understood, and often lead to counterproductive impacts on urban form. In view of the role of expectations, not only in growth or decline but in moving from settings of growth to decline and vice versa, caution should be exercised in seeking to influence investment behaviour and the expectations that are central to it.

Some contextual issues: the environments within which urban structure is evolving

Urban structural change is occurring against a backdrop of some major upheavals such as radical changes in technology — particularly communications and information technology — and in the structure of our Western economies. Because these fundamental, secular forces drive urban growth and structure, they need to be explored for the consequences they bear on future urban form. A final contextual element is government policy towards urban growth and structure.

(1) The changing technological environment. Technological innovation affects urban structure in at least three ways. First, technological change has transformed the structure of the Western economic system. Fewer and fewer people are needed to produce goods and perform repetitive secretarial and clerical tasks. Robotics

and office automation have already greatly altered the work place. Technology has shifted the occupational structure from unskilled and semi-skilled entry level positions in favour of professional and managerial skills. New technology has apparently also significantly reduced the numbers of people needed to run our economies, with unemployment remaining high despite the current economic recovery. In brief, the industrial structure, like the occupational structure, is undergoing considerable change. Traditional manufacturing industries — especially their production line components — are on the wane while service industries and those that generate and transform information are on the rise. Again, a premium is increasingly placed on managerial and professional abilities.

Second, these technological advances have dramatic implications for land use patterns, transportation and communications links, and urban buildings. Urban land use structure ultimately responds to and reflects the economic and social structures of society. Accompanying the aforementioned structural shifts in the economy, we can anticipate major shifts in land uses. The quantity of industrial land should diminish significantly. Offices should continue to grow in scale and importance. Thus in the aggregate we can expect more demand for land to accommodate office and related uses and less for industrial purposes. Due to the telecommunications and information processing revolution, the spatial distribution of the growing office sector is likely to be a pivotal issue in future discussions of urban structure. Communications technology, when combined with mini- and micro-computing, opens the possibility for replacing traditional offices by remote and dispersed work centres, frequently in the dwelling itself (Harkness, 1975; and Meier, 1962). The result could be an urban form that is even more dispersed than such spread out urban areas as Houston and Los Angeles. On the other hand, the necessity for maintaining and enhancing the flow of qualitative information via face-to-face communication might well continue present trends toward office concentration. Additionally, the considerable social aspect of work cannot be satisfied by remote work stations and telecommunications. Indeed, as Ratcliff (1949) has stressed, social functions and propinquity are perhaps the oldest rationales for urban living. Thus the ongoing tension between technological forces for dispersion and social and qualitative requirements for spatial concentration will keep the future structure of urban areas in a shaky equilibrium. That tension must be monitored to see how, if and when the equilibrium shifts.

A last area where technological innovation is likely to impact urban form is building technology itself and the opportunities to substitute capital for land. Empirical work has demonstrated that fairly significant substitution possibilities exist (Edelstein, 1983). Further technological advances in building design and construction, such as computer-aided design and new elevator and mechanical systems, should enhance those possibilities. Clearly, advances in building technology that lower building costs have important potential consequences for urban form.

(2) Governmental regulatory contexts of urban development and the changing technology of urban development controls. As the result of a growing desire, especially by local government, to intervene in shaping urban development patterns, the regulatory environment for urban development has changed greatly during the past two decades. In the process a broad array of land use and growth control mechanisms has been created, applied and tested in the courts and on the ground. The literature is vast and growing and need not be addressed here in any detail other than to predict that the last half of the 1980s will see an increased sophistication and willingness to act by local, regional and state/provincial governments in controlling and shaping urban growth (Urban Land Institute, 1975, 1977, 1980). In view of the balances between opposing forces for centralisation and dispersion discussed in this chapter, public policy could prove decisive in many instances. Thus, it is not at all unreasonable to expect that a dominant element in urban structure will be government and, in turn, the tastes and preferences of the governed, the citizens and entre-preneurs who influence local land use and development policies.

Political pressures are likely to be as divergent as the other trends and forces noted so far. For example, the growing professional and managerial class that is increasingly moving into the central city stands at odds with much of the current resident population over land use and development policies. Standing tenants, often of low income, want to maintain inner neighbourhoods as low cost housing enclaves. The managerial/professional entrants, on the other hand, want to re-habilitate and upgrade central areas and, of necessity, dislocate those unable to pay higher rents (Berry and Elster, 1983). Another potential source of political tension facing local government is the ongoing battle between local residents who seek to maintain lower neighbour-hood densities and developers and outsiders who want to build at higher densities either for greater profit or to provide increased housing opportunity. This conflict, repeated all across North America, and its resolution will lead to very different kinds of government regu-lation and, in turn, to very different kinds of urban structures.

An element that could play a perhaps deciding role is the ageing population. As many of the current opponents of land use change and higher density becomes older, their housing needs will shift. Their current resistance to changes in allowable land uses and densities, however, will largely preclude the new housing forms warranted by their altered life cycle positions. It is entirely conceivable that the present advocates for no change will become tomorrow's advocates for higher and more varied residential densities with the discovery that the current housing stock fails to match housing needs. Should this switch occur, it is likely that the political balance will swing towards higher housing densities, greater variation in housing types, and a more compact and focused urban form. Here again we face opposing forces whose final balance will greatly affect urban form and structure in the coming decades. In the interim, the jury is out and we cannot confidently argue for the domination of one set of forces or preferences over the other. In short, we face yet another lurking unknown affecting future urban structure.

Two caveats: one in time, one in space

A rather broad range of urban possibilities has been set out above. Particular stress has been laid on the forces and factors that may affect urban change. Left out of the discussion so far is urban non-change. Given the large standing stock of structures that will remain with us for many decades, more needs to be said about urban constants to place some useful bounds on our previous discussion of change.

Another feature of the argument so far has been its implicit basis in US urban issues and problems and in the research done on them. Thus, a second caveat relates to the generality of US urban experience.

(1) Urban constancy versus urban change. There are two senses in which urban constancy needs addressing. First, some human behaviours and preferences, and some built forms that respond to these human needs, obviously do not change greatly or quickly. The rediscovery of mixed use zoning merely takes us back to prezoning days, hardly an innovation in the strict sense of the word. Georgian and Victorian housing terraces have taken on new life in the form of row and garden apartments. Recent transportation 'discoveries' also support constancy. The streetcar circa 1900 has returned as the LRT of 1980. These recurring and successful land use and transportation forms dating from the turn of the century, by resisting change, provide for great stability. They are obviously highly adaptable urban form givers that can serve the twenty-first century urban dweller as well as his nineteenth-century counterpart. Underlying the durability of such land use and transportation 'innovations' is a constancy in the human spirit that likes propinquity and satisfies deep-seated social needs. To dream about radically different fantasy cities of the future

is to overlook the constants in human needs and preferences. In short, despite our stress on change, the city of the coming century is likely to look remarkably like the city of the last century.

A second reason to expect constancy against the background of change derives from the durability of urban built forms (Blumenfeld, 1975; and Spreiregen, 1967, make similar points). Boston's nonsensical street pattern, attributed to bovine commuting patterns in the seventeenth century, illustrates the durability of past forms. More permanent recent street patterns built in concrete will clearly be even more difficult to alter than have been the Boston cowpaths of 1630. When we fill these streets with buildings of 100-year-economic lives, there is further reason to expect a basic stability in urban structure notwithstanding all the dynamism discussed throughout this chapter.

(2) The American city is not the universal city. So much of the previous discussion, especially that concerning urban decline and population dispersal, was based on widely known US urban research that we frequently assume American urban issues to be universal. US cities differ in many ways from those of Canada (for example, Goldberg and Mercer, 1980; and Mark and Goldberg, 1982); if the cities of two nations inhabiting the same continent and growing out of very similar cultural experiences are so different, then it is clearly unreasonable to expect European and Asian cities, for example, to be subject to the same forces as those highlighted in the US literature. Accordingly, we must generalise from the US urban experience with caution. (Kendig, 1979, stresses this point concerning Australian neighbourhood revitalisation.)

The issues raised in this chapter have largely grown out of American observations and conjectures with some Canadian input. They may be relevant in a European and Asian setting as well. There is no reason to expect *a priori* that this should be the case, however, since there is no reason to expect that US and European and Asian cities have similar problems. Recent research by Hall and Hay (1980) and by van den Berg et al. (1982) in fact questions the relevance of US findings. Differences in scale, for example, immediately set US cities apart from their counterparts abroad where tighter land supplies have usually precluded the kind of extensive expansion that typifies even older urban areas in the US. Thus, while the foregoing issues may be of considerable intellectual interest, their relevance for cities outside the US needs to be carefully assessed before trying to generalise about urban structure and the forces that impinge upon it, say in Europe or Asia.

Summing up and sketching a research and policy agenda

Two overarching trends are at work shaping cities today and in the future. The first are the centrifugal forces dispersing population and jobs among urban areas (both metropolitan and non-metropolitan) and within urban areas. A second trend is centripetal and leads to a coalescing of activities about nodes. Dispersal and agglomeration are operating simultaneously. These forces are not competitive, but rather complementary.

These quite different factors shape cities within a larger and rapidly changing technological, social, economic and political environment. The changes have great consequences for the structure and functioning of cities over the coming decades and provide pressure for dramatic change. Against this backdrop of change, however, we must appreciate that there are also significant forces for stability and constancy. The ultimate outcome depends on the various tensions that need to be resolved, tensions that result from the pulls from the dynamic and static elements impinging upon urban structure. Deep-seated human needs for companionship and propinquity need to be played out against desires for higher living standards and privacy. Technological wizardry which can lead to greater disperson needs to be understood in the context of preferences for personal contact.

In sum, the future course of urban development is tied to an impressive array of unknowns and variables. Prediction is foolish in such an environment. Careful monitoring and study of the forces of growth and change however is prudent and necessary if we are to make effective and appropriate public policy decisions. Thus, we must address some of the more important elements that will comprise a research and policy agenda for monitoring and guiding city growth and structure into the next century.

A research agenda

A central issue that was raised at the end of our discussion related to the generality of the trends and forces noted. Two major themes permeate this research agenda: the need to assess the generality of these propositions over space (e.g. their relevance from one country and region to the next); and the need to identify the stability of urban structural forces over time. The first issue revolves around how different are the contexts within which cities develop, while the second focuses essentially on the similarities among cities and people over time. More specifically, we need to assess and establish the stability of the forces and trends set out in the body of this chapter. Is each stable over time? How do they vary over space?

Much more needs to be understood about the various behaviours discussed. What are the determinants of the behaviours of investors, households, and firms, particularly concerning their locational decisions? How do people react to government policies? How effectively do governments shape the course of urban development? In short, we need fundamental information about the functioning of urban land markets and the decision makers involved (firms, households and governments).

✓ Finally, a better understanding of the relationships between macro and micro forces impinging on urban structure is required. For example, what is the relationship between inter-regional population and job movements and intra-urban mobility, house prices and land use structure? What conscious and unconscious roles do governments play in affecting inter-regional and intra-urban mobility? Do micro-economic forces at the level of urban land and housing markets have significant feedbacks to inter-regional population and job flows (or vice versa)?

Clearly, there is no shortage of issues for research. Virtually all the factors discussed previously require deeper study and in many more locations and over longer periods of time.

Shaping urban policy to shape cities: a policy agenda

The policy requirements for the city of the next century will differ in detail from those of the city of today, but there are broad policy areas which will still need to be addressed independently of our time frame. Ideally, they should be based on the knowledge gained from research. The major policy areas include transportation and communication, land use, economic development and growth.

Transportation and communication. The trade-off between transportation and land use intensity is well established, but we must now add to our transportation policies the realisation that telecommunications substitute for travel as well as land use intensity.

Land use. More intense and effective use of scarce urban land resources is already a requirement of land use planning and control. In the future, pressures on scarce resources are likely to intensify. Land use change and adaptation in the face of more complex transportation/communication policy will be particularly challenging (Goldberg, 1981). So will coping with the more diverse needs of a changing society. Land use decisions are particularly important both because of the durability of the built forms that they shape, and because of the uncertain context within which they must be made.

Flexibility and adaptation emerge as key ingredients in future policy for they allow us to absorb some of the uncertainty that abounds in the planning environment, uncertainty rooted in the numerous behaviours and trends discussed in this chapter.

Economic development. Economic planning has largely been reserved for higher levels of government. Increasingly, however, local governments need to become involved in shaping their economic structure. For example, the City of Vancouver created the Vancouver Economic Advisory Commission to advise on economic policy matters and to complement the longstanding Vancouver Planning Commission that for decades had provided independent advice on land use and transportation planning matters. Recognition of the role of economic development and structure in forming the future city is critical for successfully translating the secular forces in our macro-economic system into meaningful and consistent policy for urban areas.

Growth. The 1960s and 1970s demonstrated that cities do indeed have some significant capabilities for regulating their scale and character. Having demonstrated the feasibility of growth control and management we must face the political issue of just how much. The recent recession has pointed out that growth was not an unquestioned 'bad' just as the 1970s showed us it was not an unquestioned 'good'. Given the perspective provided from the 1980s we now must sort the good from the bad to try to evolve growth management strategies that provide for the best of growth and stability and that simultaneously try to avoid the worst of chaotic change and stagnating regulation.

In closing, the tasks ahead are formidable. We cannot realistically expect to solve or even define all the problems and issues set out here (and others overlooked). We can acknowledge their importance, however, and get down to work to enhance our understanding and improve our policy effectiveness. The present discussion has sought to raise issues and point out directions. The more difficult task of getting on with the job remains and provides us with an exciting, if awesome, challenge.

References

Alonso, W. (1964), 'The Historic and the Structural Theories of Urban Form: their Implications for Urban Renewal', *Land Economics*, vol. 40, no. 2, pp. 227–231.

Alonso, W. (1983), 'The Demographic Factor in Housing for the Balance of this Century', *North American Housing Markets into the Twenty-first Century* (G.W. Gau and M.A. Goldberg, eds), Ballinger Publishing Co., Cambridge, Mass., pp. 33—50.

Baerwald, T.J. (1982), 'Land Use Change in Suburban Clusters and Corridors', *Transportation Research Record*, no. 861, pp. 7—12.

van den Berg, L., R. Drewett, L.H. Klaassen, A. Rossi and C.H.T. Vijverberg (1982), *Urban Europe: A Study of Growth and Decline*, Pergamon, Oxford.

Berry, B.J.L. (1976), *Urbanization and Counter-urbanization*, Sage Publications, Beverly Hills, Ca.

Berry, B.J.L. (1978), 'The Counterurbanization Process: How General?', *Human Settlement Systems: International Perspectives on Structure, Change and Public Policy* (N.M. Hansen, ed.), Ballinger Publishing Co., Cambridge, Mass.

Berry, B.J.L. and D.C. Dahmann (1977), 'Population Redistribution in the United States in the 1970s', *Population and Development Review*, vol. 3, no. 4, pp. 443—71.

Berry, B.J.L. and S. Elster (1983), 'What Lies Ahead for Urban America', School of Urban and Public Affairs, Carnegie-Mellon University, Pittsburgh, Pa (mimeographed).

Birch, D.L. (1979), *The Job Generation Process*, MIT Press, Cambridge, Mass.

Blumenfeld, H. (1975), 'Continuity and Change in Urban Form', *Journal of Urban History*, vol. 1, no. 2, pp. 131—47.

Bourne, L.S. (1982), 'Emergent Realities of Urbanization in Canada: some Parameters and Implications of Declining Growth', *Planning under Regional Stagnation* (W. Buhr and P. Friedrich, eds), Nomos Verlagsgesellschaft, Baden-Baden, West Germany.

Bourne, L.S. (1983), 'Living with Uncertainty: the Changing Spatial Components of Urban Growth and Housing Demand in Canada', *North American Housing Markets into the Twenty-first Century* (G.W. Gau and M.A. Goldberg, eds), Ballinger Publishing Co., Cambridge, Mass., pp. 51—72.

Bradbury, K.L., A. Downs and K.A. Small (1982), *Urban Decline and the Future of American Cities*, The Brookings Institution, Washington, D.C.

Brown, P.W. (1983), 'The Demographic Future: Impacts on the Demand for Housing in Canada, 1981—2001', *North American Housing Markets in the Twenty-first Century* (G.W. Gau and M.A. Goldberg, eds), Ballinger Publishing Co., Cambridge, Mass., pp. 5—31.

Burns, L.S. (1982), 'Metropolitan Growth in Transition', *Journal of Urban Economics*, vol. 11, pp. 112—29.

Clay, P.L. (1979), *Neighborhood Renewal*, D.C. Heath, Lexington, Mass.

Dantzig, G.B. and T.L. Saaty (1973), *The Compact City*, W.H. Freeman and Co., San Francisco, Ca.

deLeon, P. and J. Enns (1973), *The Impact of Highways upon Metropolitan Dispersion: St. Louis*, Research Memorandum P-5061, The Rand Corp., Santa Monica, Ca.

Dunphy, R.T. (1982), 'Defining Regional Employment Centers in an Urban Area', *Transportation Research Record*, no. 861, pp. 13—15.

Edelstein, R.G. (1983), 'The Production Function for Housing and its Implications for Future Urban Development', *North American Housing Markets into the Twenty-first Century* (G.W. Gau and M.A. Goldberg, eds), Ballinger Publishing Co., Cambridge, Mass., pp. 93—125.

Evans, A. and D. Eversley (eds) (1980), *The Inner City: Employment and Industry*, Heinemann, London.

Foley, D.L. (1964), 'An Approach to Metropolitan Spatial Structure', *Explorations into Urban Spatial Structure* (M.W. Webber et al., eds), University of Pennsylvania Press, Philadelphia, Pa., pp. 32—78.

Gertler, L.O. (1983), 'The Changing Metropolis and the Blumenfeld Blues', School of Urban and Regional Planning, University of Waterloo, Ont. (mimeographed).

Goetze, R. (1979), *Understanding Neighborhood Change*, Ballinger Publishing Co., Cambridge, Mass.

Goldberg, M.A. (1981), 'Transportation Systems and Urban Form: Performance Measures and Data Requirements', *International Symposium on Surface Transportation System Performance Proceedings*, vol. II, US Department of Transportation, Washington, D.C., pp. 259—68.

Goldberg, M.A. and J. Mercer (1980), 'Canadian and U.S. Cities: Basic Differences, Possible Explanations and their Meaning for Public Policy', *Papers of the Regional Science Association*, vol. 45, pp. 159—83.

Guttenberg, A.E. (1964), 'The Tactical Plan', *Explorations into Urban Spatial Structure* (M.M. Webber et al., eds), University of Pennsylvania Press, Philadelphia, Pa., pp. 197—219.

Hall, P.A. and D. Hay (1980), *Growth Centres in the European Urban System*, Heinemann, London.

Hansen, N.M. (ed.) (1978), *Human Settlement Systems: International Perspectives on Structure, Change and Public Policy*, Ballinger Publishing Co., Cambridge, Mass.

Harkness, R.C. (1975), *The Impact of Changing Telecommunications Technology*, Stanford Research Institute, Menlo Park, Ca.

Hoch, I. (1969), 'The Three-dimensional City: Contained Urban Space', *The Quality of the Urban Environment* (H.S. Perloff, ed.), Johns Hopkins University Press, pp. 75—135.

Hooper, D., J.W. Simmons and L.S. Bourne (1983), 'The Changing Economic Basis of Canadian Urban Growth, 1971—81', Research Paper no. 139, Centre for Urban and Community Studies, University of Toronto, Toronto, Ont.

Hoover, E.W. (1975), *Introduction to Regional Economics*, A.A. Knopf, New York, N.Y.

Hoyt, H. (1964), 'Recent Distortions of the Classical Models of Urban Structure', *Land Economics*, vol. 40, no. 2, pp. 199—212.

Jacobs, J. (1961), *The Death and Life of Great American Cities*, Vintage Books, New York, N.Y.

Kellas, H. (1983), 'Greater Vancouver: a Transit and Land Use Strategy for Managing Growth', paper presented to the Transportation Research Board Annual Meetings, Washington, D.C.

Kendig, H. (1979), *New Life for Old Suburbs*, George Allen and Unwin, Sydney, Australia.

Korcelli, P. (1976), 'Theory of Intra-urban Structure: Review and Synthesis, A Cross-cultural Perspective', *Geographica Polonica*, vol. 31, pp. 99—131.

Korcelli, P. (1982), 'Migration and Urban Change', *International Regional Science Review*, vol. 2, no. 2, pp. 193—216.

Laska, S.B. and D. Spain (eds) (1980), *Back to the City*, Pergamon Press, New York, N.Y.

Leven, C.L. (1978), *The Mature Metropolis*, D.C. Heath, Lexington, Mass.

Mark, J.H. and M.A. Goldberg (1982), 'Neighbourhood Change: A Canadian Perspective', Urban Land Economics Working Paper no. 24, Faculty of Commerce and Business Administration, The University of British Columbia, Vancouver, B.C. (mimeographed).

McKeever, J.R. and N. Griffin (1980), *Shopping Center Development Handbook*, Urban Land Institute, Washington, D.C.

Meadows, P. (1957), 'The City, Technology and History', *Social Forces*, vol. 36, pp. 141—7.

Meier, R.L. (1962), *A Communications Theory of Urban Growth*, MIT Press, Cambridge, Mass.

Moomaw, R. (1981), 'Productivity and City Size: A Critique of the Evidence', *Quarterly Journal of Economics*, vol. 96, no. 4, pp. 676—88.

Morrill, R.L. (1970), *The Spatial Organization of Society*, Wadsworth Publishing Co., Belmont, Ca.

Morris, R.S. (1978), *Bum Rap on America's Cities: the Real Causes of Urban Decay*, Prentice-Hall, Englewood Cliffs, N.J.

Mumford, L. (1961), *The City in History*, Harcourt, Brace and World, New York, N.Y.

Nelson, H.J. (1969), 'The Form and Structure of Cities: Urban Growth Patterns', *Journal of Geography*, vol. 68, no. 4, pp. 198–207.

Noguchi, T. (1982), 'Shaping a Suburban Activity Center through Transit and Pedestrian Incentives: Bellevue CBD Planning Experiences', *Transportation Research Record*, no. 861, pp. 1–6.

Norton, R.D. (1979), *City Life-cycles and American Urban Policy*, Academic Press Inc., New York, N.Y.

Passonneau, J.R. (1963), 'The Emergence of City Form', *Urban Life and Form* (W.Z. Hirsch, ed.), Holt, Rinehart and Winston, New York, N.Y., pp. 9–27.

Porell, F.W. (1982), 'Intermetropolitan Migration and Quality of Life', *Journal of Regional Science*, vol. 22, no. 2, pp. 137–58.

Ratcliff, R.U. (1949), *Urban Land Economics*, McGraw-Hill Book Co., New York, N.Y.

Schnore, L.F. (1963), 'Urban Form: the Case of the Metropolitan Community', *Urban Life and Form* (W.Z. Hirsch, ed.), Holt, Rinehart and Winston, New York, N.Y.

Solomon, A.P. (ed.) (1980), *The Prospective City*, MIT Press, Cambridge, Mass.

Spreiregen, P.D. (ed.) (1967), *The Modern Metropolis*, MIT Press, Cambridge, Mass.

Sternlieb, G. and J.W. Hughes (eds) (1975), *Post-industrial America: Metropolitan Decline and Interregional Job Shifts*, Center for Urban Policy Research, Rutgers University, New Brunswick, N.J.

Struyk, R. and F.J. James (1975), *Intrametropolitan Industrial Location*, D.C. Heath, Lexington, Mass.

Thomlinson, R. (1969), *Urban Structure*, Random House, New York, N.Y.

Tweeten, L. and G.L. Brinkman (1976), *Micropolitan Development*, The Iowa State University Press, Ames, Ia.

Urban Land Institute (1975, 1977, 1980), *Management and Control of Urban Growth*, vols I–V, Urban Land Institute, Washington, D.C.

Webber, M.M. (1963), 'Order in Diversity: Community without Propinquity', *Cities and Space* (Lowdon Wingo Jr, ed.), Johns Hopkins University Press, pp. 23–56.

Webber, M.M. (1964), 'The Urban Place and the Nonplace Urban Realm', *Explorations into Urban Spatial Structure* (M.M. Webber et al., eds), University of Pennsylvania Press, Philadelphia, Pa., pp. 79–153.

Webber, M.M. (1968), 'The Postcity Age', *Daedalus*, vol. 97, no. 4, pp. 1091–1110.

Weller, R.H. (1967), 'An Empirical Examination of Metropolitan Structure', *Demography*, vol. 4, pp. 734–43.

Witherspoon, R.E., J.P. Abbett and R.M. Gladstone (1976), *Mixed-use Developments: New Ways of Land Use*, Urban Land Institute, Washington, D.C.

Wurster, C.B. (1963), 'The Form and Structure of the Future Urban Complex', *Cities and Space* (Lowdon Wingo Jr, ed.), Johns Hopkins University Press, Baltimore, Md, pp. 73–102.

4 Analysis of episodes in urban event histories

BÖRJE JOHANSSON AND PETER NIJKAMP

Events and episodes in urban dynamics

In the past decades urban growth patterns have exhibited dramatic shifts, in both developed and developing countries, and in both market and planned economies. *Steady* growth patterns have evolved into fluctuating development paths. In addition, various subsystems within an urban system display different evolutionary patterns due to differences in adjustment speeds. Urban dynamics is nowadays marked by a complexity that is hard to disentangle by means of conventional analytical tools (see also Johansson et al., 1983).

In the context of fundamental and sometimes drastic changes in an urban system, it may be fruitful to introduce some new concepts. The first one is an *event*. In formal statistical terms an event is a subset of the sample space, so that the probability of its occurrence can be assessed by means of an underlying probability distribution. Thus an event represents a specific state from a feasible state space, with a certain probability of occurrence in a given time interval. In the framework presented in this chapter, it is especially interesting to focus attention on *changes*. Therefore, an event will be interpreted here as a distinct change in a state variable; or a distinct switch from one change pattern to another with regard to a particular variable or subsystem.

In relation to events, another term, episodes, may be introduced. An episode in urban dynamics or in urban history will be regarded here as a change pattern that is distinctive and separate from previous

43

patterns although part of a larger series of episodes in urban history. For instance, a steady change pattern or dynamic process may be termed an *episode*. Consequently, an event is a transition from one episode to another. Hence, a switch from fast growth to stagnation or to decline of a certain variable represents events for which observations on this variable can be measured at discrete time intervals. Evolutionary patterns of a dynamic system are then transformed into a series of events such that each is associated with the start of a new episode. (Formally, an event may be either a 'new' event leading to a new episode; or a 'redundant' event implying the continuation of an episode.) A whole evolution path is then divided into a series of episodes describing urban history. For instance, a change in urban finances from a state of solvency into bankruptcy may be regarded as a transition between two episodes. Urban fluctuations in the past decades may be interpreted as episodic growth patterns. With another time scale, a period of rapid variations forms an episode in contradistinction to a preceding or succeeding period of steady change.

In this chapter, the notions of events and episodes will be employed to design a formal methodological framework for studying urban evolutionary patterns and variations in those patterns.

Methodological relevance

In the past decade, many advances in the area of discrete spatial analysis have been made, for instance, by means of logit and probit analysis, generalised log-linear models and soft modelling (see, for an extensive survey, Nijkamp et al., 1984). As observations on urban events and episodes are often of a discrete nature, it is clear that discrete data analysis is a powerful tool for studying complex urban systems, witness also the great many applications in this field.

In recent years especially, panel studies and longitudinal data analyses have increasingly come to the fore, particularly in behavioural analyses of disaggregate (spatial) choice behaviour (see also Coleman, 1981). Several applications in the area of transportation and residential mobility reflect the potential of panel and longitudinal analysis for studying the determinants of individual episodes in a spatial context.

Modelling long-term processes based on discrete states, however, is far more complicated and is only recently receiving attention in social science research. For instance, discrete-state, continuous-time, stochastic models have hardly been applied in urban and regional research, though some examples can be found in Griffith and Lea (1983). The analysis of event histories in an urban context no doubt deserves more attention, especially because urban evolution in many countries is exhibiting highly unstable episodes.

Some illustrations of industrial episodes in an urban region

A typical example of successive economic/industrial episodes in an urban area would be a transition from a manufacturing base to one dominated by banking and other service activities. During this century the Gothenburg region in Sweden experienced the following episodes: textile, shipyard, and automobile industrial dominance. An urban region with an economy based on the extraction of natural resources, like coal in the Dortmund region, may experience dramatic transitions between growth, stagnation and drastic decline. The Silicon Valley in the San Francisco Bay area provides an example of a 'high technology episode' initiated during the second half of the 1960s.

For metropolitan regions one may also observe how a period of creativity and innovation is followed by a period of productivity, expansion and a fading away of creativity. From this point of view, Jane Jacobs's suggestive story about Manchester and Birmingham in the middle of the last century is revealing (Jacobs, 1969). At that time Manchester was admired for its productivity and efficiency based on large-scale specialisation. On the other hand Birmingham's economy with a multiplicity of seemingly unorganised production activities was viewed as unstructured. This environment, however, gave rise to a period of novel development characterised by combination and successful innovations; at the same time Manchester lagged behind, a casualty of its own success during an earlier period. An episode with a concentration on already established innovations logically bears fruit in the form of a transition to a phase with large-scale solutions, but an increased rigidity that excludes activities that have the potential for renewing the system. What follows is an episode of obsolescence and decline.

Urban dynamics as an event history

Urban dynamics as mutlifaceted events

Urban dynamics is related to a structure with spatial and temporal coordinates. This structure presupposes relationships between phenomena in space and time so that complex, multifaceted and nested patterns in a geographical structure of cities may emerge, sometimes leading to discontinuous space—time trajectories of the variables involved.

Consequently, due to large fluctuations caused by dissipative structures affecting the homogeneity and isotropy of space and time, the geographical structure of cities may become unstable and even exhibit bifurcations (cf. Turner, 1980). Unexpected switches in the change paths may take place especially if the subsystems of an urban system (like transportation, housing, industry, or facilities) are intertwined in a non-linear dynamic way with differences in the successive rates of change (cf. also Haag and Weidlich, 1983). Urban episodes of a stable evolution may turn into new events — sudden shocks, for example — so that the evolution of a city can be described by means of its event history.

Given the complexity involved in describing and analysing urban dynamics, special attention must be paid to the *driving forces* of *key factors* of the urban system's space—time trajectory. Key factors may be regarded as those stimuli that drive the space—time trajectory of an urban system (or of its components) without being affected in the same time period or in the same geographical area by endogenous variables describing the state of the system or of its components. There are various ways to identify such key factors of an urban system:

— an analysis of the *functional* structure of a model describing the system by focusing special attention on *predetermined* (exogenous and lagged endogenous) variables. This is the usual procedure in conventional economic modelling;

— a *causality* analysis of the interwoven structure of a complex urban system with the autonomous nodes of such a system identified by means of *graph-theoretic* approaches; for example, by calculating the causality degree of the urban system or of some of its constituents (see Blommestein and Nijkamp, 1983);

— a *mathematical* analysis of the Boolean structure of an urban system that attempts to triangularise the system as a means to derive a nested or multilevel structure exhibiting the successive driving forces (see van der Hee et al., 1978);

— a formal analysis of the *dynamic* structure of an urban system in order to identify the probability that dissipative patterns will emerge, so that internal dynamic interactions — for instance, different transition rates for intertwined phenomena — may be identified as 'change generators' for the urban system's space—time trajectory. Especially in the latter, more dynamic-oriented interpretation of key factors, the above-mentioned notions of episodes and events play a meaningful role, for co-evolution or incongruencies of episodes and events may also be analysed more precisely and related to possible singularities and bifurcations (see also Haining, 1983).

Finally, the analysis of urban episodes and events must consider the impact of *constraints* on the emergence of urban events. Here three distinctions can be made (see also Nijkamp, 1983):

- *threshold* conditions: constraints acting as necessary conditions before an urban episode can be changed and a new event takes place;
- *bottleneck* conditions: constraints that preclude the continuation of an urban episode, so that without a removal of these constraints a new urban event would come about;
- *synergistic* conditions: coupled constraints that are mutually dependent, so that a removal of one constraint has an effect only if the other one is also eliminated.

These three types of constraint are extremely relevant in an urban dynamic context; cities need a minimum endowment with facilities before they can really start growing (the threshold phenomenon); the growth of cities may draw to a close if agglomeration diseconomies such as congestion arise (the bottleneck phenomenon); and balanced urban development will occur only if private productive capital and public overhead capital are finely tuned (the synergistic phenomenon; see also Hirschman, 1958). These issues will be elaborated in the next subsections.

Industrial dynamics as an event history

In this study 'industry' embraces all kinds of production including the output delivered to markets outside the urban region; this means that the selling price is determined by factors external to the region. The viability of such production activities is then affected by the region's capability for delivering the output at prices which do not exceed those of external competitors.

The establishment of a new production activity constitutes an event which eventually gives rise to a specific industrial episode with certain genetic characteristics. An innovation generated within the region or imported production knowledge (imitation) may stimulate such an event (see also Davies, 1979). The continuation of the production requires a gradual adaptation of the productivity to the evolving standard of external competitors. This may take the form of a successive development of the product attributes as a means to retain a market share without reducing the output price. Also when some product development occurs, the overall development is frequently dominated by attempts to increase the production scale as a means of raising the productivity and thereby augmenting the ability to supply at a lower relative price.

Increased production scale has many effects. It increases the regional specialisation and this may also attract associated production activities. However, increased scale also implies a certain degree of exclusion of those activities competing for the same inputs like specific types of labour force, land, infrastructure facilities, etc. Although increased scale, with few exceptions, is accompanied by a qualitative improvement in the production process, there is usually a technological limit for the scale-dependent increase of productivity (see Wibe, 1982). Therefore, the marginal returns to scale decrease as scale rises. As a consequence, increased production scale and specialisation finally represents a dead end with stagnation and a loss of flexibility due to the specialisation. In this way a process of gradually intensified specialisation represents a typical industrial episode created by the interaction between external competition and market demand, and internal responses in the form of increased production scale.

This interaction between the urban production system and external competitors may be modelled as an endogenous process within the framework of a product cycle theory (see Andersson and Johansson, 1984). In this theory the diffusion of production knowledge to new competitors is assumed to be easier as the production scale grows with associated reduced requirements on the labour force's competence. Thus, the economic development of a region or a city can be characterised by a variety of episodes, each of which is induced by exogenous or endogenous events.

Interaction between infrastructure and industrial episodes

The typified or stylised version of industrial development described in the preceding subsection can be enriched by the case of an expanding industry that provides a breeding place from which employees leave and initiate new production based on acquired ideas and experiences. To what extent this latter process takes place critically depends on how the infrastructure develops. Infrastructure is regarded here as the stock of public capital that is supplied to regions or cities as a complement to productive capital in order to increase production efficiency (see Biehl et al., 1982; and Hirschman, 1958).

The time scales of industrial and infrastructure capital may differ considerably. Many of the extensive infrastructure systems for transportation and communication are created:

— under conditions of indivisibilities;
— with long gestation lags; and
— with built-in technological rigidities.

This implies that the turnover time of the industrial production equipment and technical solutions may be considerably shorter but more flexible than that of the infrastructure systems. Under these conditions the development of facilities and service systems, as well as provision of land, becomes subordinated to the production that dominates the urban region. Two aspects are important: if infrastructural development lags behind, incongruencies may arise to hamper the development of expanding activities; and if the design of the service systems becomes biased in favour of expanding activities, they will not provide a fertile environment for new potential production activities.

It is important to observe that attempts to link industrial with infrastructural development in a conditional probability setting may require an aggregation or clustering approach. For example, when studying a single industrial activity or sector, a subset of infrastructural systems may be grouped together, and their compound development may constitute an episode from the viewpoint of the industrial sector. Reciprocally, the development and episode of a certain infrastructure subsystem may be linked with an episode constituted by the aggregate change path of a whole set of clustered industrial sectors.

Statistical analysis of event histories

The study of spatial dynamics already has a long history. First attempts at describing space—time trajectories can be found in conventional *space—time geography* (see, for instance, Hägerstrand, 1970), in which the evolution of a spatial system and its actors was described in continuous space at both an aggregate and disaggregate level.

The next stage meant a more formalised focus on *location—allocation* problems. This episode in the history of analysing spatial dynamics was *inter alia* based on dynamic programming and optimal control theory. Most of these models were aggregate in nature.

Then more emphasis was placed on *discrete spatial* models encompassing distinct choice issues, for instance, in transportation, labour market and housing market analysis (see, among others, Clark, 1983; van Lierop and Nijkamp, 1984; and Leonardi, 1983). These are mainly disaggregate models that do not analyse the behaviour of the system as a whole or its subsystems.

In recent years, much attention has also been paid to *panel studies and longitudinal data analysis*, in which the intertemporal evolution of distinct events is analysed on the basis of discrete time intervals (see also Coleman, 1981). Most of these techniques and models focus on micro events.

Finally, the most recent development can be found in the area of *event history analysis* (see Hannan and Tuma, 1984; and Tuma and Hannan, 1984). Event history analysis examines changes and transitions in qualitative variables. It is based on information about sequences and timing of transitions and is regarded as a new tool in analysing causal hypotheses regarding qualitative spatiotemporal data.

Because event-history design has recently become an important analytical tool in both sociology and demography, it is worthwhile investigating its potential for studying spatial dynamic systems. In the social sciences, transition problems have often been described by means of *Markov models*, which are usually purely descriptive without an explicit treatment of causal relations. The underlying assumption of stationary processes is, however, not very valid, while the use of panel data in social dynamics research is not always appropriate (due to identification and consistency problems). Therefore, event history design may be meaningful, as has been demonstrated in biostatistics and reliability theory. Spatiotemporal examples of event history design can be found *inter alia* in studies dealing with the dynamics of labour markets (cf. Tuma and Robins, 1980), marital status (cf. Hannen et al., 1978) and migration patterns (cf. Sandefur and Scott, 1981).

In general, an *event history* (or sample path observation) plan records relevant information on all changes in a state variable within some observation period, so that this method may be especially suitable for studying discrete changes in the evolution of a phenomenon. An *event history* w over a certain period (τ_1, τ_2) can be represented as:

$$w\,(\tau_1, \tau_2) = [y(t) \cdot \tau_1 \leqslant t \leqslant \tau_2],$$

where $y(t)$ is the qualitative value (occurrence or not, for example) of a variable under consideration at time period t. Clearly, $y(t)$ may take any distinct value from the state space y, i.e. $y(t) \in Y$.

This can be exemplified as follows. Suppose an urban system adopts three different stages: urban growth (episode 1), urban decline (episode 2) and urban stagnation (episode 3). Then an episodic representation of the urban history may lead to a sequence of specific growth paths as illustrated in Figure 4.1.

Each jump from the one episode to the next one may be called an event n $(n = 1, \ldots, N)$ in the urban history. Thus altogether, there are N events in the urban history of Figure 4.1. These events take place at time period $(t_1, t_2, \ldots, t_N$, so that the event history of the city from period t_1 onwards can be represented as follows:

$$w(t_1, \tau_2) = [(t_1, T_1), (t_2, Y_2), \ldots, (t_N, Y_N)]$$

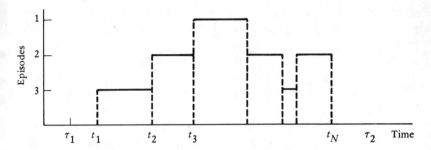

Figure 4.1   A representation of urban episodes

According to Hannan and Tuma (1984), there are three different possibilities to define statistical measures for assessing the probability of the occurrence of events:

1   *survivor function:* defines the probability that an event takes place after time t_n, given the initial conditions w_n: (Prob($T_{n+1} \geqslant t_n \mid w_n$). This probability can be estimated by means of maximum likelihood methods;

2   *waiting-time distribution function:* defines the probability that a certain event will take place based on the cumulative distribution function for the waiting time (i.e. length of intervals between successive events): Prob($U_n < t \mid w_{n-1}$). Here maximum likelihood methods can also be employed;

3   *hazard function:* defines the probability of an event at time t failing by means of a hazard rate, given that the hazard (event) has not occurred before time t. The hazard can be defined in terms of a corresponding survivor function, and can be estimated by means of a maximum likelihood technique.

An important element in event history analysis is not only the estimation of the probability that an event takes place (implying a different state of the system), but also *which* new state will be attained. Such a situation of conditional probabilities can also be illustrated as follows. Suppose that the growth of an urban subsystem is markedly reduced or stops. The succeeding potential events may be stagnation or decline. Moreover, a decline episode may or may not be coupled with an expansion phase in another subsystem. The possibility of such interdependencies illustrates the importance of a problem- or hypothesis-determined classification of events, i.e. how subsystems are aggregated or clustered in order to define a variable for which episodes are examined.

Event history analysis may in particular be used to define causality relationships between event probabilities and explanatory variables; and probabilities of simultaneous (coupled) events.

For discrete data, this type of enquiry may rely on log-linear model specifications so that positive probabilities (or positive transition rates for events) are ensured (see, for example, Arminger, 1984).

It is important to observe the time-hierarchical relation between events and episodes. A growth curve like the one in time interval (t_0, t_1) in Figure 4.2 may be treated as a series of repetitions of the same event at all points in time within the interval. In the second interval (t_1, t_2) another episode is identified, once again built up by repeated events of continuing the episode.

The probability of an event or the transition rate for events in the figure are clearly distinct from the rate of change that characterises the episode.

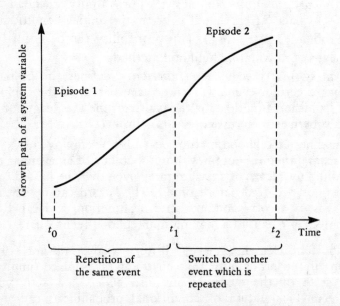

Figure 4.2 Illustration of events and episodes

Further extensions of event history analysis can be found in higher-order (nested) dynamics, in which the transition rates may also become time-dependent. In such cases, logistic specifications may be used (see Hannan and Tuma, 1984, for further details). Problems of spatiotemporal auto- and cross-correlation can be handled, especially in the framework of Lisrel V models for discrete variables (see Folmer, 1984).

So far the *spatial* aspects of event history analysis have hardly been treated. Even in panel and longitudinal analysis the spatial dimension has not been covered in a fully satisfactory way. Event history analysis may provide important insights into urban dynamics, for it:

- collects information on the sequence and timing of events in the urban evolution;
- provides a potential for testing causal hypotheses in a dynamic urban system marked by discrete events; and
- allows the inclusion of qualitative spatial data in stochastic process models for urban dynamics.

Interaction between industrial and infrastructural episodes

The breeding place principle

As discussed earlier, the regional activity structure forms an environment that may give birth to new varieties of old activities as well as qualitatively new activities or innovations. The Birmingham example illustrates novelty by combination based on richness of young activities. The Silicon Valley type of innovation development exemplifies a process in which new ideas are spun off from successful firms as a result of employees leaving to start up new firms. In this way successful firms breed new firms which eventually become strong competitors.

A specialisation-based breeding process like the recent microelectronic development in Silicon Valley or in New England has been driven by a situation where demand grows faster than output. Such a situation, if combined with a continuing inflow of a knowledge-intensive, competent and creative labour force, allows for a repeated multiplication of successful organisations. As soon as any of these requisites disappears, successful firms will prevent splitting, increase the specialisation and thereby more efficiently exclude the emergence of novelties outside the organisation (see also the principle of competitive exclusion formulated by Sonis, 1983).

When agglomerations are sufficiently large, the growth of successful organisations can follow a path along which a variety of simultaneous specialisation is retained. This is an environmental prerequisite for continuing novelty by combination. In this latter case a scale effect delays the movement towards the stage where specialisation leads to spatial exclusion.

Another basic requisite with regard to product and process development is related to infrastructure characteristics of the region. There must be an inflow and internal breeding of knowledge and knowledge-intensive employment categories. And this is related to the R & D institutions and R & D investments in the region.

Challenge and response principle in urban dynamics

The historical, often irreversible growth patterns of cities exhibit a heterogeneous nature that can be ascribed partly to locational conditions (see last section), and partly to endogenous mechanisms in the functioning of an urban system. Events such as the rise and disappearance of cities can only be understood if we are able to provide an endogenous explanatory framework for transition processes. Examples can be found in the traditional Schumpeterian lines of thought (see, for instance, Thomas, 1972) and in the more recent paradigms of self-organisation (see, for instance, Allen and Sanglier, 1979). Most of these theories, however, provide an *internal* explanation of dynamics without relating the dynamics to external developments.

In this regard, it may be useful to refer to Toynbee's *challenge and response* principle (see Toynbee, 1961), in which the author demonstrates that the historical development of societies is determined by the way in which they react to challenges, whether internal or external. Decline and disappearance is then determined by lack of adequate response relative to the response of others. In our terms, it means that the transition of one urban episode to another is dependent on the nature of public policy responses in order to meet internal and external challenges.

- *Existence of threshold values* related to endowment of infrastructure, labour force competence and scientific knowledge.
- *Lack of innovation:* if the urban production system is 'driving to maturity' new production structures, new institutional arrangements and new urban patterns are needed. Such a renewal process needs support from social overhead and R & D capital (see Nijkamp, 1983).
- *Presence of bottlenecks:* if the urban economy is reaching a saturation phase, the drive to maturity is drawing to a close due

to capacity constraints (congestion, old infrastructure, lack of R & D activities, etc.) (see for a formal approach to this phenomenon based on individual discrete choice models, Miyao and Shapiro, 1981). Drastic events such as the construction of new infrastructure, the design of new physical plant and the introduction of advanced technology are then necessary.

The above-mentioned challenges and responses for the episodes of an urban history are represented in Figure 4.3.

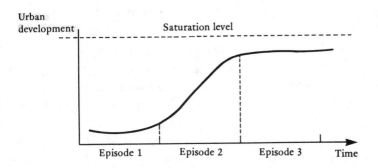

Figure 4.3   Episodes in a challenge—response view of urban history

External challenges may be subdivided into the following categories:

— *progress of other cities:* in general, an urban economy is small compared to the national or international economy, so that cities have to compete with each other for exports to a nationwide or international market. The economic success of a city is then determined by its export-base orientation. If other cities grow faster, investors/decision makers in a city *k* will receive signals about where and how to direct their efforts in order to keep pace or catch up with the development in other urban regions, for example by imitation or creation of adequate production facilities. 'Jealousy'-type signals may stimulate city *k* to be more innovative if its relative position with respect to others is weakening;
— *lack of coordination:* in linked economies, public policy requires coordinated policy measures between cities in a spatial system. In an economy with a decentralised institutional structure, coordination of policies can be frustrated by autonomous spatial

entities — cities, for example, that use their power to reinforce their position in the national economy or to force policy makers to provide them with more advantages than others.

Illustration of subsystem interactions

Some of the processes discussed in preceding sections are illustrated by the following prototype model (compare Batten, 1983):

$$\dot{v}_i = \mu_i v_i [N_i - v_i - \epsilon_i v_j] - \gamma_i v_i \; ; i,j = 1,2 \tag{1}$$

where v_i denotes production of type i with μ_i and γ_i as entry (expansion) and exit (depreciation or removal) rates, respectively. N_i represents a given upper limit on the production level v_i. When $\epsilon_i \geqslant 0$ for $i=1,2$, the ϵ-coefficients will reflect the competition between the two types of production. A negative ϵ_i signifies that sector i is positively stimulated by the growth of the other sector. With this model we may consider various types of episodes.

Suppose at time $t < t_o$ that $v_1(t) > 0$ and $v_2(t) = 0$. Then we consider the occurrence of entry as an event, identified by $\dot{v}_2(t_o + \tau) > 0$ as $\tau \geqslant 0$. Such an event is characterised by the episode attached to it. Three cases will be discussed,

Case 1: Exclusion through competition for the same resource. In this case we let 1 and 2 refer to different kinds of output. And v_1 and v_2, located in the same region, compete by using the same available land, infrastructure and labour force. N_1 and N_2 represent the upper limits of these resources.

For this case we may illustrate exclusion of v_2 due to specialisation in v_1 as

$$\epsilon_1 \leqslant , \epsilon_2 \geqslant 0 \tag{2}$$

$$N_2(t) = M(t) - N_1(t)$$

where $M(t)$ is the aggregate limit on total output of the firms at hand.

As long as $\dot{N}_1 \geqslant 0$ and N_1 is close to $M(t)$ there is no room for v_2 to grow. Then v_2 can only expand if $M(t)$ expands. If ϵ_1 and ϵ_2 are both positive and $N_1(t) + N_2(t) = M(t)$, a stagnating $M(t)$ implies that one of the following episodes occurs: v_2 is pushed back to zero; or v_2 will, in the course of time, squeeze v_1 out of the system and reduce it to zero as described in Figure 4.4. This type of exclusion may be significantly delayed if the infrastructure and labour supply continue to grow so that $\dot{M} > 0$.

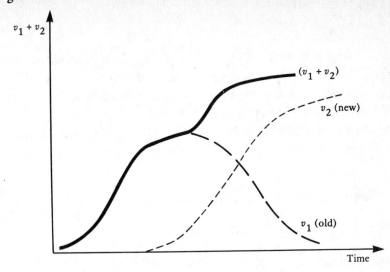

Figure 4.4   Introduction of a new activity and phasing out an old

Case 2: Competition for the same market. In this case we let 1 and 2 represent two substitutes competing for the same market, i.e.

$$M(t) = N_1(t) + N_2(t) \tag{3}$$

$$\epsilon_1 > 0 \text{ and } \epsilon_2 > 0$$

Suppose that v_2 survives. Then, just as in the preceding case, v_1 will gradually be extinguished if $M(t)$ is stagnating. In this case we must distinguish between two extremely different episodes. If both v_1 and v_2 are located in the same region, we have a process of regional renewal. If v_2 is located in a second region, however, the reduction of v_1 also brings about a regional decline.

Case 3: Synergistic reinforcement. Let v_2 represent a new type of 'infrastructure support' for the production v_1, and let ϵ_1 and ϵ_2 both be negative as an expression for mutual reinforcement.

According to (1), case 3 will allow for explosive growth if ϵ_1 and

ϵ_2 are constant. In order to illustrate the balance problem between production and infrastructure support and vice versa, we may write for $i, j = 1,2$

$$\epsilon_i = -\max [a_i, 1 - \exp (v_j - \beta v_i)] \tag{4}$$

as an example of a general relation $\epsilon_i = \epsilon_i(v_i, v_j)$. The function in (4) emphasises that when $v_j > \beta v_i$ the synergetic effect is reduced to $a_i \geqslant 0$; this means that v_j stimulates v_i stronger when v_j is below the balance level βv_i than when it exceeds this level.

Altogether, a model with a structure of (1) is able to generate a wide variety of episodes for a dynamic system.

Urban episodes illustrated by a simple model

Multi-episodes in a logistic growth process

Modelling qualitative economic changes based on nonlinear self-organising or adaptive processes has increasingly received attention during the past decade (see, for instance, Allen and Sanglier, 1979; Batten, 1983; Day and Cigno, 1978; Dendrinos, 1980; and Nijkamp and Schubert, 1983). The major aim of these contributions has been to understand the functioning of complex dynamic systems by means of models with relatively simple structures.

In this section we introduce a model that helps to illustrate some further aspects of urban episodes. We start with a simple model to which more details are added in steps. Also the initial version of the model is able to generate a multi-episode history.

First, consider a model of a sector in an urban system. As a limiting case we may conceive this sector as the entire production system of the urban economy. The increase of value added (at given prices) is assumed to depend on investments and capacity removals in the following way:

$$V(t+1) - V(t) = a(t)I(t) - \xi(t)V(t) \tag{5}$$

where for period t, $V(t)$ is value added, $I(t)$ investments, $\xi(t)$ depreciation or removal of old capacity in terms of value added, and $a(t)$ the relation between investments and new production capacity.

Assume that investments are driven by a simple acceleration behaviour so that

58

$$I(t) = \kappa(t)V(t) \qquad (6)$$

where $\kappa(t)$ may be thought of as the investment share of current production; although $\kappa(t)$ generally will oscillate around a constant value or a trend, we are treating it as a constant.

As production grows the demand for labour will also grow, pushing labour costs upwards. Growing production may also imply increased competition on markets outside the region. This implies that old production capacities with less modern production techniques will be obsolete and removed, to be replaced eventually by modern and more efficient technologies. Such a vintage process may be reflected in terms of value added as

$$\xi(t) = \lambda * V(t) \qquad (7)$$

which, together with (5)–(6), yields

$$V(t+1) = V(t) [1+a(t)\kappa(t) - \lambda * V(t)] \qquad (8)$$

Difference equations of this simple type have recently been used to analyse the dynamics of complex systems (see, for example, Beaumont et al., 1980; May, 1974; Li and Yorke, 1975; Nijkamp, 1983; Nijkamp and Schubert, 1983; and Wilson, 1981).

Before adding new components to the model, we first describe some dynamic properties of the process in (8). It adheres to a family of logistic growth processes which has been extensively analysed by May (1976). With a normalised scale such that $0 < V(t) < 1$, and with $a(t) = a$, $\kappa(t) = \kappa$, we may distinguish the following cases:

Case 1: $a \kappa < 0$; in this case $V(t)$ will gradually be reduced to zero which implies extinction of the sector in the long run.

Case 2: $0 < a \kappa < 2$; in this case there is a stable equilibrium point, and a steady state solution is guaranteed.

Case 3: $2 < a \kappa < 3$; in this case we may obtain various kinds of oscillatory solutions ranging from cyclical to chaotic behaviour as $a \kappa$ increases within the given interval.

A shift from case 1 to case 2 would represent an event leading to a new episode. With regard to case 3, variations in $a \kappa$ may generate qualitatively new episodes.

External influences

The challenge and response principle discussed earlier implies that external conditions may influence the change process in the urban region. For production which is exported and/or has to compete with imports from other regions, relative cost is of vital importance. We may use $c(t)$ and $\hat{c}(t)$ to denote the relative cost levels of the region with old and new production techniques. Then the willingness to invest is expressed by $\kappa(\hat{c}(t))$, and the depreciation rate becomes $\xi(c(t))$. (Observe that $\hat{c}(t)$ and $c(t)$ are affected by the same regional wage level.) In this case equation (8) is transformed to:

$$V(t+1) = V(t) \; [1+a(t)\kappa(c(t)) - \xi(\hat{c}(t))] \tag{9}$$

Moreover, a region lagging behind its surrounding neighbours may imitate them and import production knowledge from its environment. In order to reflect this we may let $a(t)$ change in response to the discrepancy between an aspiration level $V^*(t)$ and the regional production level $V(t)$ so that

$$a(t) = \bar{a} + a^*(V^*(t) - V(t)) \tag{10}$$

where $V^*(t)$ represents the production level (e.g. per capita production) in the relevant environment of the region.

The above remarks about external influences indicate that when interactions between the region and its environment are considered, the occurrence of new events will be much more likely and frequent than in a closed system. This becomes obvious if we insert (9) and (10) into (8), and observe that $\hat{c}(t)$ and $c(t)$ in (9) will depend on the change processes both within the region and in its environment.

A core—ring configuration

In this section, an attempt is made to extend the previous model to demonstrate how different space—time episodes of urban histories can emerge. Without loss of generality, we will assume the existence of two technologies each having its own productivity. In addition, we will also assume a segmented (i.e. dual) supply of labour as a production input.

Furthermore, it will be assumed that the agglomeration concerned may be split up into a core and a ring (see Figure 4.5; see also van den Berg et al., 1982). Due to congestion and physical inertia the technology in the core may be less flexible, while in the ring new industrial technologies may flourish.

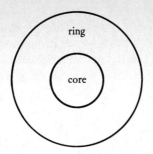

Figure 4.5   Urban agglomeration with a ring and a core

Clearly, the assumption of one core and one ring is not strictly necessary; other spatial configurations may also exist. The main argument is that different areas may favour different technologies. In particular, the availability of space will be different in the two zones, and this implies non-identical technology opportunities. Moreover, as a result of past history the technologies will in general have different vintage structures and different adjustment speeds.

The overall growth of the sector (or the entire production system as a limiting case) may be obtained as the sum of the growth in the two zones so that

$$\Delta V(t+1) = \Delta V_1(t+1) + \Delta V_2(t+1) \tag{11}$$

Let $\Delta L(t) = \sigma V(t)$ denote the labour force available for new employment in period $t+1$ for the whole urban region, and let $\Delta L_i(t) = \sigma_i V_i(t)$ be the same kind of supply in zone i. Given this, suppose that the zonal wage level $\omega_i(t)$ is affected by the tension in the labour market in such a way that

$$\omega_i(t) = \omega_i + \mu_i \Delta L_i(t) / \Delta L(t) \tag{12}$$

The change in $\omega_i(t)$ can be expected to affect the willingness to invest and the depreciation or removal rate so that $\kappa_i(t) = \kappa_i(\omega_i(t))$ and $\xi_i(t) = \xi_i(\omega_i(t))$. As a simple example we may assume that

$$\kappa_i(\omega_i(t)) = \bar{\kappa}_i - \lambda_i \sigma_i V_i(t) / \sigma V(t) \tag{13}$$

$$\xi_i(\omega_i(t)) = \bar{\xi}_i + \beta_i \sigma_i V_i(t) / \sigma V(t) \tag{14}$$

This yields for $i = 1,2$

$$\Delta V_i(t+1) = V_i(t) \left[a_i(t)\bar{\kappa}_i - \bar{\xi}_i - \sigma_i V_i(t) / \sigma V(t) (\lambda_i + \beta_i) \right] \tag{15}$$

which constitutes a model with a similar basic structure as the one in Equation (8). However, (1) constitutes a coupled system such that the development in the ring will have repercussions in the core and vice versa. Also, the two zones may show diverging change patterns and adjustment speeds. Hence, in the general case, there will be one distinct episode in each zone.

A space–time core–periphery model

The urban episodes discussed in the last section can be aligned more closely to a space–time model involving the core–periphery structure. Then an intriguing spatial competition can emerge by assuming both *intra*-urban (core *and* periphery) competition and *inter*-urban competition (or combinations of both) (see also Figure 4.6).

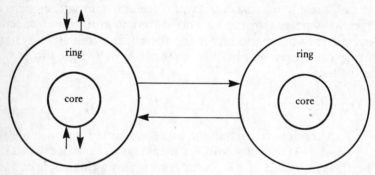

Figure 4.6   A system of cities

Then, several interesting cases can be distinguished; for instance, pure core–ring episodes (growth, decline, restructuring), interactive episodes with the outside world (such as sudden impacts of energy price), and 'internal' episodes (for example, related to technological change or substitution processes). Differences in urban growth trajectories may also be related to various resource constraints or demand limits in specific cities.

For instance, the coupling of economic development in either the core–ring pattern (*intra*-urban) or the city–city pattern (*inter*-urban) will be especially strong if we focus on the same type of production with two competing locations (either within one city or between two cities). In order to illustrate this we may rewrite the continuous model as follows:

$$V_i = a_i(t-\tau)I_i(t-\tau) - \xi_i(t) \tag{16}$$

$$a_i(t)I_i(t) = \mu_i(t)V_i(t)[N_i(t)-V_i(t)-\epsilon_j V_j(t)] \tag{17}$$

$$\xi_i(t) = \gamma_i V_i(t)\sigma_i V_i(t) / \sigma V(t) \tag{18}$$

where $(N_i - V_i - \epsilon_j V_j)$ expresses the market size which is yet uncaptured. This situation is likely to stimulate natural investment. In terms of our earlier formulations we then have

$$a_i \kappa_i = \mu_i(N_i - V_i - \epsilon_j V_j) \tag{19}$$

and

$$N_2 + N_1 = M, \text{ with } M \geqslant 0.$$

In a manner analogous to that in previous sections, the stability conditions for this more complex spatial system can be analysed.

Final comments

This chapter introduces the concept of episodes and has related their emergence to a stochastic framework in which episodes are generated and exchanged as parts of urban event histories. With the help of some examples we have also tried to illustrate how episodes may be modelled and how, in an urban region, they may form a nested network of change processes. In this perspective the concept of episodes could be thought of as an intermediary between theoretical models and empirical observations. In particular, this concept may help to develop a principle for organising observations in such a way that they can shed light on non-linear change processes in interacting subsystems.

References

Allen, P.M. and M. Sanglier (1979), 'A Dynamic Model of Growth in a Central Place System', *Geographical Analysis*, vol. 11, pp. 256–72.
Andersson, Å. and B. Johansson (1984), 'Knowledge Intensity and Product Cycles in Metropolitan Regions', IIASA WP-84-13, International Institute for Applied Systems Analysis, Laxenburg, Austria.

Arminger, G. (1984), *Measuring the Unmeasurable; Analysis of Qualitative Spatial Data* (P. Nijkamp, H. Leitner and N. Wrigley, eds), Martinus Nijhoff, The Hague.

Batten, D.F. (1983), 'A Criterion for Industrial Evolution', *Search*, vol. 14, no. 7–8, pp. 211–14.

Beaumont, J.R., M. Clarke and A.G. Wilson (1980), 'The Dynamics of Urban Spatial Structure: Some Exploratory Results Using Difference Equations and Bifurcation Theory', mimeographed paper, School of Geography, University of Leeds, Liverpool.

Berg, L. van den et al. (1982), *Urban Europe, A Study of Growth and Decline*, vol. 1, Pergamon, Oxford.

Biehl, D. et al. (1982), 'The Contribution of Infrastructure to Regional Development', Report to the European Community, Regional Policy Division, Brussels.

Blommestein, H.J. and P. Nijkamp (1983), 'Causality Analysis in Soft Spatial Econometric Models', *Papers of the Regional Science Association*, vol. 51, pp. 65–8.

Carlino, G.A. (1977), *Economies of Scale in Manufacturing Location*, Martinus Nijhoff, Boston/The Hague.

Clark, W.A.V. (1983), 'Structures for Research on the Dynamics of Residential Search', *Evolving Geographical Structures* (D.A. Griffith and A.C. Lea, eds), Martinus Nijhoff, The Hague, pp. 372–97.

Coleman, J.S. (1981), *Longitudinal Data Analysis*, Basic Books, New York.

Davies, S. (1979), *The Diffusion of Process Innovations*, Cambridge University Press, Cambridge.

Day, R. and A. Cigno (1978), *Modeling Economic Change, The Recursive Programming Approach*, North-Holland Publishing Company, Amsterdam.

Dendrinos, D.S. (1980), *Catastrophe Theory in Urban and Transport Analysis*, US Department of Transportation, Office of Systems Engineering, Document No. DOT-RSPA-DPB-25/80/20, Washington, DC.

Folmer, H. (1984), *Measurement of Policy Effects by Means of Linear Structural Equation Models*, Martinus Nijhoff, The Hague.

Griffith, D.A. and A.C. Lea (eds) (1983), *Evolving Geographical Structures*, Martinus Nijhoff, The Hague.

Haag, G. and W. Weidlich (1983), 'A Nonlinear Dynamic Model for the Migration of Human Population', *Evolving Geographical Structures* (D.A. Griffith and A.C. Lea, eds), Martinus Nijhoff, The Hague, pp. 24–61.

Hägerstrand, T. (1970), 'What About People in Regional Science', *Papers of the Regional Science Association*, vol. 24, pp. 7–21.

Haining, R. (1983), 'Spatial Structure and Spatial-Temporal Processes', *Evolving Geographical Structures* (D.A. Griffith and A.C. Lea, eds), Martinus Nijhoff, The Hague, pp. 323—46.

Hannan, M.T., N.B. Tuma and L.P. Groeneveld (1978), 'Income and Independence Effects on Marital Dissolution', *American Journal of Sociology*, vol. 84, pp. 611—33.

Hannan, M.T. and N.B. Tuma (1984), 'Dynamic Analysis of Qualitative Variables: Applications to Organisational Demography', *Measuring the Unmeasurable; Analysis of Qualitative Spatial Data* (P. Nijkamp, H. Leitner and N. Wrigley, eds), Martinus Nijhoff, The Hague.

Hee, B. van der, L. Beumer, A. van Jameson and J. Paelinck (1978), 'A Study of the Formal Structure of J.W. Forrester's Urban Dynamics Model', *Urban Studies*, vol. 15, pp. 167—77.

Hirschman, A.O. (1958), *Strategy of Economic Development*, Yale University Press, New Haven, Conn.

Jacobs, J. (1969), *The Economy of Cities*, Jonathan Cape, London.

Johansson, B., P. Korcelli, G. Leonardi and F. Snickars (1983), 'Nested Dynamics of Metropolitan Processes and Policies', Project Document 2, Regional and Urban Development Task, IIASA, Laxenburg (mimeographed).

Leonardi, G. (1983), 'An Optimal Control Representation of a Stochastic Multistage-Multifactor Choice Process', *Evolving Geographical Structures* (D.A. Griffith and A.C. Lea, eds), Martinus Nijhoff, The Hague, pp. 62—72.

Li, T. and J.A. Yorke (1975), 'Period Three Implies Chaos', *American Mathematical Monthly*, vol. 82, pp. 985—92.

Lierop, W.F.J. van and P. Nijkamp (1984), 'Perspectives of Disaggregate Choice Models for the Housing Market', *Discrete Spatial Choice Models* (D.A. Pitfield, ed.), Pion, London.

May, R.M. (1976), 'Simple Mathematical Models with very Complicated Dynamics', *Nature*, vol. 26, pp. 459—67.

May, R.M. (1974), 'Biological Populations with Non-overlapping Generations', *Science*, no. 186, pp. 645—7.

Miyao, T. and P. Shapiro (1981), 'Discrete Choice and Variable Returns to Scale', *International Economic Review*, vol. 22, no. 2, pp. 257—73.

Nijkamp, P. (1983), 'Technological Change, Policy Response and Spatial Dynamics', *Evolving Geographical Structures* (D.A. Griffith and A.C. Lea, eds), Martinus Nijhoff, The Hague, pp. 75—98.

Nijkamp, P. and U. Schubert (1983), 'Structural Change in Urban Systems', Collaborative Paper CP-83-57, IIASA, Laxenburg.

Nijkamp, P., H. Leitner and N. Wrigley (eds) (1984), *Measuring the Unmeasurable; Analysis of Qualitative Spatial Data*, Martinus

Nijhoff, The Hague.

Rostow, W. (1960), *The Stages of Economic Growth*, Cambridge University Press, Cambridge, Mass.

Sandefur, G.D. and W.J. Scott (1981), 'A Dynamic Analysis of Migration: An Assessment of the Effects of Age, Family and Career Variables, *Demography*, vol. 18, pp. 355—68.

Sonis, M. (1983), 'Competition and Environment — A Theory of Temporal Innovation Diffusion', *Evolving Geographical Structures* (D.A. Griffith and A.C. Lea, eds), Martinus Nijhoff, The Hague, pp. 99—129.

Thomas, B. (1972), *Migration and Urban Development*, Methuen, London.

Toynbee, A. (1961), *A Study of History*, Oxford University Press, London.

Tuma, N.B. and P. Robins (1980), 'A Dynamic Model of Employment Behavior', *Econometrica*, vol. 48, pp. 1031—52.

Tuma, N.B. and M.T. Hannan (1984), *Social Dynamics: Models and Methods*, Academic Press, New York.

Turner, J. (1980), 'Non-equilibrium Thermodynamics, Dissipative Structures and Self-Organisation', *Dissipative Structures and Spatiotemporal Organisation Studies in Biomedical Research* (G. Scott and J. MacMillan, eds), Iowa State University Press, Iowa, pp. 13—52.

Wibe, S. (1982), 'Engineering Production Functions — A Survey', *Umeå Economic Studies*, University of Umeå, Sweden.

Wilson, A.G. (1981), *Catastrophe Theory and Bifurcation*, Croom Helm, Beckenham.

5 Urban change: a changing process

ROLF H. FUNCK AND ULRICH C. H. BLUM

Over the postwar decades, urban development in the highly developed nations of Western Europe has been characterised by a host of conflicting tendencies that, to a considerable extent, influenced the structure and appearance of large agglomerations. West Germany is no exception. Two periods may be distinguished, and a third seems to be evolving. The first period extends from the end of the Second World War into the mid-1970s and the second, overlapping the first by about a decade, runs from the mid-1960s to the present. With respect to West Germany, major features of the first period are:

— *Continuous inflow of population* consisting of refugees from Europe who largely added to the rural population (about 1945); returning prisoners of war (1945—55); political refugees from the German Democratic Republic (until construction of the Berlin Wall in 1961); and immigration of foreign workers and their families from southern Europe and Turkey who settled mainly in the city centres of Southern and Western Germany (since 1961).
— Rapid *economic growth* with particularly high annual growth rates (1951—72) coupled with very *low unemployment* throughout the period.
— *Internal migration* from rural areas into cities (1950s and 1960s) together with *out-migration* from cores to the urban fringe (1960s and 1970s) followed by *administrative expansion* of cities into their hinterlands (1965—75).

— Accommodating these developments was a *high level of construction* in the housing, industrial and service-oriented sectors, and in transportation infrastructure.

In contrast, the second period, running from the mid-1960s to the present, has been characterised by:

— *Population decline* resulting from the drop in the natural rate of increase which, though no longer declining, is below the death rate; although the migration of foreign workers has virtually come to a halt as a consequence of policy decisions taken after unemployment began to grow in 1973, their families continue to arrive in large numbers.
— *Structural changes in the population* with respect to their age, social and ethnic characteristics.
— *Economic stagnation* with low growth rates and rising unemployment.
— *Shifting personal and social values* concerning the attractiveness of rural versus urban living, proximity to nature versus easy access to cultural and other urban activities, as well as attitudes about the importance attached to environmental impacts and the excessive energy consumption associated with a widely scattered settlement system, plus resulting mobility patterns and car use.
— Resulting *changes in urban and regional development* consisting of a return of people to city centres (but at a level that is not balanced by moves out of centres), the restoration of old urban residential areas, heavy investment in urban transit (mainly during the 1970s), and rising excess of demand for small low-rent dwellings in city centres.

The trends are embedded in the current technological changes and their effects on industrial location which tend to make job opportunities less dependent on raw materials concentrations, and increase the attractiveness of centres offering high infrastructural quality. The ageing of the urban infrastructure built during the 1950s and 1960s, and the decline in new infrastructure investment, adds another feature: the necessity for repair and maintenance that absorbs an increasing proportion of public and private expenditures.

The trends are also interwoven in a network of urban interrelationships that produce different and even opposing effects on the development of various urban agglomerations. Some cities will experience positive net migration, for others it will be negative; the economic performance of some cities will improve and will deteriorate for others; some will move up the national urban hierarchy and others will lose their position as central places.

Thus, a third period seems to emerge in which urban development is based on high technology, particularly in the information field (Funk and Kowalski, 1984), an altered focus for infrastructure investment, and a slight revival of economic and demographic dimensions. From this general description, it may be assumed that urban development does not follow a strictly monotonous growth trajectory. To the contrary, changes in growth rates over time, sudden breaks in the direction of development and — in the long run — even cyclical processes (Funck and Blum, 1985), may be expected. These urban change processes are described briefly, but systematically, in the following sections.

The urban system and the process of urban change

The city has been described as a system consisting of three subsystems (Funck and Blum, 1985). The subsystems — urban population, private and public urban capital assets, and natural resources in the urban area — are linked as shown in Figure 5.1.

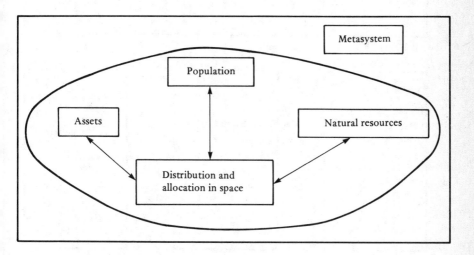

Figure 5.1   The city as a system

In the geographical sense, the city is incorporated in a metasystem that includes all other urban communities and rural areas. In its social and political meaning, the metasystem represents the prevailing technological, institutional and behavioural structures. The subsystems are realised in space which, in turn, has an economic, a geographic, and a political dimension.

Three *processes* define the interrelationships between the subsystems and with the metasystem:

1. the *economic process* in relation to which the three subsystems are identified as *production factors*;
2. the *social and cultural process*; the three subsystems in this respect are identified as *urban quality factors*;
3. the *political and administrative process*; the three subsystems are identified as *political and institutional factors*.

Taken together, the three processes and their interrelationships and interactions constitute the *process of urban development.*

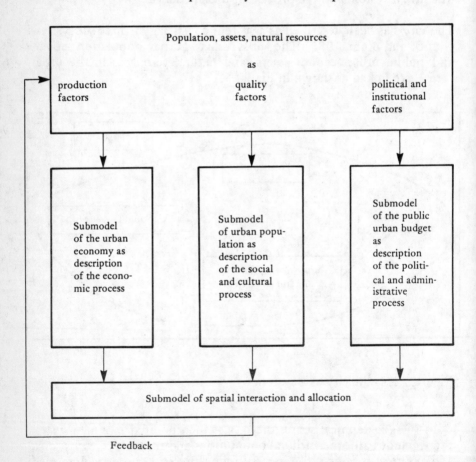

Figure 5.2   Outline of a model of urban development

The city as a special type of human settlement is characterised by the specific way in which the three processes are realised in space. Every city serves as a centre of attraction for its geographical, economic and political environment. This implies a circular relationship between the city and the larger metasystem of which it is a part. The metasystem generates exogenous impacts on the city. Examples are changes in technology, the natural environment, generative behaviour, social and cultural perception, or legal norms. In order to fully understand these relationships, the analysis of urban development should rely on a dynamic theory and models (Figure 5.2).

A number of general assumptions are required to define such a model (see Funck and Blum, 1985). Also, successfully formulating an operational urban development model requires defining adequate indicators for the various subsystems, processes and dimensions of urban space. The following indicators are suggested:

1 Production factors:
  (a) urban population:
    — size and age structure
    — educational and sectoral structure of the labour force (supply)
    — number of consumers and their preferences (demand);
  (b) urban assets:
    (i) public assets:
      — material infrastructure: capacity indicators
      — immaterial infrastructure (influence of central place ranking); average income (Funck and Blum, 1981; Blum, 1982)
    (ii) private assets; market values;
  (c) natural resources: classified by degree of spatial mobility: market values, value of resources extracted during the period analysed, or estimated opportunity costs (environmental resources).

2 Quality factors:
  (a) human resources: population distributed by age, education, and other relevant characteristics; and according to their social and cultural perception of the city;
  (b) physical assets: classified by degree of spatial mobility (supply); capacities, degree of utilisation by number of visitors, students, etc. (demand);
  (c) natural resources: classified by degree of spatial mobility;

defined socially acceptable standards and estimated actual deviation from the standards.

3   Political and institutional factors:
    (a) population: number of tax payers and amount of tax revenues;
    (b) assets and natural resources: tax base, land value changes, infrastructure equipment, etc.

4   Impact of processes on urban space:
    (a) result of urban production process: urban gross value added or gross urban product;
    (b) result of social and cultural process: level of urban attractiveness (e.g. numbers of citizens enjoying certain social or cultural services) or aggregate attractiveness of the city as indicated by the commuter balance;
    (c) result of the political and administrative process: size of urban budget and voter participation rates.

Once the necessary indicators (or variables) have been quantified the cause–effect relationships can be determined by estimating the model. Most of the relationships can best be formulated using systems of difference equations in a population model, an economic model, a fiscal model describing the public budget, and a model of spatial inter-action and allocation. The model is briefly described in the next sections. (For a more detailed description see Blum (1984).)

A dynamic model of urban development

General structure of the model

As described above, the urban system consists of three subsystems that reflect the interactions of population, assets, and natural resources. The urban system, in turn, is incorporated into a meta-system, or the rest of the world. The processes are interrelated. The construction of a public building has political, economic and cultural consequences; population is important as a production factor as well as for defining perception of urban quality; a particular zoning decision influences the economic as well as the political process.
The following assumptions are required for defining the model:

1   The urban region, consisting of three subsystems — urban population, assets, and natural resources — is incorporated into

a metasystem that includes other cities and rural areas. The city is assumed to be small compared to the metasystem and its development will not affect development patterns elsewhere.

2   Three urban processes are the result of the three elements upon which every subsystem depends. These elements consist of the economic process, the social and cultural process, and the political and administrative process.

3   The combination of the three production factors, or subsystems of population, assets, and natural resources — both in an economic process and in a social and cultural process — can be related to the urban area's quality of life.

4   Similarly, the combination of the three political and institutional factors — again, population, assets and natural resources — in a political and administrative process can be related to the level of urban power.

5   All subsystems (or factors) which, within a medium to long term, are characterised by spatial immobility are called input potentials; they constrain the input of all other attractable factors.

6   Input potentials used in the economic process are not priced at marginal cost.

7   The economic process is subject to external control — that is, from the metasystem — according to the degree to which the city is included in the system of commodity flows and thus dependent on the supply of attractable factors, the degree that companies are externally controlled, the extent of technical change, and the capability for controlling such external forces.

8   Urban space consists of geographical, economic, and political space.

9   The spatial distribution of the three subsystems maximises profits in the economic sector by maximising collective utility in the social and cultural sector and, in the political sector, by maximising long-term urban quality as well as votes within the set of restrictions valid for a certain time period.

10 Urban product is allocated between tax payments to the municipality, investment, and consumption.

11 Commuters and migrants are free to move in geographical space.

12 Two levels of interaction take place within the system. First, within every region, the processes — as well as the quantities and qualities of factors — are influenced by feedbacks from the outcomes of these processes with a one-period time lag. For example, over-investment that results in above-normal

production leads to compensating external diseconomies (process) and reduces future investments (factor). Second, within the urban system, the three processes influence each other. For example, the demand for labour fixes wages and thus the levels of real and nominal consumption.

The economic process

The economic submodel is based on difference equations including accelerator—multiplier effects, a production sector in order to account for problems of availability of production factors and especially those that are spatially immobile, plus a labour sector linking this submodel to the demographic and the social and cultural process. Furthermore, interregional links exist due to the inclusion of transportation and flows of investment capital across the city limits.

The following assumptions characterise the economic process:

1 The city and the metasystem produce goods for consumption and for investment.
2 Participants in the economic process consist of private households, private firms, and public urban institutions.
3 Investments create a capacity and an income effect.
4 Consumer demand depends on the disposable income of the urban population and the commuter balance during the preceding period.
5 *Ex post* savings must equal investments.
6 Inputs can be related to production levels by a production function of the Cobb—Douglas type.
7 Private firms maximise profits.
8 Agglomeration economies and diseconomies depend on the density of capital in a production zone. The impacts of agglomeration economies and diseconomies can be represented by a triangular distribution.

Urban income, denoted $YU(t)$, is defined as the sum of consumer demand, $CU(t)$, and urban investments, $IU(t)$. Disposable income is computed by subtracting taxes, $TU(t)$, from urban income and by adding the income of the balance of commuters given by the product of their number, $CBE(t)$, and the urban wage level, $wu(t)$. Urban investment, $IU(t)$, depends on private autonomous investment, IUA, public investment $IPU(t)$, as determined by the political process, and the change in private consumption, $CU(t) - CU(t-1)$. Hence, the first part of the model reads:

$$YU(t) - b \cdot (1+d) \cdot YU(t-1) + b \cdot d \cdot YU(t-2) \tag{1}$$
$$= IUA + IPU(t) - b \cdot TU(t-1) + b \cdot wu(t-1) \cdot CBU(t-1)$$

This non-homogeneous difference equation has cyclical, unsteady or monotonic solutions depending on the values of the marginal consumption rate b, and the value of the accelerator, d.

The most probable solutions are the cyclical ones due to b (0,1). The cyclical development is divergent if $\sqrt{b \cdot d} > 1$, constant if $\sqrt{b \cdot d} = 1$, and convergent if $\sqrt{b \cdot d} < 1$. Solving the non-homogeneous equation yields the equilibrium urban income and the urban investment multiplier, $(1 - b)$.

By assumption, urban savings equal urban investments:

$$SU(t) = IU(t) \tag{2}$$

Production factors are given by the urban labour force, $LU(t)$, the stock of private capital assets, $KU(t)$, and the stock of public capital assets, $KPU(t)$. Then

$$YU(t) = f_0 \cdot \exp(f_1 \cdot t) \cdot LU(t)^{f_2} \cdot KU(t)^{f_3} \cdot KPU(t)^{f_4}, \tag{3}$$

$$f_0, f_1, f_2, f_3, f_4, > 0$$

where f_3 and f_4 are assumed to be endogenous parameters in the sense that their values can be influenced by agglomeration economies and diseconomies.

Demand for urban labour for given levels of income, and stocks of private and public capital assets, may be computed by inverting Equation (3). If demand for labour exceeds supply, real production is reduced but nominal production is held at the level of final demand.

The first derivative of urban income with respect to urban labour yields the urban wage level:

$$wu(t) = f_2 \cdot \exp(f_1 \cdot t) \cdot f_2 \cdot LU(t)^{f_2 - 1} \cdot KU(t)^{f_3} \cdot KPU(t)^{f_4} \tag{4}$$

The return on private capital becomes:

$$gu(t) = f_2 \cdot \exp(f_1 \cdot t) \cdot f_3 \cdot LU(t)^{f_2} \cdot KU(t)^{f_3 - 1} \cdot KPU(t)^{f_4} \tag{5}$$

The return on public capital becomes:

$$ru(t) = f_0 \cdot \exp(f_1 \cdot t) \cdot f_4 \cdot LU(t)^{f_2} \cdot KU(t)^{f_3} \cdot KPU(t)^{f_4} \tag{6}$$

Urban private and public investments increase the stock of capital assets:

$$KU(t) = KU(t-1) + IU(t-1) \tag{7}$$
$$KPU(t) = KPU(t-1) + IPU(t-1) \tag{8}$$

75

Figure 5.3 describes the impact of agglomeration changes in the economic model.

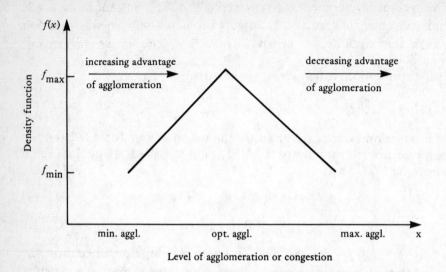

Figure 5.3   Distribution of endogenous parameters as determined by degree of urban agglomeration and congestion

If transportation conditions between places in the metasystem and the city are given, the cost of shipping goods can be included by

$$TR(t) = YT(t) \cdot d^\tau \cdot s, \quad \tau \in (0,1) \tag{9}$$

where $YT(t)$ is the value of goods shipped, d the average distance, τ a friction parameter, and s the net price. Then Equation (9) has to be accounted for in formulas (3)–(6) by a factor

$$z \cdot d^\tau \cdot s \tag{10}$$

assuming that z gives the proportion of the urban product imported or exported:

$$YT(t) = z \cdot YU(t) \tag{11}$$

76

The social and cultural process

This submodel is defined by the following properties and assumptions:

1   The urban migration balance depends on the relative quality of living in the city described by urban quality factors as perceived by the population living inside and outside the city.

2   Commuting depends on wage and employment levels in the city relative to those in the outside world.

3   Urban population size depends on size in the preceding year, on birth and mortality rates, and on the migration balance.

The migration balance, $MU(t)$, depends on the quality of life inside and outside the city, $QU(t-1)$, and on QA, the size of the city's population, $PU(t-1)$, and the size of the remaining population $PG(t-1)$, in the preceding year:

$$MU(t) = a_1 \cdot QU(t-1) - a_2 \cdot QA + a_3 \cdot PG(t-1) - a_4 \cdot PU(t-1), \qquad (12)$$

$$a_1, a_2, > 0$$

$$|a_3| \in [0,1] , |a_4| \in [0,1] \text{ as perception parameters.}$$

Both a_3 and a_4 can be considered as factors of relative attraction. Under circumstances which can be observed in most parts of the world, we would set $a_4 \in [0,1]$ and a_3 as endogenously influenced parameters which are triangularly distributed; in most cases $a_3 \in [0,1]$ would hold.

Urban quality could be measured by a composite index yielding values of quality factors weighted according to quality perception; for example,

$$QU(t) = KPU(t)^{q_1} \cdot NU(t)^{q_2} \cdot EU(t)^{q_3} \cdot LE(t)^{q_4} \cdot HU(t)^{q_5} \qquad (13)$$

$$q_1, q_2, q_3, q_4, q_5 \in IR$$

where $KPU(t)$ is the stock of public capital, $NU(t)$ the size of natural areas, $EU(t)$ the capacity of educational and training facilities, $LE(t)$ the capacity of facilities for cultural and social activities, and $HU(t)$ the structure of the urban welfare system.

The commuter balance, $CBU(t)$, depends on the labour market situation and the labour force participation rate of the city's residents $(p [0,1]$:

$$CBU(t) = \begin{cases} 0 & \text{if } LU(t) \leqslant p{\cdot}PU(t), \\ LU(t) - p \cdot PU(t) & \text{if } LU(t) > p{\cdot}PU(t), \end{cases} \tag{14}$$

where p (0,1) is the labour force participation rate.

The total model thus reads:

$$PU(t) - (1{+}g{-}m){\cdot}PU(t{-}1) + a_4 {\cdot}PU(t{-}2) \tag{15}$$

$$= a_1 {\cdot}QU(t{-}2) - a_2 {\cdot}QA - a_3 {\cdot}PG(t{-}2)$$

where g and m are the birth and mortality rates.

Depending on the values of the parameters, the solution of this non-homogeneous difference equation may either have cyclical, unsteady, or monotonic solutions. A cyclical development is most probable if the total urban population stagnates while the levels of in- and out-migration remain very high. In that case, a divergent solution is not possible as divergence depends on $a_4 > 1$, which is ruled out.

The political and administrative process

This submodel is characterised as follows:

1. Public urban revenues consist of business, property, and personal income taxes, revenues from public services and the increase of public debts.
2. Public urban capital expenditures consist of public urban investments, back-payments of loans, and payments of interest on loans; a surplus of the public urban budget is required for all publicly supported urban activities.
3. Loans are granted for two years and are repaid in the second year with interest payments due during both years.
4. Public urban investments earn revenues in the consecutive two years and are part of total urban investment.
5. Loans and investments are proportional to the surplus of the urban budget.
6. Public authorities maximise utility depending on long-term urban quality and number of votes received.

If the increase in urban public debt, $DPU(t)$, and the level of urban public investments $IPU(t)$, both depend on the size of the surplus of the urban public budget, $BPU(t)$, then

$$DPU(t) = l \cdot BPU(t) , \; l \in (0,1), \tag{16}$$

$$IPU(t) = n \cdot BPU(t), \, n \in (0,1) \tag{17}$$

Taxes, $TU(t)$, are proportional to urban income, $YU(t-1)$, the stock of private capital, $KU(t-1)$, and the size of the urban population, $PU(t-1)$, of the preceding year:

$$TU(t) = v \cdot YU(t-1) + k \cdot KU(t-1) + e \cdot PU(t-1), \tag{18}$$

$$v \in (0,1), \, k \in (0,1), \, e \geqslant 0$$

For an interest rate on public debt i, and a rate of return on public investments, $ru(t)$, derived from the economic model, the total model reads:

$$BPU(t) = DPU(t) - IPU(t) + ru(t) \cdot IPU(t-1) + ru(t) \cdot IPU(t-2) \tag{19}$$

$$- i \cdot DPU(t-1) - i \cdot DPU(t-2) - DPU(t-2)$$

$$+ v \cdot YU(t-1) + k \cdot KU(t-1) + e \cdot PU(t-1)$$

Combining Equations (16) and (19) yields:

$$(1-l) \cdot BPU(t) - (ru(t) \cdot n - i \cdot l) \cdot BPU(t-1) \tag{20}$$

$$- (ru(t-1) \cdot n - i \cdot l) \cdot BPU(t-2) + l \cdot BPU(t-2)$$

$$+ v \cdot YU(t-1) + k \cdot KU(t-1) + e \cdot PU(t-1)$$

The solution of Equation (20) is either cyclical, unsteady, or monotonic depending on the value of the parameters. Complex solutions occur if public authorities increase the level of new borrowing above the level of new investment — which is illegal in the Federal Republic of Germany — or if investments are completely unprofitable and the interest rate on public debt is high.

A utility function for public authorities may be given as

$$U(\sum_{t=0}^{T^*} QU(t) \cdot (1+c)^{-t}, V(t)), \quad c > 0 \tag{21}$$

where T^* is the time horizon of political decisions, c a social discount rate, and $V(t)$ the share of votes favouring incumbents. If we argue that local voting results strongly reflect perceived urban quality, Equation (21) can be specified by maximising the regional budget without straining the capabilities of the local taxpayer. Thus, an optimal long-term taxation strategy should be formulated.

The realisation of the three processes in urban space influences the processes themselves by changing the quantities and the structures of the subsystems and by reshaping behavioural and technological side conditions and patterns.

The quantities and the structures of the subsystems are changed at the end of each period according to the relationships established in the three submodels; the behavioural and technological patterns and relationships are reflected by the coefficients in the submodels. It is assumed that some of them are fixed and can only be affected exogenously, that is through influences from the metasystem. In the model, the respective parameters can be changed numerically as it is implemented in an interactive way on a computer. Other influences are exogenous to urban development and are subject to changes depending on the degree of urban congestion, as shown before.

Empirical evidence

The following data for a city-core were used to test the model:

Urban income (million DM): $YU(0) = 10,000$; $YU(1) = 10,200$
Urban population (persons): $PU(0) = 70,000$; $PU(1) = 68,000$
Urban budget (million DM): $BU(0) = 1,500$; $BU(1) = 1,550$
Urban private and public capital (million DM): $KU(0) = 30,000$;
   $KPU(0) = 10,000$; $IAU = 20,000$
Urban employment (persons): $LU(0) = 25,000$
Urban area (square kilometres): $FU = 50$
Parameters of the economic process (* = distributed values):
   $f_1 = 0.001$; $f_2 = 0.6$; $f_3 = 0.4 \ldots 0.6^*$; $f_4 = 0.1 \ldots 0.15^*$;
   $b = 0.7$; $d = 1 \ldots 3^*$; $z = 0.3$; $s = 0.05$; $\tau = 0.5$; $p = 0.4$;
   $i = 0.1$
Parameters of the social and cultural process:
   $a_1 = 50$; $a_2 = 50$; $a_3 = 0.05$; $a_4 = 0.05$; $q_1 = 1$; $q_2 = 0$;
   $q_3 = 0$; $q_4 = 0$; $q_5 = 0$; $g - m = 0.002$
Parameters of the political and institutional process:
   $I = 0.12$; $n = 0.15$; $v = 0.075$; $e = 0.01$; $k = 0$; $U(QU(t))$
   $= QU(t)$

Figures 5.4–5.6 show the development of the city core over a period of 100 years. Apart from a slight decline given as a side condition for the first period, urban population rose steadily. Urban income fluctuates cyclically, leading to the development of the urban budget.

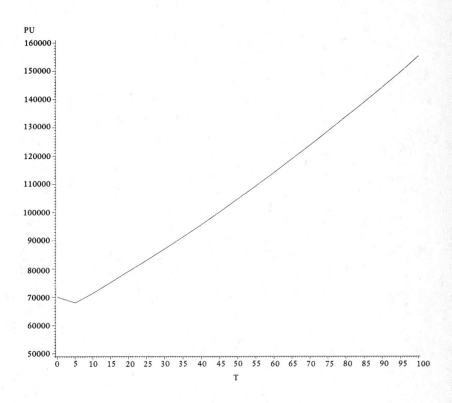

Figure 5.4   Development of urban population

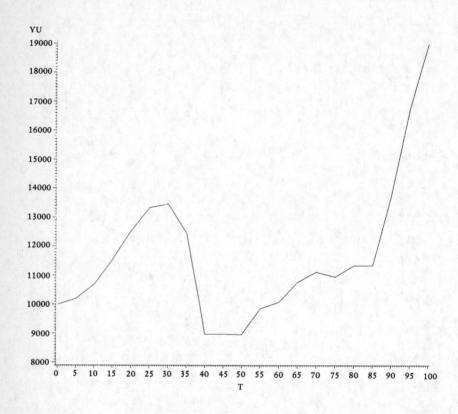

Figure 5.5   Development of urban income

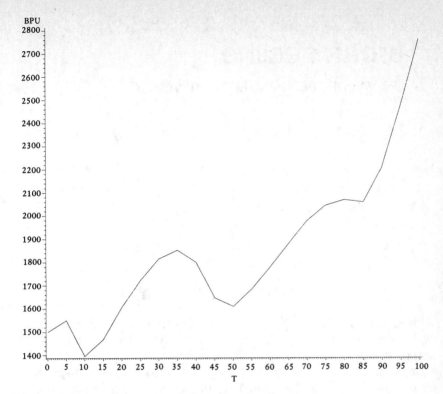

Figure 5.6   Development of the urban budget

References

Blum, U.C.H. (1982), *Regionale Wirkungen von Infrastruktur-investitionen (Regional Effects of Infrastructure Investments)*, Karlsruher Beiträge zur Wirtschaftspolitik und Wirtschafts-forschung, Karlsruhe, West Germany.

Funck, R. and U.C.H. Blum (1985), 'Processes of Urban Development', *Human Behaviour in Geographical Space* (J. Paelinck, ed.), Gower, Aldershot.

Funck, R. and J.S. Kowalski (1984), 'The role of information in regional and urban development', International Association for Regional and Urban Statistics, 14th meeting, Copenhagen.

6 The contagiousness of urban decline

LEO VAN DEN BERG AND LEO H. KLAASSEN

Although urbanisation has for decades characterised Western Europe, and indeed most of the nations of the world, developments during more recent years in many of the major urban agglomerations are more accurately described by the term '*dis*urbanisation'. One or more of the relatively large functional urban regions (or 'agglomerations') in Belgium, Denmark, the UK, Italy, The Netherlands and Switzerland are losing population. In most cases the losses are due to rapid population declines concentrated in urban centres, but population in the rings surrounding Charleroi, Liège, Liverpool and London are also declining. The fact that some cities are disurbanising while others, even those in the same region, are still urbanising or suburbanising, means that urban growth and decline can occur simultaneously at regional or national level. These are among the major conclusions of the recently completed 'CURB Project'. (The CURB Project (CURB = Costs of URBan growth) was undertaken for the Vienna Centre by research teams from 14 countries in Eastern and Western Europe. Its first results were published in van den Berg et al. (1982).)

The CURB results also show that Europe's declining cities have grown rapidly in number during the last few years. The results also support the theory that urban agglomerations tend to develop in systematic and perhaps predictable patterns, passing from overall growth during the stages of urbanisation and suburbanisation to decline in the stage of disurbanisation. If the theory is correct, the number of agglomerations that fall victim to disurbanisation may be expected to grow considerably in the years ahead. Whether that prediction will come true depends on future socio-economic conditions. Using reasonable assumptions, this chapter explores the directions of future urbanisation in Europe. In the process, special care will be given to tracing the major societal problems associated with the predicted developments. We begin that exploration by briefly considering the general theory of urban development presented in the CURB study and summarise some of its more important empirical results.

A general theory of urban development

The character of a nation's specific urban development, to be fully and properly appreciated, should be considered in the light of a general theory. Such a theory can be based on an analysis of the development of urban systems in countries with comparable levels of prosperity.

Western Europe, for many years, has held an economic position between Eastern Europe and the USA. For example, incomes in Western European countries were higher than in the Eastern European counterparts, and lower than in the USA. Recent changes in that ranking, though relevant to our predictions, are hardly so for our consideration of past developments.

In some important respects, Western Europe and Eastern Europe are closer to each other than either is to the USA. European cities are blessed with rich cultural traditions, to which their centres still bear witness. That aspect is lacking in the USA with the possible exception of New Orleans. These similarities and differences should be kept in mind when comparing urban development among the three world regions.

As is customary in research, the gradual development of theory and the emergence of empirical testing is a parallel process that in many cases converges on useful results. That is, a theory confirmed by the facts, at least to a reasonable degree, offers a reasonable explanation of the developments that have actually taken place. The process of simultaneously theorising and testing, possibly leading to revisions of the theory, will have to be initiated in some fashion. An obvious first approach is to formulate a tentative theory or hypothesis, taking into account facts that are already observed.

Of especial concern are changes in the urban spatial structure, on the assumption that some factors affect both the overall size of agglomerations and spatial distributions of population and activity within them. For the purpose of this investigation, each agglomeration has been divided into a 'core', or the central municipality, and a 'ring' consisting of all urban and rural municipalities where 15 per cent or more of the active population commute to the core.

Two questions are suggested:

1   what changes have taken place in urban structures? and
2   how have they affected the total size of the agglomerations?

Before answering these questions let us order the phenomena in a staged model of development. We observe that:

— Some cores grow at the expense of the surrounding countryside. Their often unbridled growth rapidly increases population in cores with corresponding decreases in rings. The familiar process is termed *urbanisation*.
— In other cores, population growth tends to slow down or even to decline in the absolute, while the population in ring municipalities continues to grow. As soon as the ring's growth surpasses the core's, the *suburbanisation* stage has been reached.
— Urban agglomerations where the decline of the core exceeds increase in the ring, so that total population of the agglomeration declines, have moved into the *disurbanisation* stage. The same term applies to agglomerations where the core declines faster than the ring.
— In some cases, population declines faster in the ring than in the core, or the core grows as the core declines. When growth is sufficiently strong to cause the entire agglomeration to gain population, the result is *reurbanisation*.

The staging of the phenomena suggests an embryonic theory of urban development and offers a tentative answer to the pair of questions. Indeed, urbanisation, as defined, will usually be the initial stage. Industrial development strongly attracts people from rural areas. The shift to the city will continue as long as the relative cost of transportation inhibits daily commuting.

In the course of time, living conditions in cores tend to deteriorate, housing and environmental quality declines, commuting costs fall, and incomes — particularly in the industrial sector — rise with increased productivity. Suburbanisation begins as people increasingly prefer to live further out. As transportation flows become more and more unbalanced, suburbanisation generates traffic problems, especially during peak hours. Unidirectional flows cause congestion on one side of the road and are exacerbated by public vehicles transporting passengers in a single direction. Better living is traded off against heavier traffic and longer commuting journeys. Moreover, new demands for building sites in ring areas boost land prices and drive up living costs. Generally, the larger the agglomeration, the earlier such phenomena become apparent.

These phenomena encourage relocation to somewhat smaller urban areas which boast less traffic, better priced and higher quality housing and, for workers who find local employment, shorter commuting distances.

Natural or market forces, or aggressive public policies, however, may spark renewed interest in city life and its economic and cultural potential. With population returning, the agglomeration may experience a revival that starts the development cycle anew.

Stages, according to this process, may be described as *spatial cycles*. Through time, a dynamic process is at work in which past developments help to shape future events. With spatial interaction, the evolution of large agglomerations affects that of medium-sized ones, and vice versa.

During the first phase, *urbanisation*, there is migration from rural to urban areas. The latter develop into large central places at the expense of the rural population. In the course of urbanisation, agglomerations continue along their growth trajectories, but at decreasing rates. There is, however, an end to the population decline in the surrounding rural hinterlands and it is then that the tide turns and the second phase, *suburbanisation*, begins. The growth rate of the suburban ring now exceeds that of the central cores to which they are functionally related. The core population increasingly suburbanises. As soon as the core surpasses natural growth, their population starts to drop. When the core losses exceed gains in the ring, the population of the entire agglomeration falls, leading to the next phase, *disurbanisation*. Disurbanisation continues as the cores lose even more population and growth in the ring decelerates. It becomes critical when even the ring begins to suffer losses with the core continuing its steady decline. In that situation, both core and ring lose population to smaller agglomerations not too far distant; these are termed 'emanation areas'.

The CURB investigation has shown that a substantial proportion of the agglomerations studied indeed tended to develop according to the pattern described, with some agglomerations even finding themselves at advanced stages of disurbanisation. We cannot know how these agglomerations will develop in the future but two alternatives suggest themselves: progressive disurbanisation is one possibility; the other is reurbanisation where the population losses of core and ring come to a halt or even pass into limited growth, leading perhaps to a resurgence of growth in the entire agglomeration.

The entire process is described in terms of the eight types shown in Table 6.1.

Table 6.1
The phases of urban development

Development phase		Type		Features of population change			
				Core	Ring	Agglomeration	Overall development
I	Urbanisation	1	Absolute centralisation	++	−	+	Population growth of entire agglomeration
		2	Relative centralisation	++	+	+++	
II	Suburbanisation	3	Relative decentralisation	+	++	+++	
		4	Absolute decentralisation	−	++	−	
III	Disurbanisation	5	Absolute decentralisation	− −	+	−	
		6	Relative decentralisation	−	−	− −	Population decline of total agglomeration
IV	Reurbanisation	7	Relative decentralisation	−	−	− −	
		8	Absolute centralisation	+	−	−	

Note: +, ++, +++ = population growth, slow (+) to fast (+++)

−, − −, − − − = population decline, slow (−) to fast (− − −)

Statistical evidence in Western Europe

Western Europe claims a wide variety of cities, ranging from the great capitals of London, Paris and Rome to the smaller regional cities such as Groningen, Naples and Toulouse, that differ dramatically in character, spatial structure, prosperity, and obviously in size. The following description of the development of European agglomerations can only do limited justice to the differences, let alone determine their influence on development. We can make no more than a broad analysis.

To that end we shall examine how far the processes observed in Western Europe conform with the stylised representation of urban development in the previous section, using the basic data of the CURB study. The data cover urban agglomerations in 10 West European countries (Austria, Belgium, Denmark, France, the UK, Germany, Italy, the Netherlands, Sweden, and Switzerland), for three periods, 1950–60, 1960–70, and 1970–75. Once the number of agglomerations passing through each phase of development is known for each period, the pattern of shifts over time can be derived.

Table 6.2
Urban development in Western Europe (%)

Period	Stage				Total
	Urbanisation	Suburbanisation	Disurbanisation	Reurbanisation	
1950–60	37	59	4	–	100
1960–70	8	84	9	–	100
1970–75	4	72	23	1	100

Table 6.2 shows how the position of the agglomerations shifted between 1950 and 1975. Between 1950 and 1960, 37 per cent of the agglomerations were classified as urbanising. In the next two time periods, however, the corresponding figures were only 8 and 4 per cent. Comparing 1950–60 with 1960–70 shows that the proportion of suburbanising agglomerations jumped from 59 to 84 per cent. The subsequent decrease following 1970 corresponds with the increase in the proportion of disurbanising agglomerations. The latter rose from 4 per cent in the first period, to 9 per cent in the second, then to 23 per cent in the 1970–75 period. The number of reurbanising agglomerations had by that time not (yet) shown any change of analytical consequence.

In terms of growth and decline, the data show that during the two decades between 1950 and 1970, more than 9 out of 10 agglomerations grew in population, but in the more recent five-year period the proportion fell to 3 out of 4 (Table 6.3). Evidently, urban developments in Western Europe have been accompanied by basic structural changes corresponding over time with the staging described earlier. That conclusion warrants placing some confidence in the theory's validity.

Table 6.3
Growth and decline of West European agglomerations (%)*

Period	Phase		Total
	Growth	Decline	
1950–60	96	4	100
1960–70	92	8	100
1970–75	75	25	100

*The number of agglomerations differs slightly by time period since data for all were not available. This does not significantly affect the final result, however.

The data also permit testing whether size of agglomeration and stage of development are related. Specifically, are larger agglomerations in more advanced stages than smaller ones? Because the lack of amenities and the higher social costs enumerated above are more characteristic of larger than of smaller agglomerations (which have populations of at least 200,000 persons!), the exodus would be expected to occur earlier than it would from the smaller ones. Data from 1975 give some insight into the matter (Table 6.4).

Table 6.4
Agglomeration size and urbanisation phase (%) 1975*

Size	Stage				Total
	Urbanisation	Suburbanisation	Disurbanisation	Reurbanisation	
> 1 million	–	44	56	–	100
0.5 – 1 million	–	65	35	–	100
0.2 – 0.5 million	10	70	17	3	100

*German Federal Republic excluded.

The CURB study data, because they cover Eastern as well as Western Europe, provide the opportunity for evaluating the effect of differences in prosperity on the urbanisation process. The 1970—75 data, classified between growing and declining agglomerations for major European regions, show that there is no sign of decline yet in the countries with the lowest money incomes (represented here by Bulgaria, Hungary, Poland, and Yugoslavia). In Central and Southern Europe (represented here solely by Italy and Austria), occupying a middle income position, 13 per cent of urban agglomerations were experiencing decline compared to 25 per cent in Western Europe. The assumption that prosperity, too, is a significant factor, is at any rate not refuted by these figures. While the data may not prove beyond the shadow of a doubt the validity of the — tentative — theory, they do point strongly toward its acceptability. The conclusion is corroborated by the outcomes of a recent inquiry into urban development in the countries that make up the European Community (Cheshire and Hay, 1984). That research shows that the tendencies emerging between 1950 and 1975 indeed continued into the 1975—80 period. The fact that during the latter five years the European Community counted more than twice as many disurbanising agglomerations as in the earlier period indicates that West European urban development continued to move into the disurbanisation phase.

What are the prospects for the agglomerations? Further disurbanisation or reurbanisation? Let us try, based on certain assumptions, to explore future directions of urban development.

Future trends in urban development

Three assumptions underpin our view of the urban future. First, we assume that people will increasingly regard the quality of life as an essential determinant of their wellbeing. As a consequence, the attractiveness of cities or regions as residential locations will more and more depend on the qualitative factors, such as housing and environmental amenities, that they offer.

Second, we assume that access to urban facilities and services will also continue to determine well being, and perhaps even more so than it has in past years.

Third, we assume that accessibility to work places will be less determining of residential location than it has in the past. The assumption rests on the expectation that the occupational mix will continue to shift from manufacturing jobs in favour of the more footloose, so-called tertiary and quaternary sectors. Because footloose employment tends to follow population, its spatial distribution may be expected to reflect by and large that of the population. With the rising relative importance of footloose jobs, local differences in accessibility to jobs will decline. Future migration streams will be less influenced by employment considerations. The population, then, will become more footloose with respect to job opportunities, but less so with respect to living conditions.

The foregoing argument can be presented in simple mathematical terms. We assume the existence of a welfare function such that

$$\frac{\omega_A}{\omega_S} = (\frac{\pi_A^W}{\pi_S^W})^{\lambda^W} (\frac{\pi_A^R}{\pi_S^R})^{\lambda^R} \tag{1}$$

in which

ω_A, ω_S = welfare level in large agglomerations (A) as a proportion of welfare level in smaller urban areas (S);

π_A^W, π_S^W = work potential (job opportunities) in large and smaller urban areas, respectively;

π_A^R, π_S^R = residential qualities;

λ^W, λ^R = relative weights of work and residential qualities, $0 < \lambda^R, \lambda^R < 1$.

The assumed trend relation

$$\frac{\pi_A^W}{\pi_S^W} = a(\frac{\omega_A}{\omega_S})^\beta \qquad 0 < b < 1 \tag{2}$$

means that the job opportunities (provided by the tertiary sector), depend on the relative welfare levels of the individual urban areas. Remember that tertiary activities tend to follow the population.

Combining (1) and (2) we obtain

$$\frac{\omega_A}{\omega_S} = a'(\frac{\pi_A^R}{\pi_S^R})^{\frac{\lambda^R}{1-\beta\lambda^W}} \tag{3}$$

in which $\dfrac{1}{1-\beta\lambda^W}$ is some sort of welfare multiplier.

Because $0 < b, \lambda^W < 1$, so $0 < \beta\lambda^W < 1$.

On the further assumption that $\pi_A^R < \pi_S^R$, in other words, that the residential quality is higher in smaller towns than in larger ones, we can derive:

1    $\dfrac{\pi_A^R}{\pi_S^R}$ = smaller than unity and will become increasingly so with rising energy prices;

2   λ^R = increasing; residential qualities are more and more appreciated.

3   λ^W = decreasing; work motives for living in a given area decrease in importance.

We have thus established three reasons for the ratio ω_A / ω_S to decline and consequently for people to consider moving from A to S. Now, what urban developments can we expect on that basis, starting from the present state of European development, with several large agglomerations declining and others at various stages of growth?

We have assumed that the quality of life will more and more govern people's wellbeing and their locational choices. And we know that in many large European cities the quality of life is deteriorating. Urban renewal and rehabilitation offer the hope of improving living conditions but only a privileged few will, in the near future, be able to enjoy the improvements that these programmes promise. Hence, increasing numbers will prefer leaving the older residential quarters of central cities for more amenable locations. Where will they find them? During the suburbanisation stage, people can be expected to relocate from central cities to the suburbs a few kilometres distant, retaining ready access to both urban facilities and their current jobs. Because of limits on the absorptive capacity of the suburbs, however, some will have to go further afield, beyond the urban perimeter. When population spills over into the hinterland, and declines in the core exceed growth in the ring, the agglomeration moves into the disurbanisation stage, the state to which many major European agglomerations have now been reduced. The question is: what will happen next?

According to our first assumption, many would prefer leaving central cities as a way to improve their living conditions. Based on our third assumption, many migrants will not be inhibited from leaving the agglomeration altogether, even if that requires taking another job, for shifts in industrial composition have made increasing proportions of people, as well as of jobs, footloose.

What are these migrants' destinations? Recalling our second assumption, the quality of life is influenced by accessibility to urban

93

facilities. The odds are therefore that most will choose another urban area, and one that better suits their preferences and aspirations.

Because the results of the CURB study suggest that the destinations chosen are likely to be those at earlier stages of development than the places of origin, migrants leaving disurbanising agglomerations will probably relocate in areas experiencing suburbanisation or urbanisation.

Those who favour agglomerations that are in the process of suburbanising will tend to locate in suburban rings rather than in the declining centres. Suburban municipalities will burgeon for they must cope with net immigration from their own cores, and from other agglomerations. (The influence of 'inter-metropolitan deconcentration' varies with the number of metropolitan areas involved and the number of smaller urban areas to which they decentralise.) Growing so rapidly, and given their limited housing and infrastructure capacities, the suburban municipalities will probably be developed to capacity before all those who want to move out from the core have managed to do so. A relatively large proportion of the core populations may then, in turn, consider moving to other urban areas that offer higher levels of wellbeing.

The CURB results indicate that we may expect the destination to be a small or medium-sized urban region with a rapidly growing core and the early signs of suburban growth — an agglomeration in the transition from urbanisation to suburbanisation. Thus, once more, an agglomeration entering the stage of disurbanisation will have set in motion the process of inter-metropolitan deconcentration!

From this we learn that disurbanisation at one place stimulates urban growth elsewhere. The spatial distribution of urban growth thus depends on the relative attractiveness of potential growth municipalities. Obviously, local policy can do much to enhance that potential.

The scenario based on the three assumptions portrays an urban Europe made up of agglomerations that are currently declining, will continue to decline at least in the short and medium term, and acceleration of growth in other agglomerations until they in turn also fall into decline, spilling growth over into other areas. This description suggests that a kind of urban multiplier is at work: changes in the level of living in one urban system lead to growth and decline in others. If we consider the initially declining agglomeration a 'leader' in urban development, then its direct 'followers' are the urban systems that feed on the inflow of people and industries from the declining agglomerations.

Figure 6.1 illustrates this sequence of events.

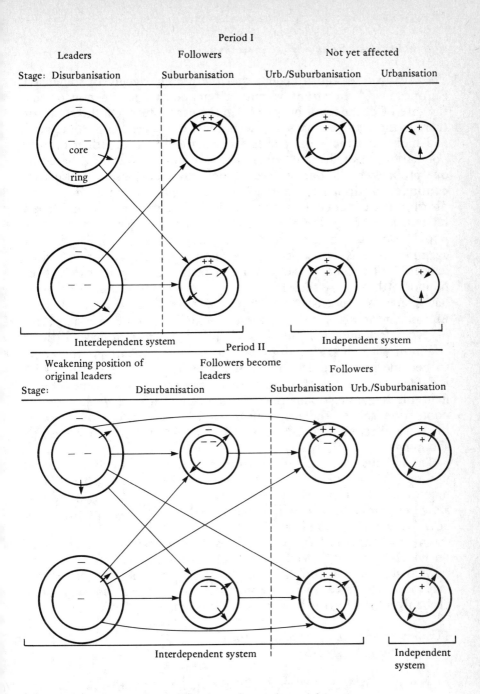

Figure 6.1 Extension of the interdependent urban system

The problems of dynamic urban systems

The future of declining urban systems

There is little reason to believe that the present decline of some large European agglomerations is only a temporary phenomenon or that the rate of decline will be slowed in the near future. On the contrary, there is the very real danger that as these urban centres become more and more unattractive as places for living and working, their rates of population loss will accelerate. That gloomy expectation is based on our probably well founded assumption that footloose activities will continue to displace industrial employment. Because the spatial distributions of footloose activity and of population tend to be closely related, loss of footloose activity will tend to follow in the wake of population loss. The out-migration of these activities implies that the agglomeration is losing its high economic-growth sectors, a serious danger. Left behind is the residual of manufacturing activities, often bound to the site by their location-specific requirements. These, as we have seen, are precisely the types of enterprises that, in Western Europe and in other parts of the post-industrial world, are stagnating or even declining. Obviously, such urbanised regions have little in common with the original growth poles; on the contrary, they tend to become growth poles in reverse, or negative growth centres. With the departure of growth sectors, the urban economy becomes dependent on stagnating industries. Via multiplier effects, decline of the population and of the economy is likely to have deleterious impacts on private and public facilities and services, such as education and shopping.

The number and quality of facilities such as shops will be affected not only by population loss but also by the selective character of migration. The relatively well paid workers employed in footloose activities move out, leaving behind the relatively poorly paid employees in the old industrial sectors.

The analysis of urban spatial cycles, together with the assumptions on which it is based, lead to the conclusion that the urban regions now in decline will probably get caught up in a negative spiral that may lead to grave social, economic, and financial consequences, probably worsening the longer the regions remain in decline.

Urban dynamics and spatial differences in the quality of urban life

At the spatial level, differences in the quality of urban life seem to increase through time. Roughly, the following development can be traced. During the urbanisation stage, better living conditions can be found in the residential neighbourhoods located at the urban fringe. During the suburbanisation stage, people move from centres to suburbs to increase their standard of living. With disurbanisation, however, people seek better places to live outside the agglomerations. Thus, as agglomerations move through stages from urbanisation to disurbanisation, more and more agglomerations are likely to decline in the future. Figure 6.1 shows how the process of urban decline shifts from local to regional scope.

A recent study (van den Berg, Boeckhout and van der Meer, 1979) shows how such a development took place in the Dutch provinces of Noord- and Zuid-Holland. Between 1960 and 1970, only one of the five agglomerations experienced decline, while total population (population in centres with more than 10,000 inhabitants) in the two provinces grew at average annual rates of 7.8 and 7.9 per cent respectively. During the next eight years, however, the number of declining agglomerations had dropped to three, but Noord-Holland's total urban population had declined by 1.2 per cent and, in Zuid-Holland, the growth rate had dropped to almost zero. In that situation, the difference in level of wellbeing between a region of urban decline and one of urban growth is considerable. While the state of disurbanisation lasts, the declining area will expand (see Figure 6.1).

Clearly, developments such as these fail to correspond with regional policy objectives that seek to equalise the spatial distribution of wellbeing. That objective can be achieved only if the quality of life in declining urban regions can be restored to levels that compete with those in urban places in high demand as residential locations.

Problems of urban growth

One of the phenomena described earlier was that the disurbanisation of one urban region may accelerate the growth of others. Relatively high growth rates will shorten the length of the growth period and hasten the approach of decline. Under the circumstances, urban growth will be costly, and the functional lifetime of (at least part of) the urban infrastructure will be shortened; there is the additional risk of overexpanding infrastructure relative to its shortened social life. The ever-present danger of overbuilding becomes a major problem when rapid growth turns into decline, as illustrated by the present situation in many European agglomerations. But the danger will be greater and the social costs higher as the growth period becomes shortened. On balance, it seems likely that future growth periods will indeed be shorter than they were in the past.

Conclusion

This chapter has presented a general description of possible urban futures derived from a set of assumptions concerning potential socio-economic developments and from the analysis of historical data for European agglomerations. Our research leads to a very bleak view of the future of agglomerations now in decline. There is the real possibility that they will develop into negative growth poles. Another conclusion, and one that derives from the CURB study, is that agglomerations, together with their cores and rings, tend to develop in systematic patterns. The immediate consequence will be a dramatic increase in the number of declining agglomerations, thus transforming them from positive to negative growth poles. Were that process to continue, decline would eventually spread to entire regions. Moreover, contrasts are expected to grow between regions marked by urban growth and prosperity and regions characterised by urban decline and poor living conditions. That brings us to a third important conclusion. The continued deconcentration of people and activities will accelerate the growth of other agglomerations, speeding up their urban development along the 'fixed' path and hastening the date when they too will have to face the realities of decline. As a consequence, the economic and social costs of urban deconcentration are expected to increase in the future.

The conclusions raise two important questions. First, is our rather bleak view of the urban future realistic? The pursuit of public policy, framed to cope with the issues of decline, could moderate the pace of urban deconcentration and effect a revival. That possibility is taken up in Chapter 8 which considers the relative impact of past re-urbanisation policies compared to other factors influencing progress through stages of development. Second, are the assumptions that undergird the theoretical and empirical analysis of this chapter realistic? A tentative answer to that question will be found in the next chapters that trace recent urban developments in Japan, The Netherlands, and the United States.

References

van den Berg, L., R. Drewett, L.H. Klaassen, A. Rossi and C.H.J. Vijverberg (1982), *Urban Europe: A Study of Growth and Decline*, Pergamon, Oxford.

van den Berg, L., I.J. Boeckhout and J. van der Meer (1979), *Stedelijke Dynamiek in Nederland (Urban Dynamics in the Netherlands)*, EUR/Netherlands Economic Institute, Rotterdam.

Cheshire, P. and D. Hay (1984), *The Development of the European Urban System, 1971—1981*, Joint Centre for Land Development Studies, University of Reading, Reading.

7 Is disurbanisation foreseeable in Japan? — a comparison between US and Japanese urbanisation processes[1]

TATSUHIKO KAWASHIMA

The 'urban problem' has two primary facets: rapid concentration of population into major urban centres; and population decline in large metropolitan areas. The former problem, urban concentration, accords with our traditional knowledge about the phenomenon of urbanisation and still characterises most developing countries. On the other hand, the problem of metropolitan decline has increasingly attracted the attention of scholars and policy makers whose interests centre around urban issues especially in the industrialised nations.[2]

A new hypothetical framework for understanding the spatial cycles of metropolitan areas and for synthesising the two apparently contrary types of urban change into one comprehensively consistent theoretical paradigm was outlined in the previous chapter and tested empirically with data on the growth and decline of European metropolitan areas. The general concept of a metropolitan area includes a central city and the suburbs, comprising juxtaposed spatial entities, with which it is functionally integrated in economic and social spheres. The spatial cycle hypothesis argues that the life cycle of metropolitan areas recurrently follows four successive metamorphic stages — urbanisation, suburbanisation, disurbanisation, and re-urbanisation — with each composed of two sub-stages depending on the relative balance of population change between central city and suburbs (Table 7.1). The second type of urban problem alluded to — decline at metropolitan level — corresponds to the disurbanisation stage in the conceptual scheme of spatial cycles.

Table 7.1
Spatial cycle hypothesis

Stage	Sub-stage	Population change* Central City (X)	Suburbs (Y)	Relative change	Metropolitan area
Urbanisation	1	+	−	X > Y	+
	2	+	+	X > Y	
Suburbanisation	3	+	+	X < Y	+
	4	−	+	X < Y	
Disurbanisation	5	−	+	X < Y	−
	6	−	−	X < Y	
Reurbanisation	7	−	−	X > Y	−
	8	+	−	X > Y	

*Plus and minus signs indicate population increase and decrease respectively.

Source: Constructed from Klaassen, Bourdrez and Volmuller (1981).

This thus focuses our scientific curiosity about whether the Japanese urban system has entered an era of disurbanisation or, if not, whether it will in the foreseeable future. To search for an answer to this question, a comparative analysis between US and Japanese urbanisation processes will be carried out using the spatial cycle framework and the ROXY index (discussed in a later section). In this analysis, we use population data by Standard Metropolitan Statistical Areas for the USA, and by Functional Urban Cores for Japan. (Functional Urban Core (FUC) is the Japanese equivalent of SMSA; see Kawashima (1972) for the definition of FUC.)

Disurbanisation in the United States

Disurbanisation preceded by population decrease in central cities

In 1981, there were 323 Standard Metropolitan Statistical Areas (SMSAs) in the USA. Table 7.2 lists the data for 1940—80 population

Table 7.2

Population changes in the US, 1940—80; 30 largest SMSAs and their central cities

SMSA	Rank (1980 SMSA Pop)	Spatial Unit	Population (1,000)				Population Growth Rate %				(Reference) PGR %	
			1960	1970	1975	1980	1960—70	1970—75	1975—80	1970—80	1940—50	1950—60
New York	1	SMSA	9,540	9,974	9,561	9,120	4.5	−4.1	−4.6	−8.6	—	A
		CC	7,782	7,896	7,482	7,072	1.5	−5.2	−5.5	−10.4	5.9	−1.4
Los Angeles—Long Beach	2	SMSA	6,039	7,042	6,987	7,478	16.6	−0.8	7.0	6.2	—	45.5
		CC	2,479	2,812	2,727	2,967	13.4	−3.0	8.8	5.5	31.0	25.8
Chicago	3	SMSA	6,221	6,977	7,015	7,104	12.2	0.5	1.3	1.8	—	20.1
		CC	3,550	3,369	3,099	3,005	−5.1	−8.0	−3.0	−10.8	6.6	−2.0
Philadelphia	4	SMSA	4,343	4,824	4,807	4,717	11.1	−0.4	−1.9	−2.2	—	18.3
		CC	2,003	1,949	1,816	1,688	−2.7	−6.8	−7.0	−13.4	7.3	−3.3
Detroit	5	SMSA	3,950	4,435	4,424	4,353	12.3	−0.2	−1.6	−1.8	—	A
		CC	1,670	1,514	1,335	1,203	−9.3	−11.8	−9.9	−20.5	14.0	−9.7
San Francisco—Oakland	6	SMSA	2,619	3,109	3,140	3,251	17.4	1.0	3.5	4.6	—	24.0
		CC	740	716	665	679	−3.2	−7.1	2.1	−5.2	20.1	−4.5
Washington	7	SMSA	2,097	2,910	3,022	3,061	38.8	3.8	1.3	5.2	—	A
		CC	764	757	712	638	−0.9	−5.9	−10.4	−15.7	21.0	−4.7
Dallas—Ft Worth	8	SMSA	1,738	2,378	2,527	2,975	36.8	6.3	17.7	25.1	—	A
		CC	680	844	813	904	24.1	−3.7	11.2	7.1	47.1	56.7
Houston	9	SMSA	1,430	1,999	2,286	2,905	39.8	14.4	27.1	45.3	—	A
		CC	939	1,234	1,357	1,595	31.6	10.0	17.5	29.3	54.8	57.4
Boston	10	SMSA	2,688	2,899	2,890	2,763	7.8	−0.3	−4.4	−4.7	—	A
		CC	697	641	637	563	−8.0	−0.6	−11.6	−12.2	3.9	−13.0
Nassau—Suffolk	11	SMSA	1,967	2,556	2,657	2,606	29.9	4.0	−1.9	2.0	—	—
		CC	n.a.	n.a.	n.a.	n.a.	—	—	—	—	—	—
St Louis	12	SMSA	2,144	2,411	2,367	2,356	12.5	−1.8	−0.5	−2.3	—	A
		CC	750	622	525	453	−17.1	−15.6	−13.7	−27.2	5.0	−12.5
Pittsburgh	13	SMSA	2,405	2,401	2,322	2,264	−0.2	−3.3	−2.5	−5.7	—	8.7
		CC	604	520	459	424	−13.9	−11.7	−7.6	−18.5	0.7	−10.8
Baltimore	14	SMSA	1,804	2,071	2,148	2,174	14.8	3.7	1.2	5.0	—	A
		CC	939	905	852	787	−3.6	−5.9	−7.6	−13.0	10.6	−1.2
Minneapolis—St Paul	15	SMSA	1,598	1,965	2,011	2,114	23.0	2.3	5.1	7.6	—	A
		CC	434	434	378	371	−10.1	−12.9	−1.9	−14.5	6.1	−7.5
Atlanta	16	SMSA	1,169	1,596	1,790	2,030	36.5	12.2	13.4	27.2	—	A
		CC	487	495	436	425	1.6	−11.9	−2.5	−14.1	9.6	47.1

Newark	17	SMSA	1,833	2,057	1,999	1,966	12.2	-2.8	-1.7	-4.4	—	A
		CC	405	382	340	329	-5.7	-11.0	-3.2	-13.9	2.1	-7.7
Anaheim–Santa Ana– Garden Grove	18	SMSA	704	1,421	1,700	1,933	101.8	19.6	13.7	36.0	—	225.6
		CC	104	166	194	219	59.6	16.9	12.9	31.9	36.4	593.3
Cleveland	19	SMSA	1,909	2,064	1,967	1,899	8.1	-4.7	-3.5	-8.0	—	A
		CC	876	751	639	574	-14.3	-14.9	-10.2	-23.6	4.2	-4.3
San Diego	20	SMSA	1,033	1,358	1,585	1,862	31.5	16.7	17.5	37.1	—	85.5
		CC	573	697	774	876	21.6	11.0	13.2	25.7	64.5	71.6
Miami	21	SMSA	935	1,268	1,439	1,626	35.6	13.5	13.0	28.2	—	88.9
		CC	292	335	365	347	14.7	9.0	-4.9	3.6	44.8	17.3
Denver–Boulder	22	SMSA	935	1,239	1,413	1,621	32.5	14.0	14.7	30.8	—	A
		CC	494	515	485	492	4.3	-5.8	1.4	-4.5	29.2	18.8
Seattle–Everett	23	SMSA	1,107	1,425	1,407	1,607	28.7	-1.3	14.2	12.8	—	31.1
		CC	557	531	487	494	-4.7	-8.3	1.4	-7.0	27.2	19.0
Tampa–St Petersburg	24	SMSA	809	1,089	1,348	1,569	34.6	23.8	16.4	44.1	—	A
		CC	275	278	280	272	1.1	0.7	-2.9	-2.2	15.7	120.0
Riverside–San Bernardino– Ontario	25	SMSA	810	1,141	1,226	1,558	40.9	7.4	27.1	36.5	—	A
		CC	84	140	151	171	66.7	7.9	13.2	22.1	34.3	78.7
Phoenix	26	SMSA	664	969	1,221	1,509	45.9	26.0	23.6	55.7	—	100.0
		CC	439	582	665	790	32.6	14.3	18.8	35.7	64.6	310.3
Cincinnati	27	SMSA	1,268	1,385	1,381	1,401	9.2	-0.3	1.4	1.2	—	24.0
		CC	503	453	413	385	-9.2	-8.8	-6.8	-15.0	10.5	0.2
Milwaukee	28	SMSA	1,279	1,404	1,409	1,397	9.8	0.4	-0.9	-0.5	—	A
		CC	741	717	666	636	-3.2	-7.1	-4.5	-11.3	8.5	16.3
Kansas City	29	SMSA	1,109	1,274	1,290	1,327	14.9	1.3	2.9	4.2	—	A
		CC	476	507	473	448	6.5	-6.7	-5.3	-11.6	14.5	4.2
San José	30	SMSA	642	1,065	1,174	1,295	65.9	10.2	10.3	21.6	—	A
		CC	204	460	556	629	125.5	20.9	13.1	36.7	39.7	214.7
Total		SMSA*	66,819	78,706	80,513	83,841	17.8	2.3	4.1	6.5		
		CC*	30,589	31,222	29,781	29,436	2.1	-4.6	-1.2	-5.7		
Average (weighted)		SMSA*	2,227	2,524	2,684	2,795	17.8	2.3	4.1	6.5		
		CC*	1,055	1,077	1,027	1,015	2.1	-4.6	-1.2	-5.7		
Average (simple)		SMSA	—	—	—	—	26.2	5.4	7.0	13.3		
		CC*	—	—	—	—	10.1	-2.8	-0.2	-2.3		
United States			179,323	203,302	215,465	226,546	13.37	5.98	5.14	11.4		

*Excluding the city of Nassau.

Sources: US Bureau of the Census (1965, pp. 17–20; 1966, pp. 17–21; 1972, pp. 21–3; 1977, pp. 19–24; 1980, pp. 12, 21–6; 1981, pp. 18–23).

changes in each of the 30 largest SMSAs and their central cities. (No SMSA data are available for the 1940–50 period.)

We see from these data that, for the 30, only Pittsburgh lost population in the 1960s although the decrease amounted only to 0.2 per cent. Population decline spread, however, with the advent of the 1970s. Between 1970 and 1975, New York, the largest SMSA, lost about 400,000 persons, or a decrease of 4.1 per cent. Others losing population during the same five-year period were Cleveland (losing 4.7 per cent), Newark (2.8 per cent), St Louis (1.8 per cent), Seattle–Everett (1.3 per cent), Los Angeles–Long Beach (0.8 per cent), Philadelphia (0.4 per cent), Boston (0.3 per cent), Cincinnati (0.3 per cent), and Detroit (0.2 per cent). With Pittsburgh also losing population (3.3 per cent) during the 1970s, as it did in the 1960s, a total of 11 SMSAs experienced population loss in the first half of the 1970s.

The second half of that decade saw Los Angeles–Long Beach, Seattle–Everett, and Cincinnati regaining population with five-year growth rates of 7.0, 14.2, and 1.4 per cent respectively. The rest of the 11 metropolitan areas, however, continued to lose population. Furthermore, with Nassau–Suffolk and Milwaukee also losing population by 1.9 and 0.9 per cent respectively, a total of 10 SMSAs registered declines during the 1975–80 period.

The data for the entire 1970–80 period show that the population decreased in 9 SMSAs out of the 13 which lost population during either the first half or the second half of the decade, excluding Los Angeles–Long Beach, Seattle–Everett, Cincinnati, and Nassau–Suffolk. This fact together with the additional information provided in Table 7.2 for the earlier 1950–60 and 1960–70 decades demonstrates that a significant reversal of past trends took place during the 1970s. In more concrete terms, the US metropolitan system had reached the fully fledged phase of disurbanisation.

It is important to note that disurbanisation did not surge abruptly on the US urban system without any warning signs. Central city population change served as a key omen of its approach. Table 7.2 shows that 14 central cities lost population during the 1950s, 15 in the 1960s, and 20 in the 1970s.[3] Thirteen central cities declined continuously during the entire three-decade period, 1950–80, and eight of these were in the SMSAs which disurbanised during the 1970s.[4] In other words, central city loss generally preceded by up to 20 years decline in the SMSAs to which the central cities belonged. This observation agrees reasonably with the spatial cycle hypothesis by implying that population loss in the central cities of large SMSAs predicts the emergence of disurbanisation.

We should not, at the same time, fail to notice that several large SMSAs gained population in the 1970s at a pace exceeding the average growth rate of national population, and their central cities followed suit. The Pheonix SMSA, which increased its population by over 50 per cent between 1970 and 1980, was a leading example. Other SMSAs that enjoyed relative growth were Houston, San Diego, Riverside—San Bernardino—Ontario, Anaheim—Santa Ana—Garden Grove, and San José.

A categorisation matrix provides a systematic overview of the current US situation involving both rapidly growing metropolitan areas, as well as the cases of disurbanisation already discussed. Table 7.3 shows various stages of urban change classified according to the population growth rates of central cities and metropolitan areas, instead of the absolute values of population change in central city and suburbs as adopted in the original spatial cycle scheme (Table 7.1).

Table 7.3
Categorisation matrix for large metropolitan areas

			Population growth rate of central city		
				Positive	
			Negative	Below national average	Above national average
Population growth rate of	Positive	Above national average	C	B	A
		Below national average	F	E	D
of					
SMSA or FUC		Negative	G	H	I

Note: FUC = Functional Urban Core

In this matrix, the population growth rates of central city and metropolitan area are both divided into three classes. The first class consists of areas with growth rates exceeding the national average; the second includes those with rates below the national average but above zero; and the third is for rates below zero. The classification yields nine cells running from A through I, each of which corresponds to at least one sub-stage of the spatial cycle scheme shown in Table 7.1. Nevertheless, this correspondence is somewhat confusing due to the fact that the growth rate is applied in Table 7.3 as a measurement for population changes while in Table 7.1 the absolute value of population change is applied for the same purpose. To make the relationships between cells and sub-stages more straightforward, we now slightly modify the conceptual framework of the spatial cycle hypothesis, but without losing its essence. We will alter the scheme described in Table 7.1, and designated as type-α scheme in Figure 7.1(a), to the scheme designated type-β in Figure 7.1(b) where the horizontal and vertical axes represent the growth rates of central city and metropolitan area respectively. (The type-γ scheme is discussed later.) Figures 7.2(a) through 7.2(c) demonstrate the resultant relationships between nine cells of the categorisation matrix and eight sub-stages of the spatial cycle scheme of type-β.

Suppose for the sake of convenience that the SMSAs falling in cell A, B, or C of the categorisation matrix are called 'actively growing SMSAs'; those in D, E, or F, 'quasi-growing SMSAs' (in the sense that population continues to grow but the growth rate is below the national average); and those in G, H, or I, 'degenerating SMSAs'. This classification roughly identifies trends in metropolitan growth or decline on the basis of the apparent changes of the SMSA populations. We can then classify the 30 largest SMSAs according to the average annual growth rates of population for 1975—80 into the three categories reported in Table 7.4 by assuming that central city boundaries remained unchanged during the five-year growth period. (Notice that in Table 7.2 the central city boundaries are variable over time.)

According to Table 7.4, 13 SMSAs grew at rates above the national average between 1975 and 1980. Eight of these belonged to Group A, two to Group B, and three to Group C. In light of the directional movement of spatial cycle flows depicted in Figure 7.2(c), the eight SMSAs in Group A (Houston, Riverside—San Bernardino—Ontario, Phoenix, Dallas—Ft Worth, San Diego, Anaheim—Santa Ana—Garden Grove, San Jose, and Los Angeles—Long Beach) are farthest from the disurbanisation stage in which the degenerating SMSAs in Group G are situated. Among the 13 actively growing SMSAs the three falling into Group C (Tampa—St Petersburg, Atlanta, and Miami) are closest to the disurbanisation stage.

As for quasi-growing SMSAs, we have zero, one, and six examples in Groups D, E, and F, respectively. As Figures 7.2(a) through 7.2(c) suggest, we cannot be quite sure to which cell — B of the second sub-stage or F of the third sub-stage — the San Francisco SMSA, in Group E at the second sub-stage, will most probably proceed in the next move. On the other hand, some of the five SMSAs belonging to Group F at the fourth sub-stage (Kansas City, Cincinnati, Washington D.C.,

Chicago, and Baltimore) are likely to disurbanise in the near future.

The 10 degenerating SMSAs (St Louis, Milwaukee, Detroit, Newark, Philadelphia, Nassau—Suffolk, Pittsburgh, Cleveland, Boston, and New York) all belong to Group G at the fifth sub-stage. There are no generating metropolitan areas in either Groups H or I. But the New York SMSA, which is closest to the sixth sub-stage,[5] seems to be taking the lead in approaching the reurbanisation stage among the 30 largest SMSAs. When New York will actually reurbanise, however, is perhaps a debatable question.

Characteristics of recent spatial changes

Drawing together the information provided in Tables 7.2 and 7.4, and accepting the basic concept of the spatial cycle hypothesis, the major

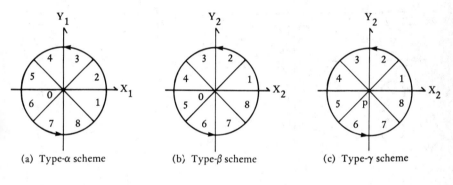

(a) Type-α scheme   (b) Type-β scheme   (c) Type-γ scheme

Notes

X_1 – population change in central city
Y_1 – population change in suburbs
X_2 – population growth rate of central city
Y_2 – population growth rate of metropolitan area
z – average growth rate of national total population
Coordinates of point P: (z,z)
Number in each fan-shaped segment: sub-stage number
Urbanisation stage   – sub-stages 1 and 2
Suburbanisation stage – sub-stages 3 and 4
Disurbanisation stage – sub-stages 5 and 6
Reurbanisation stage – sub-stages 7 and 8

Figure 7.1   Three types of spatial cycle schemes

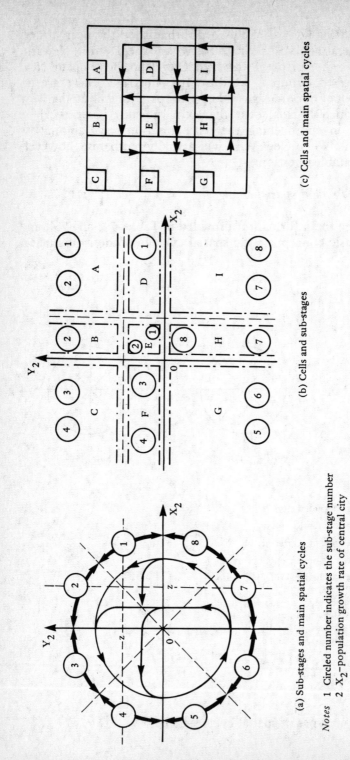

(a) Sub-stages and main spatial cycles

(b) Cells and sub-stages

(c) Cells and main spatial cycles

Notes 1 Circled number indicates the sub-stage number
       2 X_2–population growth rate of central city
          Y_2–population growth rate of metropolitan area
          z –average growth rate of national total population

Figure 7.2 Main spatial cycles of type-β scheme, its sub-stages and relation-
            ships between sub-stages and cells of categorisation matrix

108

features of the recent and possible future population changes in the 30 largest US SMSAs thus appear to be the following:

— The polarisation between metropolitan population growth and decline significantly widened as the urban system reached the full fledged phase of disurbanisation in the 1970s.
— With three pre-disurbanisation SMSAs[6] in Group C at the third sub-stage and six in Group F at the third and fourth sub-stages, the magnitude of the overall disurbanisation in the entire urban system will be continuously increased.
— All of the 13 actively growing SMSAs were located in either the South or the West, while the 10 degenerating SMSAs were in either the Northeast or the North Central regions. Moreover, all 9 pre-disurbanisation SMSAs were situated in either the North Central or the eastern part of the South. These facts indicate that the wave of population decline is permeating the South from the Northeast and the North Central regions along the South Atlantic area. Viewed more broadly, the population upsurge is sweeping from the combined Northeast—North Central region to the combined South-West regions, and travelling westward within the latter.[7]
— In terms of scale, eight out of the 10 SMSAs at the disurbanisation stage in the second half of the 1970s ranked among the nation's 20 largest metropolitan areas. If we add the five pre-disurbanisation SMSAs in Group F of the fourth sub-stage to the 10 degenerating SMSAs, then 10 of those 15 turn up among the largest. This provides persuasive evidence indeed that disurbanisation is currently concentrated in large SMSAs.

In short, the most salient characteristics of the pattern of population change revealed from our study of the 30 largest SMSAs are: the striking contrast between the population decline in the Northeast and the North Central and the population upsurge in the South and the West, with the artificial interpretation that the eastern portion of the South is considered as an extension of the combined Northeast—North Central region; and the intensive potential momentum of disurbanisation bursting into the largest metropolitan areas among those studied.

Table 7.4
Three categories and nine groups of US SMSAs

SMSA	Annual PGR 1975–80 (%)		Sub-stage of spatial cycles	Annual PGR of SMSA (%)		Region
	SMSA	Central city		1960–70	1970–75	
Category 1						
Actively growing SMSAs						
Group A						
Houston	4.91	3.28	2	3.41	2.72	South
Riverside—San Bernardino—Ontario	4.91	2.52	2	3.49	1.45	West
Phoenix	4.33	3.50	2	3.85	4.73	West
Dallas—Ft Worth	3.32	2.14	2	3.18	1.22	South
San Diego	3.27	2.51	2	2.77	3.14	West
Anaheim—Santa Ana—Garden Grove	2.60	2.45	2	7.28	3.65	West
San Jose	1.98	2.50	1	5.19	1.97	West
Los Angeles—Long Beach	1.37	1.70	1	1.55	-0.16	West
Group B						
Denver—Boulder	2.78	0.29	2	2.86	2.66	West
Seattle—Everett	2.69	0.29	2	2.56	-0.25	West
Group C						
Tampa—St Petersburg	3.08	-0.57	3	3.02	4.36	South
Atlanta	2.55	-0.51	3	3.16	2.32	South
Miami	2.47	-1.01	3	3.09	2.56	South
Category 2						
Quasi-growing SMSAs						
Group D – null						
Group E						
San Francisco—Oakland	0.70	0.42	2	1.61	0.20	West
Group F						
Minneapolis—St Paul	1.00	-0.37	3	2.09	0.46	N.C.
Kansas City	0.57	-1.08	4	1.40	0.25	N.C.
Cincinnati	0.29	-1.39	4	0.89	-0.06	N.C.

Washington	0.26	−2.17	4	3.33	0.76	South
Chicago	0.25	−0.61	4	1.15	0.11	N.C.
Baltimore	0.24	−1.57	4	1.39	0.73	South

Category 3

Degenerating SMSAs

Group G

St Louis	−0.09	−2.92	5	1.18	−0.37	N.C.
Milwaukee	−0.17	−0.92	5	0.94	0.07	N.C.
Detroit	−0.32	−2.06	5	1.16	−0.05	N.C.
Newark	−0.33	−0.66	5	1.16	−0.57	N.E.
Philadelphia	−0.38	−1.45	5	1.06	−0.07	N.E.
Nassau–Suffolk	−0.39	—	—	2.65	0.78	N.E.
Pittsburgh	−0.50	−1.57	5	−0.02	−0.67	N.E.
Cleveland	−0.70	−2.12	5	0.78	−0.96	N.C.
Boston	−0.89	−2.44	5	0.76	−0.06	N.E.
New York	−0.94	−1.12	5	0.45	−0.84	N.E.

Group H – null

Group I – null

Notes:

1 Sub-stages of spatial cycles are those appearing in type-β spatial cycle scheme described in Figure 7.1.
2 Groups A through I respectively correspond to cells A through I in Table 7.3.
3 PGR–Population Growth Rate; N.E. – Northeast; N.C. – North central.

Relative disurbanisation in Japan

FUCs approaching decline, and rapidly growing FUCs

Population data for Japan's 86 Functional Urban Cores (FUCs), and for the central cities of the 30 largest, are shown by five-year intervals from 1960 to 1980 in Table 7.5. These tabulations are the basis for the population growth rates of the 30 largest FUCs and their central cities displayed in Table 7.6.

The data show that Tokyo's central city began to lose population as early as 1965—70. The rate of loss, 0.6 per cent for the five-year period, accelerated in each of the following intervals. The rates increased to 2.2 per cent and 3.4 per cent, respectively, during 1970—75 and 1975—80. In the meantime, although the population of the FUC rose by 57.2 per cent between 1960 and 1980, the five-year rates of growth dropped from 18.3 per cent in 1960—65 to 5.5 per cent in 1975—80.

The experience of Osaka, Japan's second largest FUC, ran roughly in parallel. Decline also began in the 1965—70 period with a 5.6 per cent drop in the central city's population followed by successive declines of 6.8 per cent in 1970—75 and 4.7 per cent in 1975—80. Although the FUC increased in population by 56 per cent between 1960 and 1980, its five-year growth rate dropped steadily from 21.1 per cent during 1960—65 to only 3.1 per cent in 1975—80.

In addition, the central city of Nagasaki started losing population (0.7 per cent) in the 1975—80 period while the growth rate of the FUC began to drop. Also, Kitakyushu FUC experienced net population loss in the 1960s, largely as the result of a decreasing suburban population. Accordingly, the central cities of three large FUCs (Tokyo, Osaka, and Nagasaki) lost population between 1975 and 1980.

Turning from the three FUCs approaching decline to those experiencing rapid population growth during 1975—80, we find that, of the 30 largest, Chiba grew most rapidly (13.6 per cent), followed in order by Toyota (with a five-year growth rate of 12.2 per cent for 1975—80), Sapporo (12.0 per cent), Fukuoka (11.5 per cent), and Kagoshima (10.2 per cent). Except for Fukuoka FUC, the population of their central cities also increased by upwards of 10 per cent in the same period.

Large FUCs grouped into three categories

From the data in Table 7.6 we can construct Table 7.7 to classify — in the same manner as we did in Table 7.4 for the 30 largest US

SMSAs — the 30 largest FUCs, including both decline-approaching and rapidly growing FUCs, into nine groups (A through I) based on average annual population growth rates for the 1975—80 period.

Twenty-two FUCs grew faster than the national average. Seventeen of them (Chiba, Toyota, Sapporo, Fukuoka, Kagoshima, Sendai, Kumamoto, Utsunomiya, Hiroshima, Yokohama, Kanazawa, Oita, Niigata, Toyohashi, Okayama, Hamamatsu, and Takamatsu) belonged in Group D, and hence they were farthest from the disurbanisation stage. Tokyo, the single FUC in Group C, was at the third sub-stage of the spatial cycle scheme and, of the 22 actively growing FUCs, the one situated most closely to the disurbanisation stage.

Regarding the quasi-growing FUCs, Fukuyama was the only one belonging in Group D at the first sub-stage. For Group E, we have Wakayama where the population growth rate has continuously dropped since 1960 and, although the FUC was situated at the first sub-stage, its population between 1975 and 1980 grew the slowest of the 30 largest FUCs. Group E also included four FUCs at the second sub-stage (Kobe, Himeji, Shizuoka, and Kitakyushu). The population growth rate for two of them (Kobe and Shizuoka) has declined continuously since 1960. Group F consisted of only two FUCs, Nagasaki at the third sub-stage and Osaka at the fourth sub-stage.

The absence of any cases of degenerating FUCs in either Group G, H, or I clearly indicates that the Japanese urban system had not reached the disurbanisation phase by 1980. This implies, nonetheless, that there exists in the Japanese urban system a sub-surface momentum approaching the early phase of disurbanisation. This point is reinforced by the fact that the very biggest of the 30 largest FUCs, such as Tokyo, Osaka, and Nagoya, have experienced continuously declining growth rates. Among them, Osaka FUC appears to be closer to the disurbanisation stage than any of the others, and a near second would be Tokyo FUC.

Meanwhile, Wakayama FUC seems to be situated in a peculiar position of the spatial cycle if we adopt the type-γ scheme described in Figure 7.1(c). In that scheme, development occurs as a counter-clockwise rotation around the centre point P whose coordinates are (z, z) where z expresses the average growth rate of total national population. Wakayama emerges from this scheme as the single large FUC to have already arrived at the sixth sub-stage by 1980. The scheme also shows that other FUCs among the 30 largest were at sub-stages lower than the sixth. For example, Osaka, Nagasaki, and Shizuoka were at the fifth sub-stage, and Tokyo and Nagoya were at the fourth. The reason why I touch on the type-γ scheme here is to demonstrate the existence of a reasonable possibility, within the framework of the generalised spatial cycle hypothesis,[8] that the

Table 7.5
Population of Functional Urban Cores, Japan (FUCs), 1960–1980

FUC and CC	Rank (1980 FUC population)	Population					Nr of localities
		1960	1965	1970	1975	1980	
Sapporo	7	887,535	1,101,329	1,310,693	1,558,739	1,745,345	5
CC	–	615,628	821,217	1,010,123	1,240,617	1,401,758	–
Hakodate	50	322,970	331,804	343,406	362,637	380,514	5
Asahikawa	55	239,636	271,930	297,189	320,526	352,620	1
Muroran	71	201,221	227,200	238,137	242,941	241,428	3
Kushiro	70	178,731	198,984	214,922	231,403	242,331	3
Obihiro	73	159,846	175,329	189,643	203,004	221,662	4
Aomori	61	253,952	264,921	279,294	303,055	327,298	3
Hirosaki	67	232,842	229,993	231,520	237,813	248,963	6
Hachinohe	62	253,474	264,767	281,838	297,473	312,343	7
Morioka	48	286,736	301,530	318,532	348,174	382,814	8
Sendai	10	860,509	922,607	1,019,991	1,160,920	1,271,318	21
CC	–	425,272	480,925	545,065	615,473	664,799	–
Ishinomaki	76	188,427	187,376	191,066	197,905	204,465	6
Akita	42	401,513	404,280	415,990	438,920	466,697	13
Yamagata	45	383,092	382,153	391,335	409,933	435,632	7
Fukushima	51	319,768	325,801	338,403	358,500	376,944	8
Aizuwakamatsu	82	175,162	171,115	167,605	168,710	174,616	6
Kouriyama	49	309,223	316,187	332,688	356,581	381,819	4
Mito	31	411,235	430,161	462,343	509,530	550,432	12
Hitachi	53	318,134	331,419	335,157	348,301	360,799	6
Utsunomiya	21	564,682	583,921	625,795	697,120	752,827	14
CC	–	239,007	265,696	301,231	344,417	377,748	–
Maebashi	54	279,557	297,136	318,747	341,323	360,252	6
Takasaki	43	353,262	368,552	391,387	424,747	451,370	10
Kiryu	80	159,393	164,427	171,730	179,798	183,934	4
Chiba	12	540,852	642,330	838,299	1,077,675	1,224,611	9
CC	–	258,357	339,850	482,133	659,344	746,428	–
Tokyo	1	13,388,959	15,844,973	18,005,894	19,955,814	21,049,507	121
CC	–	8,310,027	8,893,094	8,840,942	8,642,800	8,349,209	–
Yokohama	4	2,272,380	2,901,289	3,603,704	4,258,008	4,592,642	15
CC	–	1,375,510	1,788,915	2,238,264	2,621,648	2,773,822	–

	City						
63	Odawara	233,572	263,399	283,736	302,690	311,927	9
18	Niigata	657,650	684,250	713,690	762,831	815,390	14
—	CC	325,018	356,302	383,919	423,204	457,783	—
69	Nagaoka	212,790	218,177	224,121	233,008	242,976	4
32	Toyama	477,794	480,192	493,522	522,486	547,056	11
47	Takaoka	367,534	363,314	364,085	376,284	384,157	8
24	Kanazawa	482,871	507,897	540,268	600,819	647,139	13
—	CC	313,112	335,828	361,379	395,262	417,681	—
33	Fukui	485,114	493,737	499,568	526,470	546,360	15
44	Koufu	382,963	385,021	398,003	421,891	443,777	16
40	Nagano	404,489	413,282	429,191	460,582	484,568	11
57	Matsumoto	288,435	293,499	306,225	326,626	346,645	10
13	Gifu	805,117	886,222	959,945	1,043,477	1,103,051	23
—	CC	312,597	358,259	385,727	408,699	410,368	—
14	Shizuoka	793,848	860,971	927,563	993,432	1,031,374	8
—	CC	350,897	382,799	416,378	446,952	458,342	—
15	Hamamatsu	743,710	779,062	827,403	891,775	945,941	17
—	CC	357,098	392,632	432,221	468,886	490,827	—
37	Numazu	330,878	374,868	421,513	468,590	495,140	7
58	Fuji	244,499	265,534	294,619	326,039	340,703	4
3	Nagoya	3,642,667	4,201,059	4,714,576	5,180,943	5,430,025	64
—	CC	1,697,093	1,935,430	2,036,053	2,079,694	2,087,884	—
30	Toyohashi	403,935	439,617	473,409	520,769	554,283	8
—	CC	215,515	238,672	258,547	284,597	304,274	—
29	Toyota	311,142	364,410	445,073	525,850	590,135	5
—	CC	104,529	136,728	197,193	248,774	281,609	—
52	Tsu	310,101	317,047	329,540	351,405	367,414	10
79	Ise	174,001	177,547	178,606	183,663	186,481	7
38	Otsu	302,222	322,270	356,159	424,452	488,437	8
5	Kyoto	1,511,077	1,644,808	1,809,412	1,984,788	2,085,076	15
—	CC	1,284,818	1,365,007	1,419,165	1,461,050	1,472,993	—
2	Osaka	6,855,068	8,298,236	9,521,577	10,374,705	10,694,672	68
—	CC	3,011,563	3,156,222	2,980,487	2,778,975	2,648,158	—
6	Kobe	1,441,703	1,588,300	1,740,999	1,908,784	1,988,253	8
—	CC	1,113,977	1,216,640	1,288,937	1,360,530	1,367,392	—
16	Himeji	682,238	732,534	782,646	838,691	871,119	18
—	CC	334,520	373,653	408,353	436,099	446,255	—
46	Nara	209,160	238,931	289,195	352,723	404,259	5
28	Wakayama	491,841	534,381	572,343	601,362	617,128	11
—	CC	285,155	328,657	365,267	389,677	401,462	—
75	Tottori	204,752	200,044	199,035	204,715	213,535	11

FUC and CC	Rank (1980 FUC population)	Population 1960	1965	1970	1975	1980	Nr of localities
Yonago	74	189,769	189,817	192,831	203,758	216,709	10
Matsue	68	226,178	224,096	227,877	236,758	248,093	9
Okayama	20	583,686	605,213	647,614	719,828	765,680	15
CC*	–	306,757	338,693	375,106	513,452	545,737	–
Kurashiki	36	337,115	355,369	418,465	480,215	497,686	9
Hiroshima	11	732,365	861,374	994,560	1,166,010	1,258,864	12
CC*	–	431,336	504,245	541,998	852,607	899,394	–
Kure	60	321,224	329,580	335,273	342,540	337,427	10
Fukuyama	26	475,869	491,050	544,938	604,910	622,780	7
CC*	–	183,682	204,768	255,086	329,779	346,031	–
Shimonoseki	59	331,874	332,023	328,801	336,848	340,391	5
Ube	72	242,216	220,085	211,317	221,869	229,752	4
Yamaguchi	85	136,097	130,218	130,685	135,517	145,066	3
Iwakuni	81	168,067	175,221	174,427	181,402	182,936	5
Tokushima	35	447,679	449,893	458,535	484,487	510,425	13
Takamatsu	22	594,749	595,973	617,272	667,985	705,740	21
CC	–	243,538	257,716	274,367	298,997	316,662	–
Matsuyama	34	389,653	413,531	445,917	499,017	542,284	8
Imabari	78	176,467	176,809	181,583	192,296	197,397	7
Nyhama	77	197,286	194,550	193,238	200,679	203,468	3
Kochi	41	367,439	383,774	405,169	443,577	470,870	9
Kitakyushu	9	1,518,451	1,515,708	1,501,563	1,554,303	1,604,577	19
CC	–	986,401	1,042,388	1,042,321	1,058,067	1,065,084	–
Fukuoka	8	1,089,452	1,197,739	1,348,113	1,565,142	1,744,420	24
CC*	–	661,395	749,808	853,270	1,002,214	1,088,617	–
Omuta	65	345,890	325,751	297,188	290,578	290,772	6
Kurume	39	462,451	452,729	456,193	466,017	487,704	15
Saga	64	295,715	286,643	283,571	289,675	304,956	11
Nagasaki	27	506,565	523,700	545,435	592,092	617,302	8
CC*	–	380,983	405,479	421,114	450,195	447,091	–
Sasebo	66	297,099	273,533	272,294	275,668	277,479	3
Kumamoto	19	625,931	643,565	671,565	718,481	783,397	16
CC*	–	373,922	407,052	440,020	488,053	525,613	–
Yatsushiro	86	152,094	145,623	140,809	140,019	143,279	4
Oita	25	474,068	491,972	520,798	587,009	630,798	10
CC	–	207,151	226,417	260,584	320,236	360,484	–

Miyazaki	56	247,866	257,218	274,925	310,210	349,620	6
Miyakonojyo	84	148,052	143,481	138,538	142,667	155,712	3
Nobeoka	83	148,223	147,559	151,337	157,639	161,216	3
Kagoshima	23	490,734	515,900	543,018	601,595	663,069	11
CC	–	334,643	371,129	403,340	456,818	505,077	–
Naha	17	555,764	619,847	666,131	767,619	828,563	21
CC	–	223,047	257,177	276,380	295,091	295,801	–
All FUCs	–	60,670,350	67,639,667	74,731,360	82,275,810	86,988,636	1,024

Notes:

1 Figures for population as on 1 October.
2 FUC boundaries are as in 1970 and fixed over time.
3 CC stands for central city. The population of the central city is given for the 30 largest FUCs. The boundaries of central cities are as of 1980 and fixed over time. For central cities with*, population in 1960, 1965 and 1970 is given for the 1970 boundary of that city, and population in 1975 and 1980 is given for the 1980 boundary of that city.
4 Eighty-six FUCs cover 8,596,511 ha which is 23 per cent of the national territory. The total population residing in FUCs as a fraction of the national total population was 74.31 per cent in 1980.
5 The number of localities composing each FUC is as in October 1970.
6 Total population of the 30 largest FUCs was 44,985,418 (1960), 51,580,237 (1965), 58,034,287 (1970), 64,481,476 (1975), and 68,235,026 (1980).

Table 7.6
Population growth rates of the 30 largest Functional Urban Cores (FUCs) and their central cities (1960–1980)

FUC	Rank (1980 FUC population)	Spatial unit	Population growth rate 1960–65	1965–70	1970–75	1975–80	1975–80 (annual)	Rank among 30 FUCs 1975–80 PGR	1980 Pop.
Tokyo	1	FUC	18.3	13.6	10.8	5.5	1.07	5	1
		CC	7.0	-0.6	-2.2	-3.4	-0.69		
Osaka	2	FUC	21.1	14.7	9.0	3.1	0.61	3	2
		CC	4.8	-5.6	-6.8	-4.7	-0.96		
Nagoya	3	FUC	15.3	12.2	9.9	4.8	0.94	8	3
		CC	14.0	5.2	2.1	0.4	0.08		
Yokohama	4	FUC	27.7	24.2	18.2	7.9	1.52	1	4
		CC	30.1	25.1	17.1	5.8	1.13		
Kyoto	5	FUC	8.9	10.0	9.7	5.1	0.99	13	5
		CC	6.2	4.0	3.0	0.8	0.16		
Kobe	6	FUC	10.2	9.6	9.6	4.2	0.82	10	6
		CC	9.2	5.9	5.6	0.5	0.10		
Sapporo	7	FUC	24.1	19.0	18.9	12.0	2.29	2	8
		CC	33.4	23.0	22.8	13.0	2.47		
Fukuoka	8	FUC	9.9	12.6	16.1	11.5	2.19	12	7
		CC*	13.4	13.8	17.5	8.6	1.67		
Kitakyushu	9	FUC	-0.2	-0.9	3.5	3.2	0.64	30	9
		CC	5.7	0.0	1.5	0.7	0.13		
Sendai	10	FUC	7.2	10.6	13.8	9.5	1.83	18	11
		CC	13.1	13.3	12.9	8.0	1.55		
Hiroshima	11	FUC	17.6	15.5	17.2	8.0	1.54	6	10
		CC*	16.9	7.5	57.3	5.5	1.07		
Chiba	12	FUC	18.8	30.5	28.6	13.6	2.59	4	12
		CC	31.5	41.9	36.8	13.2	2.51		
Gifu	13	FUC	10.1	8.3	8.7	5.7	1.12	11	13
		CC	14.6	7.7	6.0	0.4	0.08		
Shizuoka	14	FUC	8.5	7.7	7.1	3.8	0.75	16	14
		CC	9.1	8.8	7.3	2.5	0.50		
Hamamatsu	15	FUC	4.8	6.2	7.8	6.1	1.19	21	15
		CC	10.0	10.1	8.5	4.7	0.92		
Himeji	16	FUC	7.4	6.8	7.2	3.9	0.76	17	16
		CC	11.7	9.3	6.8	2.3	0.46		

City	No.	Type							
Naha	17	FUC	11.5	7.5	15.2	7.9	1.54	9 –	17 –
		CC	15.3	7.5	6.8	0.2	0.05		
Niigata	18	FUC	4.0	4.3	6.9	6.9	1.34	22 –	18 –
		CC	9.6	7.8	10.2	8.2	1.58		
Kumamoto	19	FUC	2.8	4.4	7.0	9.0	1.75	28 –	19 –
		CC*	8.9	8.1	10.9	7.7	1.49		
Okayama	20	FUC	3.7	7.0	11.2	6.4	1.24	24 –	20 –
		CC	10.4	10.8	36.9	6.3	1.23		
Utsunomiya	21	FUC	3.4	7.2	11.4	8.0	1.55	25 –	21 –
		CC	11.2	13.4	14.3	9.7	1.86		
Takamatsu	22	FUC	0.2	3.6	8.2	5.7	1.11	29 –	22 –
		CC	5.8	6.5	9.0	5.9	1.15		
Kagoshima	23	FUC	5.1	5.3	10.8	10.2	1.96	20 –	24 –
		CC	10.9	8.7	13.3	10.6	2.02		
Kanazawa	24	FUC	5.2	6.4	11.2	7.7	1.50	19 –	26 –
		CC	7.3	7.6	9.4	5.7	1.11		
Oita	25	FUC	3.8	5.9	12.7	7.5	1.45	23 –	28 –
		CC	9.3	15.1	22.9	12.6	2.40		
Fukuyama	26	FUC	3.2	11.0	11.0	3.0	0.58	27 –	23 –
		CC*	11.5	24.6	29.3	4.9	0.97		
Nagasaki	27	FUC	3.4	4.2	8.6	4.3	0.84	26 –	27 –
		CC*	6.4	3.9	6.9	-0.7	-0.14		
Wakayama	28	FUC	8.6	7.1	5.1	2.6	0.52	15 –	25 –
		CC	15.3	11.1	6.7	3.0	0.60		
Toyota	29	FUC	17.1	22.1	18.1	12.2	2.33	7 –	29 –
		CC	30.8	44.2	26.2	13.2	2.51		
Toyohashi	30	FUC	8.8	7.7	10.0	6.4	1.26	14 –	30 –
		CC	10.7	8.3	10.1	6.9	1.35		
Average (weighted)		FUC	14.7	12.5	11.1	5.8	1.14		
		CC**	10.5	5.1	4.2	1.3	1.26		
Average (simple)		FUC	9.7	10.1	11.4	6.8	1.33		
		CC**	13.6	11.6	10.4	5.0	0.98		
Japan			5.2	5.5	7.0	4.6	0.90		

Notes:

1 CC stands for central city.
2 See note 3 of Table 7.5 for the central cities with *.
3 **excluding Fukuoka, Hiroshima, Kumamoto, Okayama, Fukuyama and Nagasaki cities.

Table 7.7
Three categories and nine groups of FUCs

FUC	Annual PGR 1975–80 (%)		Sub-stage of spatial cycles	Annual PGR of FUC (%)	
	FUC	Central city		1960–70	1970–75
Category 1					
Actively growing FUCs					
Group A					
Chiba	2.59	2.51	2	4.47	5.17
Toyota	2.33	2.51	2	3.65	3.40
Sapporo	2.29	2.47	1	3.97	3.53
Fukuoka	2.19	1.67	2	2.16	3.03
Kagoshima	1.96	2.02	1	1.03	2.08
Sendai	1.83	1.55	2	1.71	2.62
Kumamoto	1.75	1.49	2	0.71	1.33
Utsunomiya	1.55	1.86	1	1.03	2.17
Hiroshima	1.54	1.07	2	3.12	3.22
Yokohama	1.52	1.13	2	4.72	3.40
Kanazawa	1.50	1.11	2	1.12	2.16
Oita	1.45	2.40	1	0.95	2.41
Niigata	1.34	1.58	1	0.82	1.34
Toyohashi	1.26	1.35	1	1.59	1.95
Okayama	1.24	1.23	2	1.05	2.13
Hamamatsu	1.19	0.92	2	1.06	1.52
Takamatsu	1.11	1.15	1	0.36	1.60
Group B					
Naha	1.54	0.05	2	1.82	2.89
Gifu	1.12	0.08	2	1.78	1.67
Kyoto	0.99	0.16	2	1.82	1.87
Nagoya	0.94	0.08	2	2.61	1.90
Group C					
Tokyo	1.07	−0.69	3	3.01	2.08
Category 2					
Quasi-growing FUCs					
Group D					
Fukuyama	0.58	0.97	1	1.36	2.11
Group E					
Kobe	0.82	0.10	2	1.90	1.86
Himeji	0.76	0.46	2	1.39	1.39
Shizuoka	0.75	0.50	2	1.57	1.39
Kitakyushu	0.64	0.13	2	−0.11	0.68
Wakayama	0.52	0.60	1	1.52	0.99
Group F					
Nagasaki	0.84	−0.14	3	0.73	1.67
Osaka	0.61	−0.96	4	3.34	1.73
Category 3					
Degenerating FUCs					
Group G – null					
Group H – null					
Group I – null					

Note: Sub-stages of spatial cycles are those appearing in type-β spatial cycle scheme described in Figure 7.1.

population growth rate of the Wakayama FUC in Group E at the first sub-stage in the type-β scheme would continuously drop until eventually it turned negative, probably in the not too distant future. Recall that Wakayama FUC's growth rate has both dropped constantly since 1960 and was the lowest among the 30 largest FUCs during the 1975–80 period. A similar possibility might also characterise some other FUCs in Group E after a careful study of their patterns of urban change.

ROXY index analysis

As suggested earlier, the 'larger'[9] FUCs are growing relatively slower than the other 30 largest. One indicator for quantitatively measuring how evenly or unevenly the growth rates are distributed between larger and smaller FUCs is the ROXY index, as defined by Kawashima (1981).[10] Put another way, the ROXY index comprehensively measures the acceleration or deceleration of spatial concentration or deconcentration of population in conjunction with the relative share of population per unit. Though it is a rather rough-hewn measurement device, the ROXY index would therefore be useful for drawing a comprehensive picture of how the speed of population growth or decline varies among spatial units of different sizes.

Table 7.8 shows the ROXY indices for the 30 largest FUCs and all 86 FUCs calculated for four consecutive five-year periods. In this table we see that:

– The ROXY index for the 30 largest FUCs continuously fell from 89.2 during 1960–65 to –19.3 during 1975–80 with the positive sign turning negative around 1970. This implies that before 1970 the population growth rates of 'larger' FUCs generally exceeded those of 'non-larger' FUCs, but also that the discrepancy in rates between the two size groups of FUCs was narrowing. For a while around 1970, population growth in the 30 FUCs became more balanced. After 1970, however, the rates of 'non-larger' FUCs generally exceeded those of 'larger' FUCs and, at the same time, the discrepancy in rates between the size groups was widening.
– The ROXY index for the 86 FUCs remained positive throughout the entire 1960–80 period, implying that, during this 20-year period, the larger FUCs generally grew faster than those with smaller populations. The ROXY index, however, continuously decreased from 121.0 for the 1960–65 period to nearly zero (0.5) for 1975–80, implying that the discrepancy in population growth rates between larger and smaller FUCs constantly narrowed during the two decades.

Table 7.8
ROXY index (type II) for urbanisation in Japan

Group of spatial units	Period			
	1960—65	1965—70	1970—75	1975—80
30 FUCs	89.2	42.8	-6.1	-19.3
86 FUCs	121.0	84.5	39.5	0.5

Note:

ROXY index = $[\dfrac{\text{growth ratio (weighted average)}}{\text{growth ratio (simple average)}} - 1.0] \times 10000$

where growth ratio (weighted average) [per annum]

$$= \sum_{i=1}^{n} p_i^{t+1} / \sum_{i=1}^{n} p_i^{t}$$

growth ratio (simple average) [per annum]

$$= \sum_{i=1}^{n} [p_i^{t+1} / p_i^{t}] \times \frac{1}{n}$$

p_i^{τ} — Population level of spatial unit i at time τ

n — Number of spatial units.

Table 7.9
ROXY index (type II) for urbanisation in the US

Group of spatial units	Period		
	1960—70	1970—75	1975—80
30 SMSAs	-68.5	-59.0	-53.5

For comparison purposes, Table 7.9 furnishes ROXY index values for the 30 largest US SMSAs during the 1960—70, 1970—75, and 1975—80 periods. This table shows that the index remained negative throughout the entire 20 year period, but that its absolute value gradually decreased. This implies that, since 1960, the rates of growth (or decline) of 'non-larger' SMSAs exceeded (or were exceeded by) those of 'larger' SMSAs, but that the discrepancy in growth (or decline) rates between 'larger' and 'non-larger' SMSAs was narrowing over time.

The above analysis leads to the following conclusions. First, in the Japanese urban system of 86 FUCs, population was generally still concentrating into the large FUCs even during the most recent 1975–80 period. The speed of spatial concentration, however, has continuously decelerated since 1960. From the trend in the values of the ROXY index, it is quite probable that values have turned negative in recent periods such as 1980–85. That is, the smaller FUCs will in general begin to grow faster than the larger FUCs — for the first time in Japan's postwar history. This phenomenon corresponds to the disurbanisation stage in the spatial cycle scheme of type-γ and might be referred to as relative disurbanisation to indicate the general emergence of a *lower* population growth rate. Thus, the early 1980s would perhaps be viewed as epoch-making years in the history of the Japanese urban system.

Second, in the 30 largest FUCs of the Japanese urban system the smaller ('non-larger') FUCs began to grow faster than the largest FUCs in the early 1970s, and the absolute value of the negative ROXY index has steadily increased. If we bravely assume that the Japanese urban system will generally follow along the path of its US counterpart — which would be regarded as an 'advanced country in the sphere of urbanisation' — and if we compare Tables 7.8 and 7.9, the ROXY index for the 30 largest FUCs will possibly decline to values ranging from, say, -50 to -100 in the future, and then once again gradually increase in value. This would imply that some large FUCs would most probably start to lose population in the foreseeable future.

To sum up the analysis of this section, there appear to be possible shifts of this order in the Japanese urban system:

— The urban system of 86 FUCs will possibly reach the relative disurbanisation stage in the 1980s.
— Higher growth rates will be observed for 'non-larger' FUCs, thus increasing the discrepancy between the two size groups of the 30 largest FUCs.
— Osaka FUC will reach disurbanisation during the first half of the 1980s at the earliest.
— Tokyo, Nagasaki, Wakayama, Shizuoka, and Nagoya are among the 'disurbanisation reserve' FUCs, some of which will start losing population even within the decade of the 1980s.

Conclusion

Returning to our initial question, the answer derived from the investigation carried out on the Japanese urban system, using spatial cycle analysis and ROXY index analysis, would be, 'Yes, disurbanisation is foreseeable in Japan'. It should be kept in mind, however, that the validity of this answer must be carefully checked through studies on, for example, urban agglomerations and disagglomeration economies (including amenity agglomeration economies), age structure of urban populations, transportation and communication network systems, spatial distribution of industrial activities, product cycle of industry, regional development policies, regional tax systems, cost of living, and technological innovation, all of which will affect the promotion or hinder the arrival of disurbanisation.

Notes

1 Preliminary versions of this chapter were presented at the Second International Congress of Arts and Sciences, Erasmus University, Rotterdam, The Netherlands, in June 1984 and at the Sixth Advanced Summer Institute in Regional Science, University of Bamberg, in the Federal Republic of Germany, in August 1984. The author would like to thank participants of those meetings for helpful comments on earlier drafts of this chapter. Partial financial support for the research from the Tokyo Marine Kagami Memorial Foundation is also gratefully acknowledged.

2 For a discussion of population decline in the large metropolitan areas of Europe and the USA, see, for example, Alden (1981), Beale (1975), Berry (1978), van den Berg and Klaassen (1979, 1984), van den Berg et al. (1982), Gordon (1979), Hall and Hay (1980), Kawashima and Korcelli (1982), Klaassen and Paelinck (1979), Korcelli (1982), and Leven (1978).

3 The boundaries of central cities were not fixed but variable over time. However, city boundaries usually change due to merger. Therefore, in most cases, the area of the central city would expand whenever it changed. From this point of view, the decrease in the populations of central cities shown in the table would fairly reflect the actual loss of central city population, which could have been observed had the boundary remained fixed.

4 It should be noted that, in the case of New York, the decreases in the population of SMSA and central city began simultaneously in the 1970–75 period.

5   This is because the rate of population decline in the SMSA, divided by that in the central city, is highest for the New York SMSA among the ten disurbanising SMSAs.

6   SMSAs in Groups C and F will be termed 'pre-disurbanisation SMSAs' since they are straightforwardly approaching disurbanisation cell 6, as shown in Figure 7.2(c).

7   Westward movement of the wave of population upsurge does not necessarily mean that the SMSAs located along the west coast are all among the fastest growing of the 30 largest.

8   The generalised spatial cycle hypothesis involves the concepts of the three types of spatial cycle schemes illustrated in Figure 7.1 as well as other types of schemes that could directly grow out of the original spatial cycle scheme.

9   The word 'larger' indicates the FUCs that are relatively large even among the 30 largest FUCs; the 'non-larger' FUCs refers to FUCs that are relatively small among the 30 largest FUCs.

10 Precisely, the ROXY index used in this chapter is the ROXY index (Type II) which is a slightly revised version of the original (Type I) developed by T. Kawashima (1982); the relationship between the two types of ROXY indices is:

ROXY index (Type II) = [ROXY index (Type I) −1.0] x 10,000.

For a discussion of the basic features of the ROXY index, see Kawashima (1985).

References

Alden, J. (1981), 'A Cross-National Study of Metropolitan Problems in Industrialized Countries: Experiences of the USA and West Europe', Institute of Science and Technology, Cardiff (mimeographed).

Beale, C. (1975), 'The Revival of Population Growth in Nonmetropolitan America', Economic Research Service Series ERS 605, US Department of Agriculture, Washington, D.C.

Berry, B.J.L. (1978), 'The Counterurbanization Process: How General?', *Human Settlement Systems: International Perspectives on Structure, Change and Public Policy* (N.M. Hansen, ed.), Ballinger, Cambridge, Mass.

van den Berg, L. and L.H. Klaassen (1979), 'The Process of Urban Decline', paper delivered at the meeting of the International Association of Regional and Urban Statistics, Reims (France).

van den Berg, L., R. Drewett, L.H. Klaassen, A. Rossi, and C.H.T. Vijverberg (1982), *Urban Europe: A Study of Growth and Decline*, Pergamon, Oxford.

van den Berg, L. and L.H. Klaassen (1984), 'Economic Cycles, Spatial Cycles, and Transportation Structures in Urban Areas', *Foundations of Empirical Economic Research Series 1984/1*, Netherlands Economic Institute, Rotterdam.

Gordon, P. (1979), 'Deconcentration without a "Clean Break", *Environment and Planning A*, vol. 11.

Hall, P. and D. Hay (1980), *Growth Centers in the European System*, Heinemann, London.

Kawashima, T. (1982), 'Recent Urban Trends in Japan: Analysis of Functional Urban Regions', *Human Settlement Systems: Spatial Patterns and Trends* (T. Kawashima and P. Korcelli, eds), International Institute for Applied Systems Analysis, Laxenburg, Austria.

Kawashima, T. and P. Korcelli (eds) (1982), *Human Settlement Systems: Spatial Patterns and Trends*, International Institute for Applied Systems Analysis, Laxenburg, Austria.

Kawashima, T. (1985), 'ROXY Index: An Indicative Instrument to Measure the Speed of Spatial Concentration and Deconcentration of Population', *Gakushuin Economic Papers*, vol. 22, no. 2, Gakushuin University, Tokyo.

Klaassen, L.H. and J.H.P. Paelinck (1979), 'The Future of Large Towns', *Environment and Planning A*, vol. 11.

Klaassen, L.H., J.A. Bourdrez and J. Volmuller (1981), *Transport and Reurbanization*, Gower, Aldershot, England.

Korcelli, P. (1982), 'Patterns of Urban Change', *Options*, International Institute for Applied Systems Analysis, Laxenburg, Austria.

Leven, C.L. (ed.) (1978), *The Mature Metropolis*, D.C. Heath, Lexington, Mass.

US Bureau of the Census (1965, 1966, 1972, 1977, 1980, 1981), *Statistical Abstract of the United States*, US Government Printing Office, Washington, D.C.

8 Urban revival?

LEO VAN DEN BERG, LEO H. KLAASSEN AND JAN VAN DER MEER

Introduction: some theoretical considerations

Spatial deconcentration became the dominant urban development trend in the Netherlands during the 1960s (van den Berg, Boeckhout, and van der Meer, 1979). Many central cities and entire agglomerations suffered losses of people and jobs. The major Randstad agglomerations – Amsterdam, The Hague, and Rotterdam – declined into 'disurbanisation'. The agglomerations that disurbanised not only lost their inhabitants and activities, but also faced the problems and consequences of rising unemployment, deteriorating facilities and services and, particularly in the central cities, public deficits created by their shrinking tax bases.

This chapter asks the question, will disurbanisation persist through the 1980s or are there signs of an urban revival? Statistical evidence will provide some insight into a possible answer.

First, however, some general considerations relating to urban development, and in particular the stage approach, as presented in recent literature will be reviewed (van den Berg, Drewett, Klaassen, Rossi, and Vijverberg, 1982). In the context of this chapter, it is important to recall that the rising incomes enjoyed during past decades, together with the relative decline in transportation costs, made longer distances easy to overcome by car and, in the process, broadened the urban population's range of residence and workplace choices. With the expectation of continued income increases and travel cost decreases, many households made the decision to relocate further from their workplaces. In principle, that freedom of choice opened the door to suburbanisation.

Push factors played a supporting role. Smaller families boosted the demand for the types of housing that were unavailable in the central cities. Increased crime, a heightened sensitivity to environmental degradation, worsened housing opportunities and the poorer quality of education offered in older central cities further stimulated flight to the suburbs.

In summary, events after the Second World War have brought about the easy and abundant transportation that transformed urban constellations into non-traditional urban forms. With the arrival of the 1970s, so many of the more affluent residents had left or were leaving for higher amenities areas elsewhere that the population of entire agglomerations began to decline and disurbanisation was well underway.

The 1973 oil crisis was responsible in large part for triggering a reversal of the trends that had characterised the previous quarter of a century. The abrupt and steep price increases that drastically raised the cost of car travel became an anomaly in a spatially decentralised society. Long commuting distances, shopping in suburban districts located far from traditional town centres, travel to remote holiday resorts, visits to relatives and friends living at great distances, are phenomena consistent with low transportation costs. The substantial rises in energy costs helped to provoke a worldwide recession that led to income stagnation or decline. This chain of events, together with a generally gloomy outlook for the future, created an inevitable tension between current and projected consumer budgets, and the desire to maintain a high standard of living. The commitment to travel by car, and to the life style and spatial patterns that accompanied it, was seriously compromised. Households faced the alternatives of either moving closer to work, staying where they were if they already lived close to their jobs, or finding new employment closer to home. A scarcity of jobs in a relatively tight labour market eliminated the last option for most, at least for the medium term. The remaining two options tended to slow the rate of central city decline and perhaps even to generate some new growth.

Generally, the middle- and upper-income groups of the population have enjoyed the greatest freedom in choosing their residential locations. Regular and continued income gains brought those choices within reach of ever-increasing numbers of poorer households. If incomes had continued to rise, these households would have followed the patterns established by their more prosperous cohorts. Faced however with the prospect of rising fuel and energy costs, many undoubtedly postponed their plans for moving. That decision perhaps checked the outflow and even restored modest growth in the central cities.

New and more aggressively pursued urban public policies, aimed at turning the tide by luring people back to the major cities and containing those who lived there, played a supporting role. Building housing instead of offices, improved traffic circulation schemes, traffic-protected streets, and pedestrian malls, were among the efforts designed to restore some of the old glory to once-declining centres, making them once again more attractive as places to live. Given the trend towards smaller families, no miracles were to be expected, but it was assumed that measures such as these, combined with dwindling emigration, would slacken the flight from central cities.

These are the considerations that will be examined and tested in this chapter. As background, the principal results of earlier investigations covering the 1950—74 period will be briefly reviewed before contrasting them with more recent developments. The chapter concludes with some speculations about the implications of the findings for future urban development in The Netherlands.

Urban development, 1950—74

Recent research (van den Berg, Drewett, Klaassen, Rossi and Vijverberg, 1982) has demonstrated clearly the relation between the level and pace of economic development on the one hand and the process of urbanisation on the other. During the process, urban regions pass successively through the stages of urbanisation, suburbanisation, and disurbanisation.[1] The process is represented graphically in Figure 8.1.

In the research into urban dynamics in the Netherlands, 24 agglomerations were classified by development stage. Table 8.1 shows the sample arranged by size class and region. Regional divisions are shown in Figure 8.2. Figure 8.3 illustrates the dynamics of urban development in The Netherlands, indicating how large, medium-sized, and small agglomerations moved from one stage to the next during the 1950—74 period. The three largest appear to have been in the vanguard during the entire period, always positioned at a more advanced stage of development than the others, which consistently followed in their tracks. The medium-sized and small agglomerations have only recently started to pass from spatial concentration (the urbanisation stage) to spatial deconcentration (suburbanisation stage) and the moves were still few in number. The three largest agglomerations suburbanised from the 1950—60 period onwards; the persistent out-

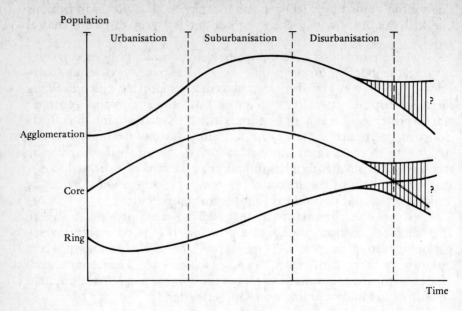

Figure 8.1   Urban development stages

Table 8.1
The sample of Dutch agglomerations

Size	Region		
	Randstad	Emanation zone	Peripheral zones
more than 500,000 inhabitants	Amsterdam (12) Rotterdam (16) The Hague (15)		
250,000 to 500,000 inhabitants	Utrecht (9)	Arnhem (6) Eindhoven (22)	Groningen (1) Enschede/H* (5) Heerlen/K* (23)
100,000 to 250,000 inhabitants	Leiden (14) Hilversum (13) Amersfoort (8) Dordrecht/Z* (17) Haarlem (11)	Nijmegen (7) Breda (19) Alkmaar (10) Tilburg (20) Den Bosch (21)	Leeuwarden (2) Zwolle (4) Emmen (3) Maastricht (24) Vlissingen/M* (18)

*H = Hengelo, K = Kerkrade, Z = Zwijndrecht, M = Middelburg

Note: Numbers in brackets identify the locations of agglomerations on the map of The Netherlands shown in Figure 8.2.

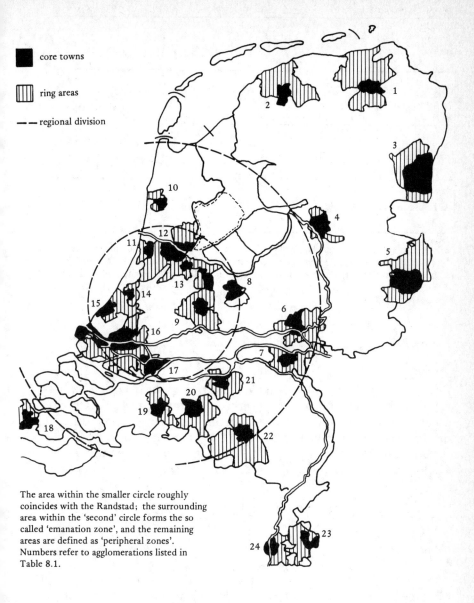

core towns

ring areas

regional division

The area within the smaller circle roughly
coincides with the Randstad; the surrounding
area within the 'second' circle forms the so
called 'emanation zone', and the remaining
areas are defined as 'peripheral zones'.
Numbers refer to agglomerations listed in
Table 8.1.

Figure 8.2   The sample of Dutch agglomerations

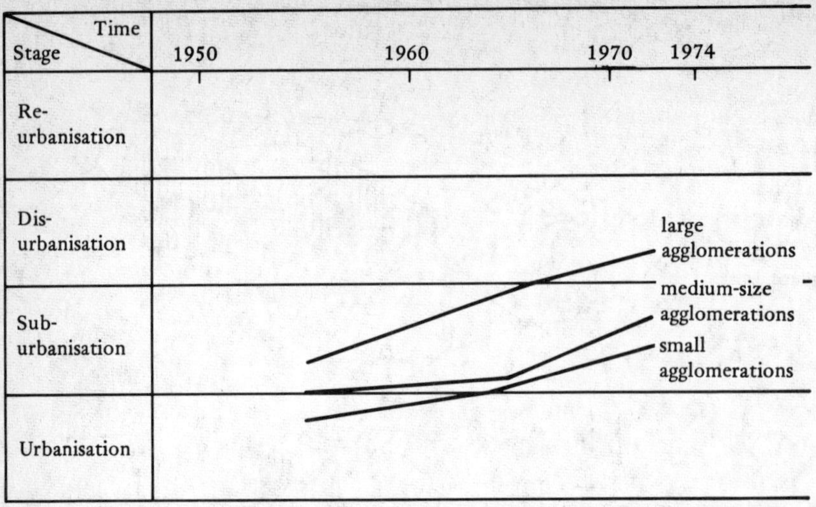

Stage \ Time	1950	1960	1970	1974
Re-urbanisation				
Dis-urbanisation				large agglomerations
Sub-urbanisation				medium-size agglomerations / small agglomerations
Urbanisation				

For technical reasons, the Haarlem agglomeration could not be arranged by phase. The population of its ring (Bloemendaal and Heemstede) has been declining since the 1960s. Natural growth has also been negative since then. Because the population of these municipalities is so old in general, there has been no normal growth. A feasible division by phase of urbanisation could not be carried through.

Figure 8.3 Urban change by phase, The Netherlands, 1950—74

flow of population culminated in negative growth during 1970—74. A difference can also be observed in the speed at which the agglomerations changed position from one stage to another; the diagram shows, for example, that the large agglomerations moved fastest and, by the early 1970s, had begun to disurbanise while the smaller units in the sample were still in the suburbanisation stage.

The development of the agglomerations since 1970

General trends

The most recent demographic developments of the Dutch agglomerations can best be viewed against the backdrop of three periods, 1970—74, 1974—78, and 1978—82.

In 1982, 51 per cent of the Dutch population lived in the sample of agglomerations selected for this analysis. The data in Table 8.2 show that the fraction has declined steadily since 1950 with growth rates

Table 8.2
Annual growth rate of the 24 selected Dutch agglomerations
in percentages of the total agglomeration population, 1950—82

	1950—60	1960—70	1970—74	1974—78	1978—82
Cores	+0.82	+0.19	−0.66	−0.47	−0.10
Rings	+0.51	+0.81	+0.90	+0.64	+0.51
Agglomerations	+1.32	+1.00	+0.24	+0.17	+0.41
Netherlands	+1.38	+1.35	+1.03	+0.75	+0.70

of the entire nation exceeding those for the agglomerations. The gap widened particularly during the 1970s. The picture begins to change, however, between 1978 and 1982 when a tendency appears for agglomerations to increase their relative share of the national total.

The recent turn-around is attributable in large part to the rapidly diminishing outflows from the central cities. This is apparent in the data displayed in Table 8.3 showing growth rates for cores, rings, and agglomerations arrayed by size. During the most recent period, 1978—82, the outflow from the large agglomerations reversed and the medium-sized units reached a growth rate equal to the national average (which, incidentally, was only half what it was in the 1950s and 1960).

Although the central cities still exerted a negative influence on growth of the collective agglomerations between 1978 and 1982, their development was generally positive. The reduced volume of population loss in the three largest cores was particularly remarkable. During the period, only nine cores registered losses compared to twice that number between 1970 and 1974 (see Appendix Table A8.1).

In sharp contrast to the changes occurring in the central cores, the contribution of the suburban rings to overall agglomeration growth declined steadily throughout the period. The ring zones of the largest agglomerations, however, were an exception. Their contribution to overall growth increased both proportionally and absolutely during the most recent period. Closer inspection of the data shows that this was the result of the spectacular growth of a very few suburban rings, most of which government had designated as growth nuclei. The growth of Amsterdam's ring (12,000 persons between 1978 and 1982) was largely accounted for by growth in the outlying muncipalities of Haarlemmermeer (+5,000) and Purmerend (+5,300). Much of the increase in the Rotterdam ring (50,000) reflects the growth of Spijkenisse (+14,000), Hellevoetsluis (+9,100), and Cappelle a/d

Table 8.3
Annual population growth of cores, rings, and total agglomerations, by size classes, The Netherlands, 1970–82

Size	1970–1974			1974–1978			1978–1982		
	Cores	Rings	Agglomerations	Cores	Rings	Agglomerations	Cores	Rings	Agglomerations
Annual percentage change									
> 500,000	-1.38	+0.86	-0.52	-1.02	+0.61	-0.41	-0.55	+0.66	+0.12
250,000–500,000	-0.32	+1.11	+0.79	-0.39	+0.93	+0.54	+0.14	+0.56	+0.70
100,000–250,000	+0.05	+0.78	+0.83	+0.22	+0.44	+0.66	+0.26	+0.24	+0.53
All agglomerations	-0.66	+0.90	+0.24	-0.47	+0.64	+0.17	-0.10	+0.51	+0.41
Annual absolute change (x 1,000)									
> 500,000	-42.3	+26.5	-15.8	-30.8	+18.2	-12.5	-16.2	+19.6	+3.5
250,000–500,000	-6.0	+20.9	+15.0	-7.6	+18.0	+10.5	+2.7	+11.2	+13.8
100,000–250,000	+1.2	+16.7	+17.9	+5.0	+9.7	+14.6	+6.0	+6.0	+12.1
All agglomerations	-47.2	+64.1	+17.0	-33.4	+45.9	+12.5	-7.5	+36.7	+29.3

IJssel (+7,400). In the ring around The Hague, the population of suburban Zoetermeer increased by 19,000, which is more than the growth of the ring as a whole (including Zoetermeer). The ring surrounding Utrecht, one of six medium-sized agglomerations, has also stabilised with its total growth of 27,000 divided among Nieuwegein (+18,000), Maarssen (+6,700) and Houten (+4,200). Here, too, its remaining eight suburban communities sustained net population losses. In sum, a limited number of suburban areas accounted for 60 per cent of the net ring growth of 147,000 (or 89,000) recorded between 1978 and 1982; the remaining 40 per cent was distributed over the approximately 220 remaining ring municipalities (also see the appendix table). The conclusions are:

- the rate of population loss experienced by the three largest agglomerations decreased after 1974 and reversed into positive gains from 1978 onward;
- population in the rings of the large agglomerations continued to expand at modest levels, but growth has diminished since 1974 in the rings of the other agglomerations;
- the core cities of the other agglomerations also developed positively; negative growth decreased and positive growth was reinforced;
- although rings still accounted for most of the growth in medium-sized and small agglomerations, their contribution to total agglomeration growth clearly diminished.

Natural increase and migration

To reveal the underlying sources of the changes described above, we turn next to an examination of the extent to which natural population growth and migration in cores and rings have contributed to the overall development of the agglomerations. The results vary somewhat by size of agglomeration as the data in Table 8.4 show.

The recent, positive development of the largest agglomerations appears to be due mainly to the drop in the numbers leaving central cities which, in 1970, was still very large and influential. The remaining three demographic components — natural growth in cores and in rings, and migration in rings — made only modest and negative contributions to overall agglomeration growth.

The changes occurring in the mid-range group were similar to those in the largest agglomerations. The gains from natural growth diminished rapidly after the 1970—74 period, particularly in the cores. Especially since 1978, net migration to the rings has contributed less and less to growth. Only migration to the cores accounted for the

Table 8.4

Annual population growth by components of natural increase and migration, in percentages of total population, by size classes, The Netherlands, 1970–82

Agglomerations	Periods	Natural growth			Migration			Total agglomerations
		Cores	Rings	Agglomerations	Cores	Rings	Agglomerations	
Large agglomerations	1970–1974	+0.09	+0.32	+0.41	−1.47	+0.54	−0.92	−0.52
	1974–1978	−0.09	+0.24	+0.14	−0.93	+0.37	−0.56	−0.41
	1978–1982	−0.05	+0.21	+0.16	−0.50	+0.45	−0.05	+0.12
Medium-size agglomerations	1970–1974	+0.39	+0.44	+0.83	−0.71	+0.67	−0.04	+0.79
	1974–1978	+0.13	+0.31	+0.44	−0.52	+0.62	+0.10	+0.54
	1978–1982	+0.11	+0.27	+0.38	+0.03	+0.29	+0.32	+0.70
Small agglomerations	1970–1974	+0.50	+0.26	+0.76	−0.46	+0.52	+0.06	+0.83
	1974–1978	+0.22	+0.17	+0.39	+0.00	+0.27	+0.27	+0.66
	1978–1982	+0.22	+0.16	+0.37	+0.05	+0.11	+0.16	+0.53

increases registered in the total agglomerations. From 1970 to 1974, the annual rate of agglomeration growth of 0.79 per cent was still entirely due to natural increase (0.83 per cent). Between 1978 and 1982, however, nearly half the annual growth of 0.7 per cent was due to net migration to the agglomerations.

The story repeats itself with essentially the same trends observed for the small agglomerations as for the others. The contribution of ring zones to agglomeration growth, relatively small in comparison to the medium-size group, is explained by differing ratios between the sizes of cores and rings (for the core/ring relations, see Table A8.1).

The analysis of the contribution of migration and natural growth to agglomeration development leads to the following conclusions:

— sharp reductions in net out-migration cut population losses in the large central cities, but reductions in the rate of natural increase had the opposite effect;
— dwindling natural increase of the population and a rapid fall-off in net migration combined to reduce radically the share contributed by the suburban rings to the growth of medium-sized and small agglomerations;
— the stabilised growth of the large agglomerations' suburban rings seemed to be due principally to an overall balance struck between in- and out-migration, but with ring growth concentrated in a very few suburban communities; six out of the total of 58 ring municipalities accounted for more than three-quarters of the total growth of 78,000 persons during the period;
— the positive developments in the cores of medium-sized and small agglomerations were due to the reversal of departure surpluses to settlement surpluses.

Inflows and outflows of migrants

The use of net flows complicates the task of assessing the relative importance of migration *vis-à-vis* natural increase as factors in total growth. A changing net balance reveals nothing about the magnitudes of its components. Consequently, the movements or gross flows of in- and out-migrants into and out of the four largest central cities will have to be examined.[2] Hopefully, cautious conclusions for the other central cities may be drawn from the results of this limited sample.

Consistent with the previous tables, Table 8.5 shows the proportional contribution to growth, taking as the base the total agglomeration population at the beginning of each period, and helps to identify the sources of the considerable drop in the negative effect of migration on overall growth. A falling departure rate was the

Table 8.5

Gross migration flows, central cities of the four largest
agglomerations, in percentages of their total population
(in percentages of the base year), The Netherlands, 1970—82

Period	Rotterdam			Amsterdam		
	In-migration	Out-migration	Balance	In-migration	Out-migration	Balance
1970—1974	2.01	3.18	-1.17	2.73	4.08	-1.35
1974—1978	2.03	2.91	-0.88	3.02	3.81	-0.79
1978—1982	1.92	2.32	-0.40	2.77	3.31	-0.54
	The Hague			Utrecht		
1970—1974	2.49	4.27	-1.78	3.29	4.67	-1.38
1974—1978	3.03	3.82	-0.79	3.02	4.45	-1.43
1978—1982	2.90	3.13	-0.24	3.07	3.46	-0.39

principal source. Increases in arrivals during the period 1978—82 compared with the period 1970—74, on the other hand, had only a minor
effect in Amsterdam and The Hague, and no effect at all in Rotterdam
and Utrecht. The relative stability of the in-migration rate was partly
explained by the rising proportion of foreign migrants who, in the
four large central cities, represented an average of 36 per cent between
1978 and 1982, up from 31 per cent during the 1970—74 period.

The analysis shows that rates of in-migration to the large central
cities remained almost constant; and departures were rapidly diminishing. Taken together, these two results indicate the strongly waning
relative importance of migration as a factor feeding population growth
that, for the four large central cities sampled, was compensated for in
part by foreign migration — those arriving from abroad and settling in
the large centres, and those leaving for destinations abroad — which
remained steady in volume. Except for foreign migration, population
flows from and to the four large central cities dropped steadily from
181,000 (1970—74) to 167,000 (1974—78), and finally to 141,000
(1978—82).

Conclusions

The data presented above allow us to complete Figure 8.3 through
the period 1978—82. The results are shown in Figure 8.4 for regions

138

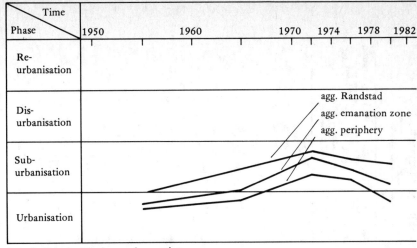

* Excluding the Haarlem agglomeration

Figure 8.4   Urban change by phase, The Netherlands,
1950–60 to 1978–82, by region*

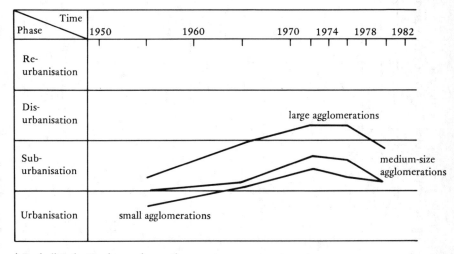

* Excluding the Haarlem agglomeration

Figure 8.5   Urban change by phase, The Netherlands,
1950–60 to 1978–82, by size class*

Table 8.6

Agglomerations classified by urbanisation stage and size class, The Netherlands, 1970–82

Size class	Period	Urbanisation		Suburbanisation		Disurbanisation	
		Absolute concentration	Relative concentration	Relative deconcentration	Absolute deconcentration	Absolute deconcentration during decline	Relative deconcentration
> 500,000	1970/74					Rotterdam Amsterdam Den Haag	
> 500,000	1974/78					Rotterdam Amsterdam Den Haag	
> 500,000	1978/82				Rotterdam Den Haag	Amsterdam	
250,000–500,000	1970/74			Enschede/H	Utrecht Eindhoven Arnhem Heerlen/K Groningen		
250,000–500,000	1974/78			Eindhoven Enschede/H	Utrecht Arnhem Heerlen/K Groningen		
250,000–500,000	1978/82		Enschede/H Groningen	Eindhoven Arnhem Heerlen/K	Utrecht		

				Hilversum
100,000—250,000	1970/74	Dordrecht/Z Emmen	Amersfoort Alkmaar Zwolle Vlissingen/M	**Nijmegen** **Tilburg** Den Bosch Breda Maastricht Leeuwarden Leiden
100,000—250,000	1974/78	Dordrecht/Z Leiden Emmen Alkmaar Zwolle Vlissingen/M	Den Bosch Leeuwarden	**Nijmegen** **Tilburg** **Breda** **Maastricht** **Amersfoort** Hilversum
100,000—250,000	1978/82	Tilburg Den Bosch Dordrecht/Z Maastricht Emmen Alkmaar Zwolle Vlissingen/M	Leiden Amersfoort	**Nijmegen** Breda Leeuwarden

Hilversum

(Randstad, emanation zone, and periphery) and in Figure 8.5 for the agglomerations arranged by size class.

Since 1974, spatial concentration has tended to increase across all regions, principally so in the periphery and least in the urbanised Randstad. Because Amsterdam, Rotterdam, and the Hague dominate the Randstad, a closer study of their recent evolution, and a comparison with the medium-sized and small agglomerations, seems useful. Like Figure 8.3, Figure 8.5 portrays the development of the three size groups but with the time period extended through 1982.

The diagram shows how urban development reversed its course during the 1970–74 period. From 1950 to 1974, development was marked by increasing spatial deconcentration, with urbanisation passing into suburbanisation, and suburbanisation into disurbanisation. That process had come to a halt by 1974 and the current picture differs significantly. At present, urban agglomerations are no longer spatially deconcentrating but, on the contrary, concentrating.

The new urban development trend occurs with the larger as well as with the medium-sized and smaller agglomerations. Table 8.6 indicates the positions of the individual agglomerations. (The agglomerations are classified according to the scheme shown in Figure 6.1.)

The future

The data and analysis presented in the previous section confirm the theory developed in the introduction. Increasing prosperity, good prospects for the future, and low transport costs foster spatial deconcentration as reflected in slower population growth or even population loss of the central cities. Stagnation, gloomy prospects, and rising transportation costs check the propensity for deconcentration and encourage concentration. We have seen that the concentration of population in agglomerations results chiefly from reduced outflows from the centres, but not (yet) by increased in-migration. Apparently, many people have postponed plans to move out, perhaps until the return of better times.

What are prospects for the future? Until 1974, disurbanisation dominated urban development; since then we have observed a striking 'return' trend. Will that trend continue in the short and medium terms, or is another turn-around likely?

How cities will develop probably depends very much on the economic cycle, mirrored in average consumer incomes, unemployment rates and the proportion of people who receive social payments, expenditure patterns, and the cost of living. Worse economic conditions in the near future will probably be reflected in reduced travel demands for public as well as for private transport and reduced residential mobility as households stay where they are rather than moving farther from work or, given limited job opportunities, changing jobs.

Current public policy aims at striking a better balance between public transport revenues and actual costs. With higher fares and possibly lower service levels as likely outcomes, transportation costs measured in money terms can be predicted to rise. Although energy prices may continue to drop, the public sector's worsening financial situation makes higher tax levies on cars and fuel highly probable.

With locations closer to services and employment in increasing demand, preferences will shift for living in town or, for those now living in suburbs or beyond the metropolitan fringe, to relocate nearer centres. In theory, absolute concentration would be the final outcome. In practice, however, the trend will be checked by space availability. Any movement towards densification – to the 'compact city' – is bound to run into spatial limitations after some time. (We ignore the possibility of occupancy intensification by, for example, sub-letting, doubling-up, or the return of large families.) Sooner or later, the central city will be built and occupied to capacity. Presumably the nearest rings, because they are the most strongly oriented to the central city, will then accommodate the spillovers. These are likely to be the growth nuclei that are currently increasing most rapidly in population, unless they, too, have already filled up.

On the other hand an economic recovery accompanied by falling transportation costs and energy prices relative to disposable income may spark a return to the situation that prevailed until about 1975. Deconcentration would be expected with out-migration from the central cities, and from the suburbs, including the growth nuclei, to the areas immediately beyond.

The term 'revival' in the title of this chapter refers not only to a return to an earlier era of metropolitan expansion, but to a growth in quality stimulated by public policy in an effort to counter the negative consequences of population loss. The introduction of re-urbanisation policies in some of our large cities has apparently met with a measure of success as evidenced by a modest reversal of population trends. The current centripetal tendencies also result, however, from the recession which has improved the competitive position of the largest agglomerations' central cities in their struggle to retain their existing residents and attract migrants. The (slight) revival, because it is a general phenomenon that applies to those with policies, as well as those without them, is probably due mainly to present economic conditions.

That conclusion addresses the question put in this chapter's title.

Most likely, the deterioration of the general economy and the pessimism generated by an extended recession has merely postponed urban decline. This is not to say that the resources that supported the re-urbanisation policies of the more aggressive municipal governments have been wasted, nor that they have been ineffective in stimulating local urban revival. But with economic revival, the policies may be under considerable strain to retain the advantages gained.

Notes

1 The typology of stages refers to the development of functional urban regions or agglomerations, composed of a core municipality and a ring of one or more suburbs that in 1971 had a commuting relation with the core involving at least 15 per cent of the local professional population. The stages are defined as follows: 'urbanisation' occurs when the core grows more than the ring and the population of the entire agglomeration increases; there is 'suburbanisation' when the population of the ring grows more than the core and the total agglomeration continues to grow; 'disurbanisation' is the stage when the core population declines sufficiently to entail the decline of the total agglomeration. Finally, 're-urbanisation' occurs when, with the agglomeration still declining, the core population once more increases in proportion to that of of the entire agglomeration.

2 Repeating the exercise for all 250 municipalities included in the analysis would have been a chore beyond the scope of the present chapter; moreover, for the most recent period, the origin of migrants is unknown.

References

van den Berg, L., I.J. Boeckhout and J. van der Meer (1979), 'Stedelijke Dynamiek in Nederland' ('Urban Dynamics in the Netherlands'), *Economische-Statistische Berichten*, no. 3220.

van den Berg, L., R. Drewett, L.H. Klaassen, A. Rossi and C.H.T. Vijverberg (1982), *Urban Europe: A Study of Growth and Decline*, Pergamon, Oxford.

Appendix

Table A8.1
Demographic development in the agglomerations, by size class, 1970 and 1982 (x 1,000)

Area and Population size / Time	> 500,000						250,000–500,000						100,000–250,000					
	N^K	Cores	N^R	Rings	N^A	Total	N^K	Cores	N^R	Rings	N^A	Total	N^K	Cores	N^R	Rings	N^A	Total
Level 1970	3	2231	3	835	3	3066	6	1107	6	774	6	1882	15	1581	15	563	15	2145
Δ 1970/74 (pos.)	0	–	3	+106	0	–	1	+4	6	+84	6	+60	6	+25	14	+68	13	+80
(neg.)	3	-169	0	–	3	-63	5	-28	0	–	0	–	9	-21	1	-1	2	-9
Level 1974	3	2062	3	941	3	3003	6	1083	6	858	6	1941	15	1586	15	630	15	2216
Δ 1974/78 (pos.)	0	–	3	+73	0	–	2	+2	6	+72	6	+42	8	+35	15	+39	14	+65
(neg.)	3	-123	0	–	3	-50	4	-32	0	–	0	–	7	-15	0	–	1	-7
Level 1978	3	1939	3	1014	3	2953	6	1053	6	930	6	1983	15	1606	15	669	15	2274
Δ 1978/82 (pos.)	0	–	3	+78	2	+17	5	+17	6	+45	6	+55	10	+34	14	+25	13	+58
(neg.)	3	-65	0	–	1	-6	1	-6	0	–	0	–	5	-10	1	-1	2	-10
Level 1982	3	1874	3	1092	3	2966	6	1064	6	975	6	2038	15	1630	15	692	15	2322

N^K : number of cores; N^R : number of rings; N^A : number of agglomerations

9 Regional dynamics

LEO H. KLAASSEN

Introduction: a quadripartition of regions

This chapter explores the possibility that cycles have characterised recent Dutch regional development. Income and employment data covering the 1950–75 period are used to test empirically the proposition. The data are displayed in Appendix Tables A9.1–A9.3. The regions are shown in Figure 9.1 and the types are defined as follows:

BCR = big cities, Randstad
RTR = remaining cities, Randstad
RR = rural Randstad
UEA = urban emanation area
REA = rural emanation area
UP = urban periphery
RP = rural periphery

The regions are divided into four categories according to two criteria. The regions are first split by income level at the *beginning* of the study period, between those that are higher than or equal to the national average, and those below the average. The two categories are further divided according to the second criterion, which is the rate of change in income *during* the period; regions are distinguished between those growing at or above the national rate, and those that have grown more slowly. The result is the schematic division of regions shown in Table 9.1.

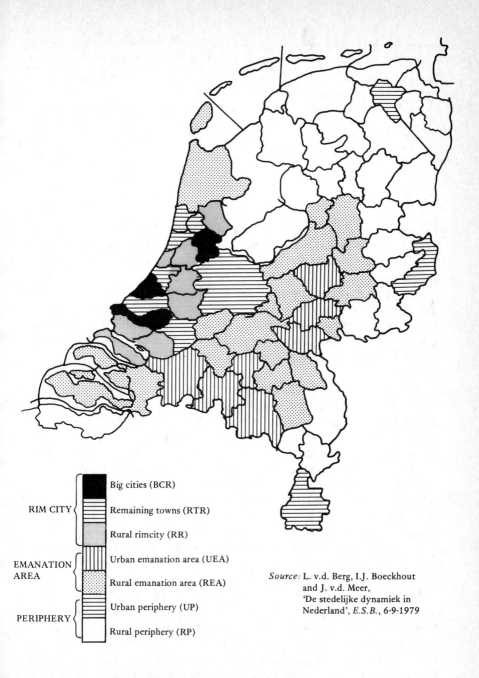

RIM CITY

- ■ Big cities (BCR)
- ≡ Remaining towns (RTR)
- ▨ Rural rimcity (RR)

EMANATION AREA

- ▥ Urban emanation area (UEA)
- ▦ Rural emanation area (REA)

PERIPHERY

- ▤ Urban periphery (UP)
- □ Rural periphery (RP)

Source: L. v.d. Berg, I.J. Boeckhout and J. v.d. Meer, 'De stedelijke dynamiek in Nederland', *E.S.B.*, 6-9-1979

Figure 9.1   Regional division of The Netherlands

Table 9.1
Schematic division of regions

	Level, initial period	
Change during period	≥ average	< average
≥ average	Prosperous area (1)	Potentially prosperous area (4)
< average	Potential development area (2)	Development area (3)

This four-way division reflects not only the position of a region at a given moment but also its change in position during the period following. A dynamic element has thus been introduced into the comparison of regions.

The prosperous areas enjoy an enviable position for both the levels and increases of their incomes exceed the national average. Its regions are steadily becoming richer and, to the extent that income measures quality of life, living conditions are good and improving. The opposite holds for the developing areas with below average income level and growth.

The intermediate cases are particularly interesting and possibly less stable. Areas with development potential have above average incomes but below average growth rates and thus run the risk of becoming development areas when that situation persists. The outlook is more favourable for potentially prosperous areas. Although their incomes are relatively low, growth is above average so that if growth rates are maintained, the areas have the potential for joining the ranks of the prosperous areas. Indeed the potential development areas (2) in the table will tend to move towards (3) in the course of time, and the potentially prosperous areas (4) will tend to move towards (1).

The hypothesis is tested with data for income level and growth for the 1950–60 and 1960–75 periods. The results for the two time periods are shown in Tables 9.2 and 9.3.

During the earlier period, 1950–60, the RTR (remaining towns of the Randstad) were situated in (1), the most favourable position. Regions in (2) characterised by a good starting point but unfavourable growth, were the large Randstad cities and towns in the urban periphery. The rural periphery occupied (3), the worst position. The rural Randstad and the entire emanation area, concentrated in (4), start from a less favourable point but have good prospects for growth.

Table 9.2
Relative income position, Dutch regions, 1950—1960

Change 1950—1960	Level, 1950	
	≥ average	< average
≥ average	Prosperous area (1) Remaining towns of Rimcity	Potentially prosperous area (4) Rural Rimcity of emanation area
< average	Potential development area (2) Big cities of Rimcity, urban periphery	Development area (3) Rural periphery

Table 9.3
Relative income position, Dutch regions, 1960—1975

Change 1960—1976	Level, 1960	
	≥ average	< average
≥ average	Prosperous area (1) (no cases)	Potentially prosperous area (4) Rural Rimcity of emanation area
< average	Potential development area (2) Big cities and remaining towns of Rimcity	Development area (3) Periphery

The second table, reflecting later developments in 1960—75, shows that regions have either retained their positions from the previous period or have shifted position in a counter-clockwise direction. The RTR moved from Stage (1) to (2), and the peripheral areas shifted from (2) to (3), both categories of areas having worsened their positions. As far as income is concerned, the Randstad (or Rimcity) towns are moving towards the status of developing areas and the urban periphery into the category development area.

Table 9.4
Relative labour-reserve position, Dutch regions, 1960–1965

Change 1960–1965	Level, 1960	
	≤ average	> average
≤ average	Prosperous area (1)	Potentially prosperous area (4)
	Rural emanation area of Rimcity	(no cases)
> average	Potential development area (2)	Development area (3)
	Urban areas in emanation area and periphery	Rural periphery

Table 9.5
Relative labour-reserve position, Dutch regions, 1965–1975

Change 1965–1975	Level, 1965	
	≤ average	> average
≤ average	Prosperous area (1)	Potentially prosperous area (4)
	Rural emanation area	Rural area in periphery
> average	Potential development area (2)	Development area (3)
	Rimcity	Urban areas in emanation area and periphery

Tables 9.4 and 9.5 represent the positions of the various regions with respect to their employment during 1960–65 and 1965–75. Although the periods differ from those used to investigate income, the changes in position follow essentially the same pattern. The Randstad and the rural emanation area were among the prosperous areas (1) during the first period, 1960–65, with the urban periphery and the urban emanation area occupying (2) and the rural periphery in (3), the worst position. (4) is empty for there were no potentially prosperous areas in that period. The counter-clockwise movement is

evident from a comparison with the situation in the second period, 1965—75. The Randstad, in moving from (1) to (2), lost its status as a prosperous area and became a potentially developing area. The urban emanation area and the urban periphery shifted from (2) to (3), moving from potential into genuine developing area status. The rural periphery, shifting from (3) to (4), moved into the category of potential prosperity. There were not only shifts of position from (2) to (3) and from (4) to (1) as expected, but also from (1) to (2) and probably from (4) to (1) as well. To investigate that point more closely it seemed useful to ascertain, using more detailed data, what shifts in position occurred during five-year periods since 1950. The results for income and employment are shown in Tables 9.6 and 9.7.

Regional cycles

From the evidence presented in Tables 9.6 and 9.7, it appears that all changes in regional position were in the *same* direction. Regions either remained in the same position throughout the analysis period or they shifted one position *to the right* during successive time intervals. In terms of employment, the entire Randstad ranked as prosperous in the first period considered, but declined to the status of a developing area during both subsequent periods. The urban periphery began in 1960—65 as a potential development area, became an actual development area in 1965—70, and finally a potentially prosperous area in the last period. Judged in income terms, the urban periphery shows approximately the same development, but the Randstad (excluding its rural area) has remained as a potential development area since 1960—65. The emanation area maintained its status as a potentially prosperous area (stage 4) throughout the period.

The results lead to three general conclusions. First, in any five-year period, regions shifted by no more than one position. Second, regions either remained in the same position or they moved to the next subsequent one. Finally, no moves to a previous position occurred.

The results are presented graphically in Figure 9.2. The curve describes the area's position with respect to the national average. A rising line shows positive relative growth and a falling line, a negative one. The overall cycle indicates the stages through which the regions pass.

Regions move through this cycle at differing speeds. Neither the very prosperous of Stage 1, nor the strongly underdeveloped regions of Stage 3 are likely to reach the next stage in their development quickly. Because they are on either a high or a low level relative to the

Table 9.6
Shift in position of regions, by income, 1950–75

Period	Position					
	1	2	3	4	1	2
1950–1955	BCR RTR	UP	RP	UEA RR REA		
1955–1960	RTR	BCR	UP	RP UEA RR REA		
1960–1965	–	BCR RTR	UP	UEA RR REA RP		
1965–1970	–	BCR RTR	UP	UEA REA RP	RR	
1970–1975	–	BCR RTR		UEA UP REA RP		RR

Table 9.7
Shift in position of regions, by labour reserve, 1960–75

Period	Position			
	1	2	3	4
1960–1965	BCR RTR RR REA	UEA UP	RP	–
1965–1970	REA	BCR RTR RR	UEA UP	RP
1970–1975	–	BCR RTR RR REA	UEA	UP RP

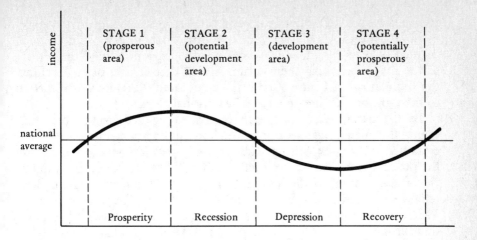

Figure 9.2   Regional development stages

national average, more time is required for them compared to the others to cross the threshold of the average.

In the 1970–75 period, the position of five regions remained the same, as measured by both the income and employment criteria. These were the three Randstad regions (BCR, RTR, and RR) – all to be found in position 2 as potential development areas – and the regions of the periphery (RR and RTR), both classified as potentially prosperous areas. The emanation area cannot be classified unequivocally, however. As for income, it is potentially prosperous and on a line with the periphery. For employment, the rural emanation area counts as a potential development area and the urban emanation area as a developing area. The position of the emanation area deserves further investigation; characteristic tendencies and influences from outside the Randstad interact here in a manner that is unclear. Further, subdivision of this rather heterogeneous area may permit a more definitive interpretation.

Policy implications

Though the conclusions to be drawn from the previous sections are as tentative as the investigation is broad, it is nonetheless intriguing to interpret their implications for regional policy. To that end, let us first assume that, in the interests of promoting regional stability and

153

equality, it would be desirable for all regional positions to move eventually on to the horizontal line of Figure 9.2, or into the centre of the diagram in Table 9.1. The aim of regional policy could then be defined as realising a spiral movement of all regions around the centre of the diagram, taking them ultimately to that centre, or, as levelling the undulation in Figure 9.2 until, in due time, all regions had shifted to the right on the line denoting the national average.

To the extent that policy can accelerate regional growth and thus eventually higher aggregate incomes and employment rates, it should certainly do so, exploiting each region's development potential in the process. For the rest, regional policy will have to take into account the fundamental dynamics of regional development, placing less reliance on traditional instruments to change any region's situation. This conclusion may not be very strong, but it recognises the reality that urban and regional development has its own characteristic, inherent dynamics. It remains for research to investigate the issue further, and to determine the implications for appropriate policy.

Appendix

Table A9.1
Shares of population per regional type,
relative to national total, The Netherlands, 1950–78

Regional type	1950	1955	1960	1965	1970	1975	1978
1 Big cities	23.6	23.4	22.7	21.6	20.0	17.9	17.1
2 Urban	16.2	16.3	16.7	16.9	17.3	17.3	17.2
3 Rural	5.1	5.0	5.1	5.3	5.8	6.5	6.7
Rimcity	(44.9)	(44.8)	(44.5)	(43.9)	(43.1)	(43.7)	(41.0)
4 Urban	12.8	13.1	13.4	13.7	14.0	14.1	14.2
5 Rural	15.8	15.8	16.0	16.3	16.9	18.0	18.6
Emanation	(28.6)	(28.9)	(29.4)	(30.0)	(30.9)	(32.1)	(32.8)
6 Urban	7.8	8.0	8.0	8.1	7.9	7.7	7.6
7 Rural	18.7	18.4	18.1	18.0	18.1	18.5	18.6
Periphery	(26.5)	(26.3)	(26.1)	(26.1)	(26.0)	(26.2)	(26.2)
The Netherlands	100.0	100.0	100.0	100.0	100.0	100.0	100.0
Urban	60.5	60.8	60.8	60.4	59.1	57.0	56.1
Rural	39.5	39.2	39.2	39.6	40.9	43.0	43.9

Source: Central Bureau of Statistics, 'The Population of the Municipalities of the Netherlands' (The Hague, various years).

Table A9.2
Shares of income by regional type, relative to national total and to population shares, The Netherlands, 1950—75

Regional type	Shares (in %)						Indices***					
	1950	1955	1960	1965	1970*	1975**	1950	1955	1960	1965	1970	1975
1 Big cities	28.5	28.5	26.8	25.3	23.4	20.2	121	122	118	117	117	113
2 Urban	17.6	18.2	18.7	18.8	18.8	18.7	109	111	112	111	109	108
3 Rural	4.7	4.7	5.0	5.3	6.0	6.6	93	95	99	100	103	102
Rimcity	(50.8)	(51.4)	(50.5)	(49.4)	(48.1)	(45.5)	(113)	(115)	(114)	(113)	(112)	(109)
4 Urban	11.3	11.9	12.3	12.9	13.2	13.7	88	91	92	94	95	97
5 Rural	13.8	13.8	14.1	14.6	15.6	16.8	87	87	88	89	92	93
Emanation area	(25.1)	(25.7)	(26.5)	(27.5)	(28.9)	(30.5)	(88)	(89)	(90)	(92)	(93)	(95)
6 Urban	7.9	7.8	7.7	7.6	7.2	7.3	100	98	96	94	91	95
7 Rural	16.2	15.1	15.3	15.5	15.8	16.7	87	82	85	86	87	90
Periphery	(24.1)	(22.9)	(23.0)	(23.1)	(23.1)	(24.0)	(91)	(87)	(88)	(89)	(88)	(92)
Total	100.0	100.0	100.0	100.0	100.0	100.0	100	100	100	100	100	100
Urban	65.3	66.4	65.5	64.7	62.6	59.9	108	109	108	107	106	105
Rural	34.7	33.6	34.5	35.3	37.4	40.1	88	86	88	89	91	93

*interpolation between 1969 and 1974.
**extrapolation of 1969 and 1974.
***indices are the income share divided by the population share (see Table A9.1).

Source: Central Bureau of Statistics, The Hague.

Table A9.3

Shares of the registered labour reserve by regional type, relative to national total and to population shares, The Netherlands, 1950–75

Regional type	Shares (in %)				Indices**			
	1960*	1965*	1970*	1975*	1960	1965	1970	1975
1 Big cities	19.3	16.3	19.1	19.5	85	75	96	109
2 Urban	7.8	6.4	9.0	9.2	47	37	52	53
3 Rural	2.2	2.1	2.6	3.0	44	40	45	46
Rimcity	(29.3)	(24.7)	(30.8)	(31.7)	(66)	(56)	(71)	(76)
4 Urban	12.2	16.3	17.1	19.1	91	119	123	135
5 Rural	15.5	15.5	13.9	15.4	97	95	82	85
Emanation area	(27.7)	(31.8)	(31.0)	(34.4)	(94)	(106)	(101)	(107)
6 Urban	6.4	11.1	12.2	11.9	80	138	154	154
7 Rural	36.6	32.3	26.0	22.0	202	179	144	119
Periphery	(43.0)	(43.4)	(38.2)	(33.9)	(164)	(166)	(147)	(129)
Total	100.0	100.0	100.0	100.0	100	100	100	100
Urban	45.7	50.0	57.4	59.6	75	83	97	105
Rural	54.3	50.0	42.6	40.4	139	126	104	94

*five-year moving averages.
**indices are the labour-reserve share divided by the population share (see Table A9.1).

Source: Ministry of Social Affairs, The Hague.

157

10 Urban and regional income development in The Netherlands: an integrative approach

LEO VAN DEN BERG, LEO H. KLAASSEN AND JAN VAN DER MEER

It has become the tradition in spatial research to more or less artificially distinguish regional from urban studies, with the latter tending to focus on activities within urban and metropolitan areas. Upon close examination of even intra-metropolitan developments, however, it soon becomes evident that what happens in these areas largely reflects what takes place at the more macro regional level, but also that urban developments give strong impulses to regional evolution. Consider, for example, staged development that runs somewhat as follows.

Rapid metropolitan growth is fed by migrations of workers streaming from smaller cities and settlements. With growth, the largest cities approach some limit to further development and population begins to spill over into adjacent areas. Income as well as population grows in the overspill areas. Growth spreads in ever-widening circles until urban decentralisation eventually leads to dispersal of the entire system. Because spread effects transmit urban changes to regional level, the urban system manifests itself not only as a coherent system of 'settlements', in the widest sense of that term, but also as an integral part of the regional system that embraces non-urbanised regions as well.

This concept of interwoven systems, and the spatial spread of growth and decline, forms the basis for the quantitative analysis of the 1950—78 period reported in this chapter. Data are analysed by the regions shown in Figure 8.2 (Chapter 8).

Urban income and spatial economic development

In the analysis to follow, local income is defined as the total amount of income received by the resident population of an area, and consists of earnings from various sources including the income transfers received from social funds. Income can be earned in part outside the area's borders; inversely, income earned locally by out-of-towners may leak away to other regions.

An area's income position is determined by several forms of payment: income per capita of the population is distinct from that of employed income earners, and from those who rely on social payments. The balance among income recipients by type of income received influences the area's overall income, and will depend for example on the balance between persons employed and those who rely on social benefits, such as unemployment compensation. The higher the share of the employed population in the total population, the higher will be per capita income. Relatively large numbers of benefit recipients depress average incomes, but if the share of earners is relatively large, per capita income can still be high. This situation may characterise areas experiencing high rates of out-migration where single-person households, for example, replace those moving elsewhere.

In communities with a large proportion of benefit recipients, or low average wages or employment rates, both the per capita income and the income by benefit recipient will be relatively low and lower even when the non-active portion of the population receives little or no income from social funds.

Studying the development of local income requires insight into the evolution of these factors at the various stages that might characterise development of the settlement system. These stages are

— inter-metropolitan contraction;
— intra-metropolitan dispersal;
— inter-metropolitan dispersal; and a return to
— inter-metropolitan contraction.

Concentration of the urban system
(inter-metropolitan contraction)

Concentration is typical of regions with economies that depend on basic industries. The specific requirements of mining, shipbuilding, and the steel industry, for example, dictate where they will locate. Expansion of industry and of employment will be spatially concentrated in industrial growth poles. By exerting a strong attraction on the population of surrounding non-industrialised areas, the population of the poles grows rapidly. Local income rises because total employment expands and the wages paid by new industry generally exceed those paid to employees in their former occupations. Moreover, in this development stage, relatively little income leaks to other regions since most of the newly recruited workers have settled in the growth pole. Urban areas at this stage tend to constitute more or less closed labour markets.

Multiplier effects further increase incomes. Migrating workers will be accompanied by other family members who may or may not join the labour force. Although they make no direct contribution to the economy if they do not find work, indirectly they stimulate income growth through their consumption of private and public goods which, via the multiplier, positively affects both local income and employment.

Growth poles will also attract people who fail to find work. growing numbers of the unemployed can only contribute to local income if they receive social payments that, like wages, have multiplier effects.

Based on these arguments, the areas can be expected to have above average incomes for they act as motors for regional development. Whether this is in fact true warrants further study for the locality's economic position will depend in large part on the stage of development in other regions.

Urban dispersal (intra-metropolitan dispersal)

The stage of urban dispersal is characterised by the migration of families from city centres to suburbs. Young families with children are particularly likely to change residence without changing jobs. With increased suburbanisation and commuting, the character of the centre gradually shifts from a place to live to a place for work.

An important consequence of suburbanisation is that an increasing part of locally earned income leaks to neighbouring municipalities as the closure of the concentrated agglomeration erodes. Even with no increase in suburban employment, income rises. The suburb and centre become closely linked, both economically and functionally, constituting true 'functional urban regions'. Such an agglomeration, growing in population and employment, may stimulate the larger regional economy, increasing its income in the process.

Meanwhile, since the most productive members of the labour force also tend to be the most mobile and likely to relocate in the suburbs, the centre is left with those who are more vulnerable to job loss. The proportion of benefit recipients rises, and average incomes are likely to drop. With shifts in the employment structure and the possibility of growth in total employment, however, income may remain stable or increase.

Suburban developments are the mirror image of those in the city centres: rapid population growth, a relatively small number of earners, and a high income per worker (but one constrained by the relatively limited number of employed workers relative to the size of the total population).

System dispersal (inter-metropolitan dispersal)

During dispersal of the urban system, decentralisation has progressed so far that population and jobs in the larger agglomerations are moving to other regions. As a result, the importance of the agglomeration as a donor region decreases and other regions take on that function. Urban dispersal becomes more general and regional development moves in a downward, self-reinforcing spiral. In the extreme, these are the effects of:

— the best qualified workers leaving;
— many employees, reduced in absolute and relative numbers, becoming benefit recipients; and
— most of the remaining work concentrating in low-wage jobs.

Obviously, such developments have substantial income effects on expulsion and attraction areas alike. In general, income will drop steeply in the former and rise in the latter. With per capita income initially higher in the expulsion areas than elsewhere, at first there will be income levelling among regions. Within the expulsion area, however, most of the decline will be concentrated in the central cities whose precarious economic position is evident not only by declining income but also, and in particular, in the progressively decreasing share of income paid as wages.

Indeed, the economic foundation of the agglomerations suffering from dispersal has been seriously eroded. The economy is artificially supported by social payments that for a short period may help to avert fiscal crisis. In the long run, however, only a policy aimed at fundamental economic restructuring can foster recovery.

Renewed concentration (inter-metropolitan contraction)

Successful reurbanisation requires improving the competitive position of the urban regions with respect to other regions. Only then can new industry and human resources be attracted. Successful restructuring will stimulate renewed income growth and the generation of new activities. In short, this critical stage will be marked by the growth of employment and of income in total, per capita of the population, and per earner. Whether this stage of renewed contraction will ever be realised, only the future will show.

Changes in urban income, 1950–78

Regional economic conditions and population size will be central to the analysis as possible explanatory variables of income development.[1] A functional trichotomy of the Netherlands areas, based on regional economic considerations, is defined as:

- *the Randstad*, the most intensively urbanised section of The Netherlands, comprising the nation's three largest agglomerations;
- *the periphery*, the economically weaker frontier of the nation on which the central government has focused its socio-economic development policy since the 1950s; and
- *the emanation zone*, the transitional zone between Randstad and periphery, and comprised of areas receiving spillovers of people and industries from the large urban agglomerations.

The division into three parts — the traditional economic gravity points, the surrounding regions benefiting from emanation effects during decentralisation periods, and the economically weaker peripheral areas — probably applies to many countries comparable in their economic development to The Netherlands.

The 24 major agglomerations have been further divided into three size classes — those with more than 500,000, those between 250,000 and 500,000, and those between 100,000 and 250,000 inhabitants. Together they accounted for 51 per cent of the Netherlands population in 1982 and 58 per cent in 1950.

This section examines how income has developed in these agglomerations, giving special attention to the divergent development of their cores and rings. In the previous section we pointed out how, because of the flight of younger, relatively better educated and higher-income families, the central cities were left with an over-representation of small households, old-age pensioners and low-income earners. That picture of lower average incomes in the central cities and higher ones in the suburbs is most evident from an analysis of income by earner, as Table 10.1 shows.

The share of national income earned in the agglomerations dropped from nearly 62 per cent in 1950 to about 55 per cent in 1978. Figure 10.1 shows in index numbers the development of average income for

Table 10.1
Income per head of population and per income earner,
The Netherlands, 1978 (in guilders)

Agglomeration	Income per head		Income per earner	
	Core	Ring	Core	Ring
Amsterdam	14,600	15,000	25,800	33,600
Rotterdam (including Schiedam and Vlaardingen)	13,900	13,700	26,700	32,600
The Hague	15,300	16,400	28,300	36,600
Average	14,500	14,800	26,700	34,000

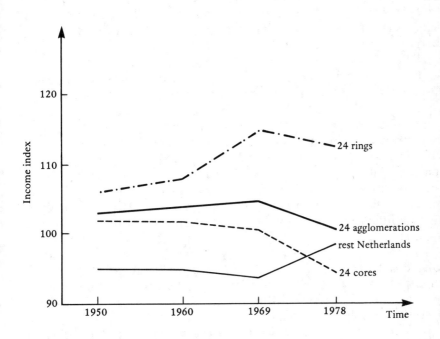

Figure 10.1 Income per earner (index); by agglomerations, cores, rings and rest of The Netherlands, 1950—78 (Netherlands = 100)

an earner living in the agglomerations, or in either their cores or rings, or in the rest of The Netherlands. Although incomes earned in the agglomerations still exceed those earned in the remainder of the country, since 1969 there has been a tendency towards convergence on the national average. The picture is less clear within the agglomerations; since the 1950s, the average incomes in the cores and rings have progressively moved apart.

Spatial developments have influenced these tendencies. Until the late 1960s, income in the largest agglomerations was considerably above those in the medium-sized and small agglomerations. Yet, since 1969, incomes in agglomerations of all sizes have converged on the national average and the differences between the largest agglomerations and all others have narrowed (Figure 10.2).

At regional level, matters differ slightly (Figure 10.3). The higher Randstad and emanation zone incomes have tended to converge towards the national average and the below average incomes in the emanation zone remained relatively unchanged during the 1970s.

Comparing Figure 10.4, which shows agglomeration income by core and ring components, with Figure 10.2, reveals that the convergence has by no means occurred within those components. The incomes in rings surrounding the largest agglomerations dropped sharply after 1969, reversing their historical climb during the 1950s and 1960s. The rings of the smaller agglomerations, however, fared far better as their incomes continued to rise throughout the entire 28-year period. Although income dropped markedly during the 1960s for cores of all sizes, the timing of changes was clearly related to size. The reversal from growth to decline occurred first — in 1960 — among the largest agglomerations. Incomes for the next largest group, those with 250,000—500,000 population, rose sluggishly during the 1960s and dropped beginning in 1969. The smallest agglomerations enjoyed fairly rapid income growth between 1960 and 1969 before their incomes declined. Thus, relative declines were initiated in the largest metropolitan set and gradually filtered down the hierarchy to the smallest units.

The regional picture is identical with that by size class as far as the comparison of rings and cores is concerned (Figure 10.5). Income in Randstad cores declined fastest, followed by those at the periphery and the emanation zone. Income in the rings, except for the Randstad, continued its rise.

Income developments in the ring areas are especially illustrative of the processes expected during the stages of spatial concentration, suburbanisation, and disurbanisation. During the 1950s and 1960s, incomes rose relative to the nation in the rings of the Randstad and emanation zone. This would be expected during the suburbanisation

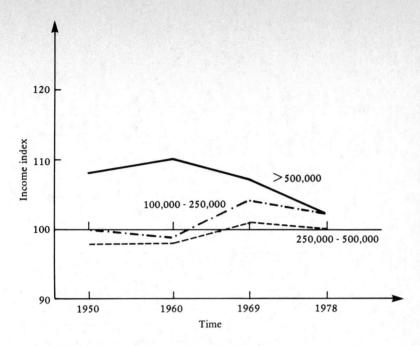

Figure 10.2   Income per earner (index); agglomerations by size class, The Netherlands, 1950–78 (Netherlands = 100)

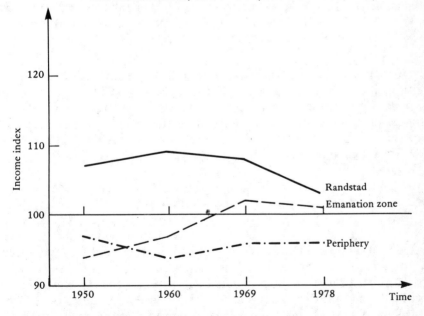

Figure 10.3   Income per earner (index); agglomerations by region, The Netherlands, 1950–78 (Netherlands = 100)

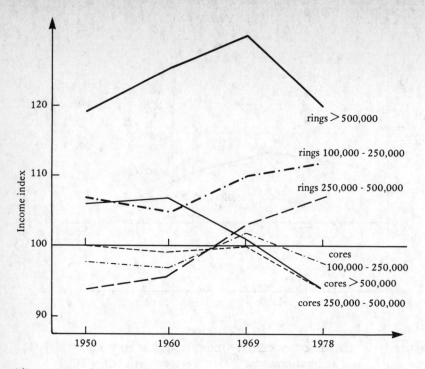

Figure 10.4   Income per earner (index); cores and rings by size class,
The Netherlands, 1950—78 (Netherlands = 100)

stage. During the next decade, a period characterised by disurbanisation, incomes predictably declined in the Randstad rings and rose,
but at slowed rates, in the rings of the emanation zone. In line with
processes expected during the stage of spatial concentration, periphery
incomes dropped at first and then rose. Levels in these areas, however,
remained below average.

Urban income and regional economic development

It will be recalled from the analysis in the previous chapter that
regions passed through four well defined development stages running
from prosperity, through recession and depression, to recovery, with
a return to prosperity from whence it is assumed the cycle is repeated
with staging in the same order (see Chapter 9, Figure 9.2). The
analysis of average income per capita showed that five regions, among
them the three rural ones, remained in the same stage throughout the

166

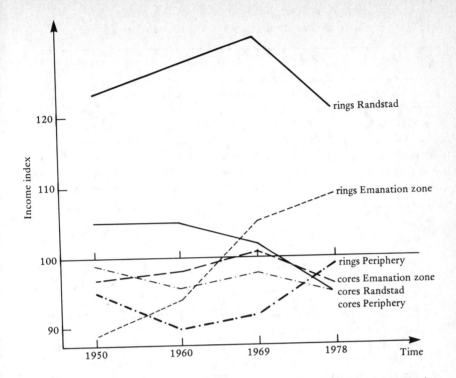

Figure 10.5 Income per earner (index); cores and rings by region, The Netherlands, 1950—78 (Netherlands = 100)

periods 1950—60 and 1960—75, the medium-sized urban regions in the Randstad passed from stage 1 to 2, and those in the periphery from stage 2 to 3. Table 10.2 summarises the results, where numbers in brackets denote development stages.

One region, the urban periphery, crossed the threshold of the national average. *Very* prosperous or *very* underdeveloped regions, it was found, were slow to reach the next development stage. Incomes in the urbanised regions of the Randstad, for instance, remained well above the national average though dropping somewhat in recent years, while the incomes of the urban and rural emanation zones increased but remained below the national average. The periphery lagged behind the other two. In general, the pattern of income change suggests regional convergence on the national norm.

The analysis of income in this chapter will follow the same framework as in Chapter 9 but with several important changes and expansions:

Table 10.2
Summary of Dutch regions by development stage, income per capita, 1950–60 and 1960–75

Regional type	1950–1960		1960–1975	
Large cities Randstad	recession	(2)	recession	(2)
Remaining towns Randstad	prosperity	(1)	recession	(2)
Rural Randstad	recovery	(4)	recovery	(4)
Urban emanation zone	recovery	(4)	recovery	(4)
Rural emanation zone	recovery	(4)	recovery	(4)
Urban periphery	recession	(2)	depression	(3)
Rural periphery	depression	(3)	depression	(3)

- the variable examined is income by earner rather than income per capita; because the former better represents the spread between higher and lower incomes;
- the units of analysis consist of 24 agglomerations and the 'remainder' of the Netherlands;
- splitting agglomerations into their core and ring components allows more detailed investigation of the spatial elements of income development; and three time periods, 1950–60, 1960–69, and 1969–78, are considered.

The income changes serve as the basis for characterising the various categories of agglomerations, cores, and rings by the stages of regional economic development just dealt with. This is shown in Table 10.3, which simultaneously presents the changes in urban population development expressed in stages, borrowed from van den Berg and van der Meer (1981).

Agglomerations

The income development of the three Randstad agglomerations deserves the most attention since together they account for such a large proportion of total income receipts. During the 1950s, they were the only regions to be classified as prosperous (Stage 1); as for the other agglomerations, those in the remaining Randstad had above average incomes but were not growing, and those in the emanation and peripheral zones stood below the national average (Figure 10.3). Evidently, Randstad agglomerations, and in particular the three

Table 10.3
Comparing urban development and income development

			1950–1960	1960–1969/1970	1969/1970–1978
Large Randstad agglomerations	Urban development		Suburbanisation	Sub–disurbanisation	Disurbanisation
	development of income	aggl.	prosperity	recession	recession
		core	prosperity	recession	recession–depression
		ring	prosperity	prosperity	recession*
Remaining Randstad agglomerations	Urban development		Urbanisation	Urb.–suburbanisation	Suburbanisation
	development of income	aggl.	prosperity	prosperity	recession
		core	recovery	prosperity**	recession–depression
		ring	prosperity	prosperity	recession*
Emanation-zone agglomerations	Urban development		Urbanisation	Urb.–suburbanisation	Suburbanisation
	development of income	aggl.	recovery	recovery–prosperity**	recession
		core	recovery	recovery–prosperity**	recession–depression
		ring	recovery	recovery–prosperity	prosperity
Peripheral agglomerations	Urban development		Urbanisation	Urbanisation	Suburbanisation
	development of income	aggl.	depression	recovery	recovery
		core	depression*	recovery	depression
		ring	depression	recovery	recovery

* on a relatively *high* level.
** on a relatively *low* level.

largest, were the most prosperous in that period but, as history has shown, they were not to maintain that position for long.

The relative decline of the three largest began in the 1960s. In terms of income, they were overtaken by the five small Randstad agglomerations and closely approached by three medium-sized agglomerations, Utrecht, in the Randstad, and two others located in the emanation zone. During this period, the downward development of the peripheral agglomerations was halted and reversed. Their income level remained relatively low but still above that in the mostly non-urban 'rest of the Netherlands'. Indeed, the 1960s witnessed positive income development of all agglomerations, save the three largest.

A decade later, however, income growth had come to a stand-still in all groups of agglomerations. The peripheral ones maintained their relatively low incomes while in all others income declined. Income in all the agglomerations converged towards the national average with the exception of the relatively prosperous small Randstad agglomerations.

For the first time since the initial period of urbanisation, income in the larger Randstad agglomerations appears to be moving towards a level below the national average. Changes in the emanation zone are nearly parallel, the only differences being that incomes are lower during the entire period, and the rate of decline is less steep. Quite possibly, their future income levels will exceed those of the large Randstad agglomerations. Developments in the periphery are obscure. Their incomes have closely paralleled national income and, except for this, no obvious trend is discernible.

The cores

The greater part of the agglomerations' total income is produced in their cores, as is evident from the following:

	share of cores %	share of ring zones %
1950	77.7	22.3
1960	74.8	25.2
1969	70.4	29.6
1978	63.7	36.3

The cores' declining share of the total is reinforced by the changes evident in Table 10.3. Except for the small Randstad agglomerations, the cores of all groups of agglomerations were classified as development areas — that is, as depressed — during the 1970s. The comfortable position occupied by the three large Randstad agglomerations in the 1950s deteriorated drastically during the next two decades. Elsewhere, the positive income development of the cores persisted from the 1950s through the 1960s, then declined there as well. Only the cores of the small Randstad agglomerations managed to keep just above the national average. The trend makes further decline — that is, continued status in stage 3 — the probable development for the 1980s. Indeed, income in the agglomerations' cores has sunk below that of the ring zones and the 'rest of the Netherlands'.

The rings

Developments in the ring zones have been the opposite of those in the cores. The Randstad rings in particular have remained quite prosperous in spite of declines starting with the 1960s, and incomes in the suburban rings of the small Randstad agglomerations ranked by far the highest of the Netherlands throughout the whole period. Particularly impressive have been the remarkable increases in average incomes in the ring areas of the emanation zone agglomerations, especially during the 1960s. Nevertheless, as an inheritance of their bad initial position in the 1950s, these areas are still lagging far behind the Randstad rings.

Incomes in the rings of the periphery and emanation zones have shown dramatic growth. The peripheral rings were clearly depressed (stage 3) in the 1950s and their incomes were the lowest in the entire Netherlands in 1960, but a subsequent cautious pick-up stimulated their vigorous recovery in the 1970s. By the end of the analysis period, their incomes had surpassed those of all cores and were exceeded only by the remaining ring zones.

There is good reason to assume that the peripheral ring areas will join the high income emanation rings in stage 1 (prosperity) in the years ahead. The Randstad ring zones will remain in stage 2 (recession) with incomes in the three large agglomerations' rings converging fastest on the national average.

Summary

The development of income mirrors more or less the spatial and temporal spread of high and low incomes. Incomes appear to evolve along similar lines throughout the nation, all but independently of size or geographic position. There is, however, a 'leader—follower' sequence in the spatial transmission of stages, with the large agglomerations in the Randstad leading the smaller ones in terms of income change, and the latter in turn being followed first by the emanation zone and then by the periphery. In sum, the results provide considerable support for the hypothesis that regional development is cyclical in nature with spatial lags.

Urban development stages related to regional income dynamics

During the entire 28-year study period, the development of the large Randstad agglomerations was consistently more advanced than that of any other Dutch agglomerations. In turn, the smaller Randstad agglomerations and the emanation zone agglomerations led those located in the periphery. From this, the factors of size and geographic position emerge as key variables explaining the stages of urbanisation.

The assumption that urbanisation is accompanied by a rising urban income is confirmed by evidence for the remaining Randstad agglomerations and the emanation zone agglomerations up to 1970. The transition from urbanisation to suburbanisation marks the critical point when prosperity is reached. The suburbanisation stage persisted longest and initially was not characterised by rising income in the peripheral agglomerations. Their relatively weak economic position offers one explanation. Following 1960, income in these agglomerations began to grow. Developments in the remaining Randstad and emanation agglomerations between 1950 and 1960 were comparable to those in the peripheral agglomerations during the next ten years, again confirming the significance of time differences in explaining the urban development process. The same applies to the suburbanisation and disurbanisation stages. During the transition from one to the other, e.g. large Randstad agglomerations, cores were becoming depressed while rings remained prosperous. This agrees with our *a priori* expectations concerning the nature of these stages.

Income development after 1969 suggests that all other agglomerations follow the stages initiated by the Randstad agglomerations. Although shifting from urbanisation to suburbanisation in the 1970s, income in the periphery failed to exceed the national average, contrary to expectations. Nor is this likely to occur in the years to come, in view of the development of the cores.

Conclusions

Recent studies of economic development in the urban and rural regions of the Netherlands have concluded that regional income differences have tended to disappear since 1950 (among others, see Klaassen and Molle, 1981). Incomes in the initially prosperous Randstad and the lagging other parts of the nation were expected to converge on each other. The extension of the analysis reported in this chapter, with its distinctions drawn between cores and rings, indicates that levelling out has in fact not occurred at the intraregional level. Average income levels have actually tended to widen between cores and rings of agglomerations as Figure 10.4 particularly well illustrates. In the 1950s, regions differed among themselves but cores and rings tended to develop in the same direction. In the 1970s, however, the regional differences had more or less disappeared while the cores and rings had started to diverge. Note in particular:

- the fast decline in the relative average income of the large agglomerations;
- the slower decline in the relative average income of other Randstad and emanation zone agglomerations;
- the stable but relatively low average income in peripheral agglomerations; and
- the fairly rapid rise of relative average income in non-urban regions.

During the 1950s, the central cities of the three large Randstad agglomerations enjoyed very favourable income positions. Income was higher only in the Randstad's rings. Since then, however, the superior position of those central cities has eroded compared to the rest of the nation. The same applies to the cores of medium-sized agglomerations in the Randstad and the periphery. All other categories of cores and rings (and 'the rest of the Netherlands') reached a higher income per earner by the end of the analysis period. The Randstad ring zones have clearly remained in the vanguard as to income level, although their lead has lost its edge. The greatest improvement was achieved by the rings of the emanation areas: from by far the lowest average income in 1950, their ranking now approached the high level of the Randstad ring zones.

These conclusions seem to confirm the assumed connections between changes in urban demographics and urban income on the one hand and urban and regional dynamics on the other.

Note

1 Income data analysed in this chapter were obtained from *Income Distribution: Regional Data*, published irregularly by the Central

Bureau of Statistics, The Hague, from data supplied by the tax administration. The publication reports income per head of the population and by income earners, for local areas and regions of the Netherlands. The income definition applied is 'taxable income' which includes social transfers and excludes non-reportable items. By income earner or tax payer is understood 'anyone for whom a declaration of any income has been received for purposes of income taxation'. Incomes of working wives are added to their husbands'.

Because of tax system changes and improved registration, the series is not strictly comparable over time as regards the definitions of 'income' and 'income earner', but there are no better data available. Although the inconsistencies are minor and probably have no serious effects on the results of the analysis reported in this chapter, they should nonetheless be interpreted with some caution. The population data have been arranged as accurately as possible with the current municipal definitions serving as the basis. The utmost temporal comparability has been aimed at by, among other things, taking into account revisions in municipal boundaries.

References

van den Berg, L. and van der Meer, J. (1981), 'Urban Change in the Netherlands', *Dynamics of Urban Development* (L.H. Klaassen, W.T.M. Molle and J.H.P. Paelinck, eds), Gower, Aldershot.

Klaassen, L.H. and W.T.M. Molle (1981), 'The Urban—Rural, Centre—Periphery Dichotomy Revisited: The Case of the Netherlands', Foundations of Empirical Economic Research, Netherlands Economic Institute, Rotterdam.

11 Cyclical patterns in US regional development[1]

LELAND S. BURNS

The long-term development of the US economy has been distinguished by secular growth, often at dramatic rates, but also by sharp fluctuations between prosperity and recession of no less spectacular dimensions. All of this is well known. Less is known, however, about the spatial structure of development over time and particularly of the unevenness of regional economic growth and of its oscillations, frequently masked by long-term changes. Yet these swings are as characteristic at sub-national levels, whether measured at regional or metropolitan scale, as they are of the entire nation.

The research reported in previous chapters has demonstrated how sub-national economies fluctuate between periods of growth and decline, of prosperity and depression, and of expansion and contraction. This holds true no less for US regions and states, as the analysis in this chapter demonstrates. Consider, for instance, the following:

– The loss of the textile industry to the Deep South during the interwar period marked the beginning of the long-term decline of New England's formerly expanding and thriving economy. More recently, after successfully retooling its economy to the demands of a technological era specialised in producing information-intensive services, and with the aid of large-scale defence contracts, the economy has turned around. For example, in Massachusetts, New England's largest labour market, the unemployment rate in 1985 was under 4 per cent, the nation's lowest; yet only ten years before the figure stood at over 11 per cent, the highest of all states.

— With the substitution of oil for coal production, Appalachia's once thriving mining economy turned sour and the region soon became the nation's largest and most severely depressed. With the change in relative factor prices precipitated by the energy crisis of the early 1970s, much of the economy sprang back to life.

— Following massive plant closures, few jobs remain today in the formerly booming multi-state industrial region that provided the nation with the steel required to win its wars, and to build its oil derricks, railways, cars, and many of the other critical products undergirding the nation's productive plant. The region, now appropriately dubbed the 'Rust Bowl', includes major parts of New York, Pennsylvania, Ohio, and Indiana. Lacking replacement industry to broaden an economic base built largely on nineteenth century technology, there seems little hope for restoring prosperity.

— After many decades of growth, Pittsburgh, a one-industry 'town' with steel production as its mainstay, became in the 1960s the nation's first large metropolitan area to lose population in the postwar period, later to be followed by a host of other large agglomerations; Pittsburgh's economic restructuring — import substitution at metropolitan level — promises a renaissance of growth.

— In the wake of substantial losses of jobs and industry to outlying areas, New York City hovered on the brink of municipal bankruptcy in 1975, but with the successful resolution of severe financial problems, ended the 1981 fiscal year with a sizeable surplus, the first in a decade. Commercial redevelopment has helped New York to re-emerge as a major centre offering financial services to the world.

— Cleveland and Detroit, major cities that faced severe fiscal crises brought on in large part by their economic dependency on the declining car industry, have also succeeded in bailing out their public economies, and face somewhat happier prospects for the future.

— A combination of cyclical factors, such as the current oil glut, recent overbuilding, and the devaluation of the Mexican peso have brought hard times to Houston, Texas, the nation's leading metropolitan growth area in the 1970s.

Earlier chapters have shown that the growth and decline of metropolitan populations follows an international pattern, with the spatial diffusion of effects related to levels of economic development. (For comparisons between parts of Europe, see Chapter 6; and for USA—Japan comparisons, see Chapter 7.) This chapter continues that theme by demonstrating how regional economies, like those of nations, experience broad swings in the course of their development, and how their cycles occur in spatially regular ways, in waves crossing the nation's landscape.

The data in Table 11.1, showing the ratio of per capita income growth in each region relative to the nation, reveal two important empirical regularities. First, the ratios rise and decline in cyclical fashion. Each series has at least one peak, or maximum value, and a trough, or minimum, just as in the cycles that characterise the economic behaviour of sectors and nations. Second, the peak values tend to move from east to west. The two north-eastern regions, New England and the Middle Atlantic, and the East South Central region each peaked during the 1950s, followed by the East North Central and South Atlantic regions in the next decade. The Mountain region reached its peak in 1967–72 followed by later peaks in the West South Central and Pacific regions.

This chapter examines the cyclical nature of US regional development during the 1950–80 period and, in the process, seeks answers to the questions: what are the characteristics of the cycles and what factors account for cyclical variations in regional development? In tracing the oscillations of US regional development, the chapter complements and extends the work of the previous two.

The next section describes the data and the regions that serve as observation units. The third section considers the framework in which this analysis is carried out and reconciles it with the frameworks used in evaluating Dutch regional cycles. The fourth section deals with trends in per capita regional income, the major indicator explained cyclically. Later sections present empirical results from testing income change in the cyclical framework, identify the determinants of amplitude and volatility, and estimate their importance. A concluding section summarises and draws out the policy implications.

Data and regions

The broad term 'regional' may be defined in a variety of ways, but the definition used here accords with official designations for purposes of data collection and reporting. The research is based on data for per capita personal income collected and reported by the US Department of Commerce for states and regions, defined according to the Census Bureau's regional system. The nine regions are composed of the 50 states, the smallest area disaggregate dealt with here, plus the District of Columbia (Figure 11.1).

Several reasons governed the choice of personal income as the

Table 11.1

Five-year per capita income growth rates, ratio of nine regions to US, 1950–55 to 1973–78
(five-year moving averages; current dollars)

Period	New England	Middle Atlantic	East North Central	West North Central	South Atlantic	East South Central	West South Central	Mountain	Pacific
1950–55	1.092	.987	1.004	.738	1.042	1.223	1.046	.761	.907
1951–56	1.105	1.010	.899	.869	1.043	1.279	1.065	.789	.894
1952–57	1.113	1.034	.850	.826	1.064	1.311 p	1.107	.828	.910
1953–58	1.114	1.078	.801	.931	1.059	1.268	1.089	.863	.896
1954–59	1.117 p	1.089 p	.756	1.063	1.048	1.261	1.072	.964	.899
1955–60	1.100	1.053	.740	1.154 p	1.097	1.261	1.020	1.043	.927
1956–61	1.070	1.031	.841	1.097	1.099	1.224	.933	1.005	.949
1957–62	1.040	1.014	.874	1.151	1.112	1.197	.902	.960	.940
1958–63	1.003	.967	.933	1.153	1.140	1.228	.930	.909	.910
1959–64	.964	.933	1.004	1.123	1.157	1.213	.949	.851	.887
1960–65	.952	.926	1.022 p	1.088	1.161	1.212	1.023	.809	.868
1961–66	.951	.924	1.011	1.074	1.165	1.205	1.086	.810	.854
1962–67	.960	.922	.999	1.073	1.163	1.197	1.107	.847	.857
1963–68	.980	.941	.959	1.040	1.170	1.180	1.116	.901	.879
1964–69	.991	.962	.924	1.017	1.182	1.177	1.117	.973	.886
1965–70	.984	.966	.915	1.031	1.187 p	1.172	1.079	1.052	.893
1966–71	.962	.953	.917	1.109	1.186	1.172	1.053	1.118	.889
1967–72	.938	.945	.921	1.125	1.176	1.182	1.067	1.154 p	.894
1968–73	.906	.925	.952	1.151	1.141	1.176	1.084	1.145	.913
1969–74	.889	.901	.980	1.149	1.097	1.166	1.120	1.112	.948
1970–75	.883	.887	1.005	1.128	1.047	1.145	1.170	1.069	.980
1971–76	.894	.891	1.013	1.041	1.006	1.124	1.210	1.038	1.026
1972–77	.914	.890	1.021	1.020	.974	1.086	1.220 p	1.015	1.053
1973–78	.955	.903	1.009	.991	.967	1.053	1.217	1.014	1.057 p

Note: p = peak value

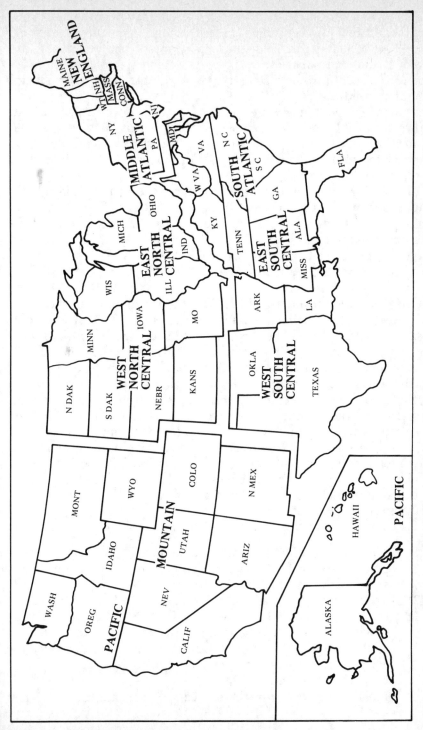

Figure 11.1 US states and regions

principal indicator for assessment. First, the data are available in a long, consistent, and detailed series. Second, per capita personal income is probably the best single measure of the quality of life. Third, because personal income tends to fluctuate congruently with business cycles, income data serve as a reliable proxy for general economic conditions.[2]

Ideally, a region might be defined in such a way that the area shows reasonable internal homogeneity but, when taken as a whole, is distinguished from its neighbours. The criteria work in some respects for some regions that follow the Census Bureau definition, but not at all for others.

The East North Central region embraces the manufacturing belt. The economy of the adjacent West North Central (or Mid-West) region, aptly termed 'the nation's bread basket', depends on agricultural production. Both satisfy the criteria well in terms of employment specialisation. If regional cycles are found, they should be closely associated with either durable manufactures or farm output.

Other regions fare less well on these standards. The South Atlantic region embraces the metropolitan District of Columbia in the north but most of the remaining parts are agricultural. The vast Mountain region, extending from the Mexican border on the south to Canada on the north, covers an area almost half the size of Europe and, in climate and terrain, it is just as diverse. About the only features shared by the states that make up the Pacific region is their common status as frontiers — they were among the last states to be admitted to the Union — and their borders along the Pacific Ocean; yet thousands of miles separate two of the five, Alaska and Hawaii, from the rest.[3]

Because so many US regions are internally heterogeneous and lack the integrity required of the formal definition, the analysis relies primarily on states rather than regions as observation units. It is interstate variations in the cyclical pattern of income growth that the analysis seeks to explain.

That variable to be investigated is obtained as follows:

1   The raw, unadjusted data are annual estimates of per capita personal income[4] by state, running in a continuous time-series from 1948 to 1982.

2   To remove erratic annual fluctuations, the raw data for the states, regions, and US total are first smoothed to five-year moving averages, thus shortening the time series to 1950—80.

3   Each regional and state per capita income figure is divided by US per capita income to yield an estimate of 'relative income' for each data point.[5]

4   Finally, five-year growth (or change) rates are calculated per

state and region, spanning the 1950—55 to 1975—80 analysis period. Changes in these rates provide the empirical base for measuring cycles, and later for estimating their determinants.

Subsequently, the terms 'income' and 'income growth' will connote state and regional per capita income data adjusted as described.

The analytical framework

With only minor alterations, the analysis of this chapter is carried out in the framework used for the investigation of regional cycles in The Netherlands (henceforth 'the Dutch analysis') and described in the previous two chapters. That research demonstrated how regional income oscillates over time between periods of prosperity and recession connected by intervals of decline and recovery, as in conventional business cycle analysis. Just as prosperity is marked by high and rising positive indicators such as income, depressions are characterised by low income and negative growth ((1) and (3), Table 9.1). The regions are respectively labelled 'prosperous' and 'development areas'. 'Potentially prosperous' and 'potential development areas' are those in transition from prosperity to depression (4) or vice versa (2). It was postulated there, as it is here, that during the process of development, regions progress through a sequence of stages. Although the sequence could begin at any stage, progress had to be made through stages 1, 2, 3, 4, 1, etc. in that order. Empirical testing with income and employment data for the Dutch regions covering five-year intervals running from 1950—55 to 1970—75 confirmed that, as hypothesised, the dynamic sequence characterised development.

Although the concept for testing for US regional cycles is the same, the measurement method differs in degree. First, as noted, the units of observation are states and regions and the time-series is continuous rather than, as in the Dutch analysis, for discrete time intervals. Second, the analysis uses a coordinate system that identifies each region's stage and position at a moment in time, compared to the Dutch analysis which assigned regions to one of the four stages without further definition of their position. Third, whereas the Dutch analysis identified regional growth stage by comparing level of income with its subsequent growth, this analysis defines regional position by growth rate and first differences in rates. The modification was required to facilitate regional comparisons over time. First approximations with the data showed that if a region's income ranked above (or below) the US average at the beginning of the analysis, it usually remained there throughout. Thus the time-pattern showed that US

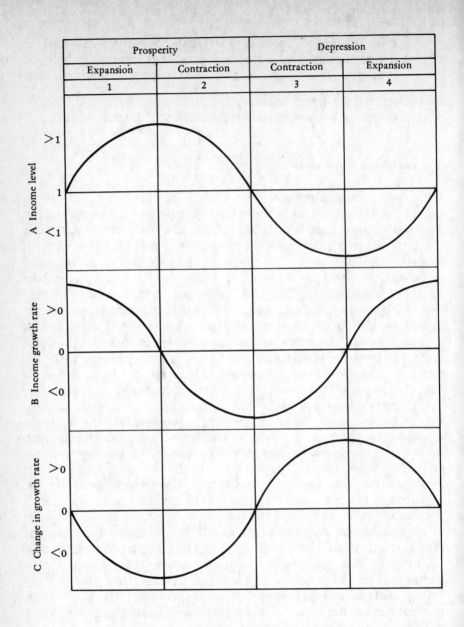

Figure 11.2   Income level, growth, and change
during prosperity and depression

Table 11.2
Correspondence between Dutch and US frameworks

State	Values of ratios: regional to nation		
	Income level	Growth rate	Changes in growth rate
1 Prosperity with expansion (PE)	> 1	> 0	< 0
2 Prosperity with contraction (PC)	> 1	< 0	< 0
3 Depression with contraction (DC)	< 1	< 0	> 0
4 Depression with expansion (DE)	< 1	> 0	> 0

Dutch framework

US framework

Table 11.3
Schematic division of development stages

	Income growth rate	
Changes in growth rate	> 0	< 0
< 0	Prosperity with expansion (1)	Prosperity with contraction (2)
> 0	Recession with expansion (4)	Recession with contraction (3)

states and regions generally moved either between stages 1 and 2, or between 3 and 4 (albeit in circular fashion as postulated), but not between 2 and 3 or 1 and 4, nor through the full spectrum of stages. The use of growth rates and their changes realigns the regions, in effect centring the time-series and making their development paths comparable without affecting fluctuations.

A graphic representation helps to clarify the differences between the two measurement schemes. The sine wave in part A of Figure 11.2, borrowed from Figure 9.2, describes hypothetical progress through the four development stages. In the first two stages, both denoted here as 'prosperity', the level of regional income exceeds the national average; the latter two stages, or 'depression', are characterised by below average incomes. Growth rates are positive in the first and last stages and negative in the two intermediate stages. As part B of the figure shows, income grows at a positive rate in stage 1, turns negative during the contraction of stage 2, remains negative through stage 3, and finally becomes positive once again during the recovery that takes place in stage 4. The changes in the growth rate, shown in part C of the diagram, follow with negative changes during the prosperity of stages 1 and 2, and with positive changes in the depression of stages 3 and 4. Comparison of parts A and C shows that the first differences in growth rates are the mirror image of the income levels. The Dutch analysis relies on stage of development definitions described in parts A and B of the figure; the US analysis draws on the changes shown in parts B and C. Table 11.2 summarises the differences between the two frameworks. Thus, although the measurement method differs in detail, the development stages are conceptually the same although titled differently. The hypothesis to be tested is also the same, as is the presumed sequence through stages (Table 11.3).

Borrowing from conventional business cycle terminology, an income growth *peak* occurs at the point of transition from stage 1 to 2 where prosperity shifts from expansion to contraction. The *trough* occurs between stages 3 and 4 as the recovering region moves from the contraction to the expansion phase.

Empirical testing

Do cycles characterise US regional development? Are fluctuations sufficiently ordered to show regular cyclical behaviour? The data shown in Figure 11.3 hint at answers. The charts showing relative regional growth rates and their changes are arranged by the nine regions. States are grouped by the regions to which they belong with the first diagram of each set displaying the regional pattern.

The smaller the swing about the intersection of the axes, the more closely the regional or state cycle approximates the national cycle; the broader the swing, the relatively greater the regional fluctuation and, of course, the greater is its dissimilarity with the national cycle. For example, the cycles for regions tend to be much closer to the intersection, as a general rule, than are those for the states of which they are composed. Regions are larger statistical units and closer to the nation in size than are states, and given their greater size, are likely to have more diversified economies.[6] With the national economy defined as the benchmark, it follows that the less the difference between regional (or state) and national cycles, the greater is regional stability.

The graphs portray for most of the regions and states considerable regularity in the cyclical development of income or, put another way, in the evolution of regions through regular and well defined states of development. With very few exceptions, all units tend to cycle through stages in the direction predicted: from stage 1 (or from another starting point), to 2, to 3, to 4, back to 1, etc. An arrow indicates the actual starting point for each.

Shifts along the diagrams' abscissa indicate secular growth. Patterns shifting from left to right denote declining relative growth rates over time. The New England and Middle Atlantic regions are particularly clear examples. Shifts to the left, as for the several Southern regions and for the states of Texas and Wyoming, characterise long-term positive growth.

Cycle duration, or longevity, can also be traced in the graphs, and in some with particular clarity. Some states and regions moved through stages sufficiently rapidly to complete at least two whole cycles; others moved so slowly that the analysis period was too short for capturing one complete cycle. Examples of the former are the East North Central region and the states of Maine, Louisiana, and Nevada. The clearest examples of the few states failing to complete an entire cycle are Vermont, Connecticut, and New York, all of which are located in New England or the Middle Atlantic regions. For the states that completed at least one entire cycle, the average duration was about 11 years.

The diagrams particularly well identify stability and distinguish often striking dissimilarities between regional and national patterns. At one extreme is the highly stable behaviour of states such as Pennsylvania (Middle Atlantic), Maryland (South Atlantic), Illinois (East North Central), Missouri (West North Central), and California

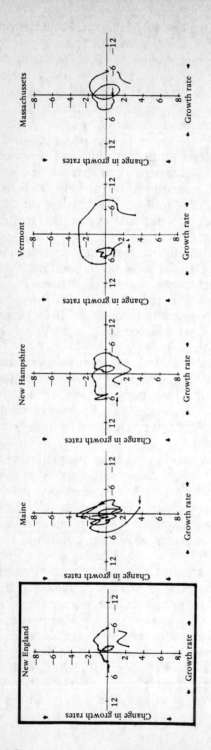

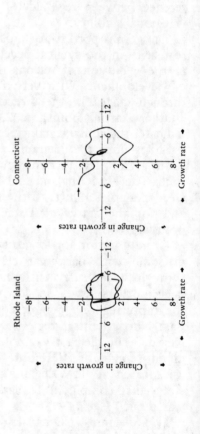

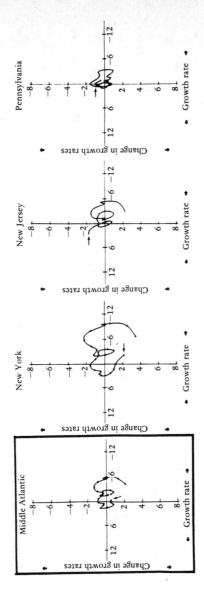

Figure 11.3 Cycles in the growth of relative per capita income, US regions and states

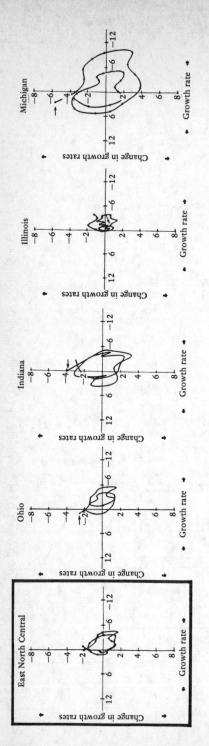

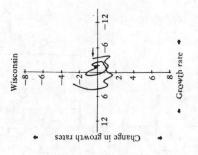

188

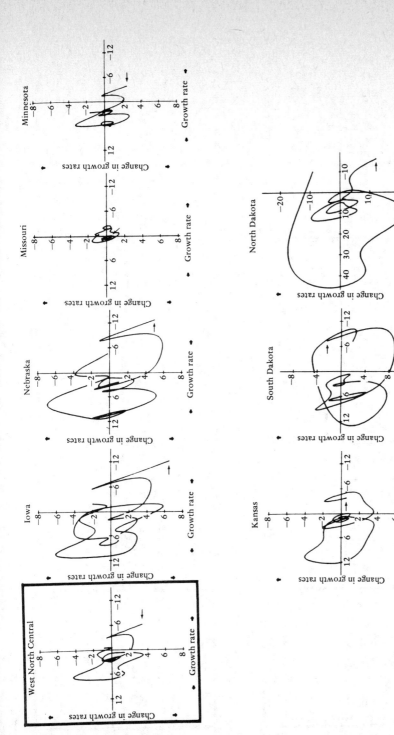

Figure 11.3 (cont.)

East South Central

Kentucky

Tennessee

Alabama

Mississippi

West South Central

Arkansas

Louisiana

Oklahoma

Texas

190

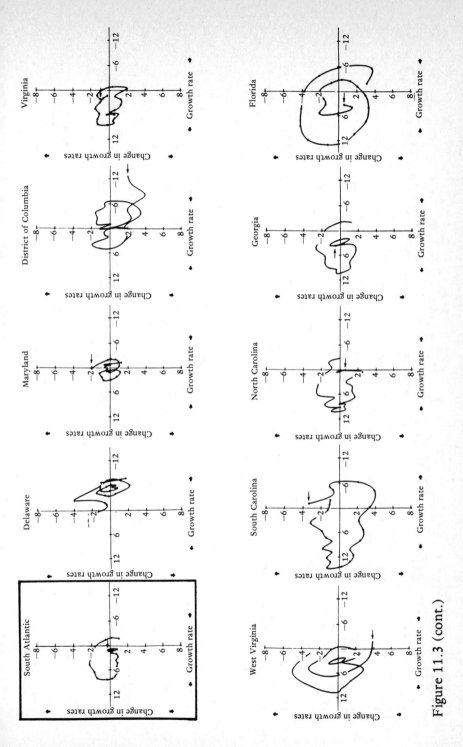

Figure 11.3 (cont.)

191

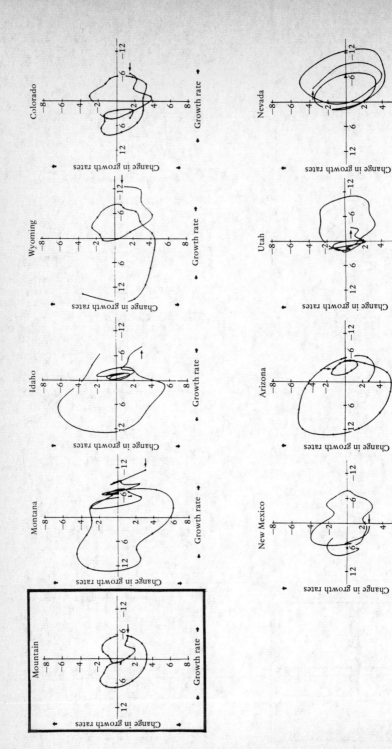

192

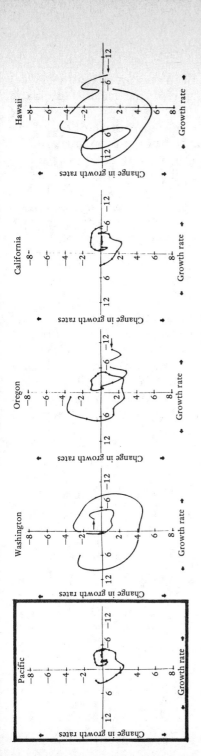

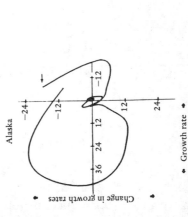

Notes:

1 Scales are identical for all regions and states except Alaska and North Dakota.

2 Because of the drastic reduction of the diagrams due to space limitations, much important detail has been lost; a complete set of the charts on a substantially larger scale is available on request from the author.

Figure 11.3 (cont.)

193

(Pacific). At the other extreme are states with wildly fluctuating economies such as those located in the rural mid-West. Iowa, Nebraska, the Dakotas, and Kansas (all West North Central), plus Alaska and Hawaii (both Pacific) furnish particularly dramatic examples.

In general, swings tend to be broader in the West and South than in the North and East regions. The fact that the economies of the West and South divisions tend to have grown more rapidly is perhaps no coincidence, but an association that will be more rigorously tested later.

The charts furnish a strong empirical base for exploring hypotheses about the determinants of change. It remains to distinguish with more precision the elements of which the cycles are composed.

Cycle components

Two components of regional cycles, volatility and amplitude, are isolated for identification and analysis. Each measures a different dimension of fluctuations.

Volatility, defined as the variation over time of the regional income growth ratio, is measured by the residuals between the actual income growth ratio for each period and those predicted from the long-term growth trend. Conceptually, differences in volatility might be shown as in Figure 11.4.

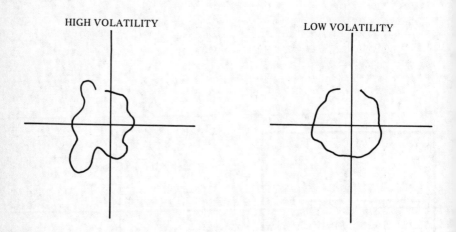

HIGH VOLATILITY   LOW VOLATILITY

Figure 11.4   Differences in volatility

Measurement varies slightly depending on whether the growth trend is significant. In cases where the true slope of the trend is zero, the deviations are taken from the mean of the series rather than from predicted values. The formula is given in the appendix.

The data mapped in Figure 11.5 reveal the geographical pattern of volatility. According to the map, the economies of states in the western half of the nation are generally more volatile than those in the east. Within the eastern portion, the states with the lowest volatility tend to be those located north of the Mason-Dixon line, the time-honoured boundary separating north from south. There also appears to be a parallel between urbanisation and volatility, with the most rural states, including Alaska and Hawaii, and those dependent on other natural resources, evidencing considerable instability. Almost uniformly, the states in the Mountain region rank as highly volatile.

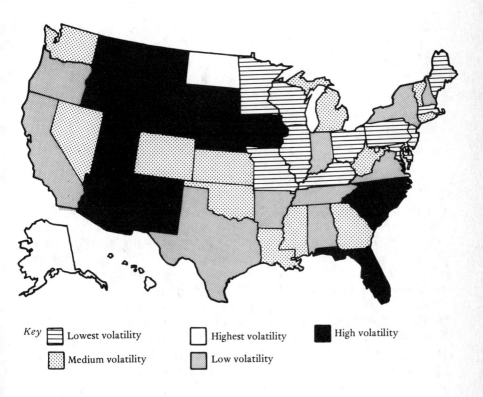

Key
▤ Lowest volatility   ▢ Highest volatility   ■ High volatility
▨ Medium volatility   ▨ Low volatility

Figure 11.5   Volatility, US states

Amplitude is defined as the average range of the swing of the income growth series around the intersection of the axes (the point in the earlier graphs that identifies the national average). Referring to the graphs that make up Figure 11.3, amplitude is obtained as the average sum of differences between each observed values for a state and period and the corresponding national figure. The formula is given in the appendix. Schematically, amplitude might appear as in Figure 11.6.

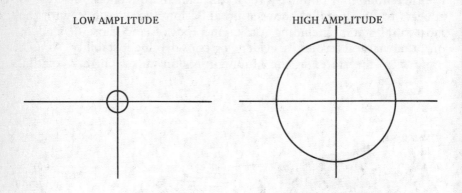

Figure 11.6   Differences in amplitude

The distribution of the amplitude data shows somewhat less geographical regularity than was the case for volatility although, with that exception, roughly the same generalisations can be made (Figure 11.7). Except for Idaho and California in the West, the lowest amplitudes were concentrated in the nation's north-east quadrant. Not coincidentally, these are the areas that enjoyed the lowest growth rates, suggesting that instability runs with high growth.[7]

There is little reason to believe that amplitude and volatility are similar. Yet an examination of the state rankings listed in Table 11.4, and a comparison of the mapped data in Figures 11.5 and 11.7 suggests, and the correlation coefficient between the two verifies (Table 11.5), that the two measures are colinear.

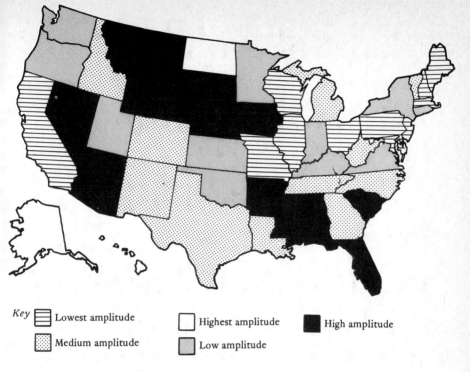

Key ▤ Lowest amplitude   □ Highest amplitude   ■ High amplitude

▨ Medium amplitude   ▨ Low amplitude

Figure 11.7   Amplitude, US states

The determinants of instability

The analysis based on the graphical representation of cycles suggests that amplitude and volatility are related to economic specialisation – and particularly to specialisation in cyclical industries – and to the secular rate of economic growth. It will be recalled that the regional income data have been normalised to national data; in this section they will be 'denormalised' to take into account regional variations, specifically the economic characteristics that describe a regional or state economy, such as its employment structure and growth rate. The 'theory' can be detailed as follows.

First, we would expect that the greater the dissimilarity between the structures of the regional and national economies, the greater will be the regional fluctuations. That is, with a regional cycle measured in relation to the national cycle, the more closely the region's industry mix resembles the nation's, the greater should be

Table 11.4

Rankings of states on volatility, amplitude and independent variables

Rank	Volatility	Amplitude	Concentration	Change, concentration	Agriculture, etc.	Manufacturing, durables	Manufacturing, non-durables	Change, employment	Change, income
1	ND	ND	DC	Wisconsin	ND	Michigan	SC	Nevada	Hawaii
2	Alaska	Alaska	ND	Maryland	SD	Connecticut	NC	Arizona	Alaska
3	Hawaii	Hawaii	Nevada	Nevada	Nebraska	Indiana	Delaware	Florida	Mississippi
4	SD	Mississippi	Alaska	Vermont	Mississippi	Ohio	Maine	Alaska	Arkansas
5	SC	SD	SD	Hawaii	Iowa	RI	NH	Colorado	Alabama
6	Nebraska	Wyoming	Wyoming	Wyoming	Idaho	Pennsylvania	RI	California	Georgia
7	Idaho	Arkansas	SC	Maine	Arkansas	Wisconsin	NJ	Utah	Tennessee
8	Arizona	SC	NM	Indiana	Montana	Illinois	Georgia	NM	Kentucky
9	Florida	Montana	Montana	DC	Kansas	NH	Tennessee	Hawaii	Oklahoma
10	Wyoming	Alabama	NC	Virginia	Kentucky	Massachusetts	Massachusetts	Maryland	Louisiana
11	Iowa	Nevada	Mississippi	Louisiana	Minnesota	NJ	Pennsylvania	Texas	SC
12	Montana	Iowa	Nebraska	Montana	Wyoming	Oregon	NY	Delaware	Virginia
13	NM	Nebraska	Michigan	Oregon	SC	Vermont	Alabama	Washington	NC
14	NC	Arizona	Hawaii	Ohio	NC	Washington	Virginia	NH	Florida
15	Utah	Florida	Idaho	Illinois	Wisconsin	California	Wisconsin	Virginia	ND
16	Washington	Delaware	Connecticut	Missouri	Vermont	Alabama	Missouri	Wyoming	WV
17	Nevada	Georgia	Florida	NY	Alabama	NY	Illinois	Oregon	Vermont
18	Michigan	Vermont	RI	Florida	Tennessee	WV	Ohio	Connecticut	Texas
19	Louisiana	Louisiana	WV	Colorado	Oklahoma	Missouri	Connecticut	Georgia	NH
20	Georgia	NC	Delaware	Washington	Georgia	Arkansas	Kentucky	Louisiana	Kansas
21	Colorado	NM	Iowa	NM	Missouri	Kentucky	Mississippi	Idaho	Minnesota
22	Mississippi	WV	Wisconsin	Tennessee	Hawaii	Maryland	Arkansas	NC	NM
23	Vermont	Texas	Arizona	Connecticut	NM	Mississippi	Maryland	NJ	Maryland
24	WV	Idaho	Utah	Texas	Texas	Tennessee	Louisiana	SC	Massachusetts
25	Kansas	Tennessee	NH	Massachusetts	Louisiana	Maine	Maine	WV	Colorado
26	Oklahoma	Michigan	Arkansas	Alaska	Colorado	Minnesota	Indiana	Indiana	Maine
27	Connecticut	Colorado	Oklahoma	NH	Arizona	Iowa	Hawaii	Minnesota	Missouri
28	Arkansas	Kentucky	Maine	NJ	Virginia	NC	Minnesota	Michigan	Connecticut

29	Texas	Oklahoma	Georgia	Delaware	Oregon	Kansas	Vermont	Vermont	NJ
30	DC	Virginia	Louisiana	Pennsylvania	Florida	Virginia	Iowa	Indiana	Iowa
31	Oregon	Oregon	Ohio	Minnesota	Indiana	Georgia	Texas	Wisconsin	Pennsylvania
32	Indiana	Washington	Indiana	Georgia	Utah	Arizona	California	Ohio	SD
33	RI	DC	Kentucky	RI	Washington	Utah	Kansas	Kansas	Arizona
34	NH	NY	Colorado	Michigan	Maine	Texas	Michigan	Massachusetts	Nebraska
35	California	Kansas	Massachusetts	Utah	Nevada	SC	Washington	Montana	Wisconsin
36	Alabama	Utah	NJ	California	Delaware	Delaware	Nebraska	Illinois	Indiana
37	Virginia	Connecticut	Tennessee	Arizona	Alaska	Colorado	Idaho	Maine	Wyoming
38	Tennessee	RI	Ohio	Idaho	WV	Oklahoma	Oklahoma	Alabama	Washington
39	NY	Minnesota	Maryland	Nebraska	California	Idaho	Florida	RI	Utah
40	Kentucky	Indiana	Texas	WV	Illinois	Florida	Colorado	Kentucky	Idaho
41	Maine	NH	Minnesota	Alabama	Ohio	Louisiana	Utah	Nebraska	Illinois
42	Minnesota	California	Virginia	Iowa	Michigan	Montana	Oregon	Missouri	NY
43	Massachusetts	Massachusetts	Alabama	Kansas	NH	Nebraska	Alaska	Arkansas	Michigan
44	Delaware	Ohio	Pennsylvania	Oklahoma	Montana	Hawaii	SD	NY	California
45	Ohio	Maine	New York	NC	Arkansas	NM	DC	Pennsylvania	Ohio
46	Wisconsin	NJ	Vermont	SC	Idaho	Pennsylvania	RI	California	Georgia
47	Maryland	Wisconsin	California	SD	Connecticut	SD	Arizona	DC	DC
48	NJ	Illinois	Oregon	Kentucky	NJ	Alaska	Montana	Mississippi	Oregon
49	Pennsylvania	Maryland	Illinois	ND	Massachusetts	Wyoming	NM	SD	Nevada
50	Illinois	Pennsylvania	Washington	Arkansas	RI	ND	ND	ND	Delaware
51	Missouri	Missouri	Missouri	Mississippi	DC	DC	Nevada	WV	Montana

Note: DC = District of Columbia, NC = North Carolina, ND = North Dakota, NH = New Hampshire, NJ = New Jersey, NM = New Mexico, NY = New York, RI = Rhode Island, SC = South Carolina, SD = South Dakota, WV = West Virginia.

Table 11.5
Correlation matrix

		1	2	3	4	5	6	7	8	9
1	Amplitude	1.000								
2	Volatility	.884	1.000							
3	Concentration	.617	.551	1.000						
4	Change, concentration	-.308	-.145	-.077	1.000					
5	Agriculture, etc.	.543	.418	.298	-.420	1.000				
6	Manufacturing, durables	-.554	-.446	-.540	.105	-.460	1.000			
7	Manufacturing, non-durables	-.319	-.333	-.278	-.073	-.280	.311	1.000		
8	Change, employment	.131	.175	.059	.239	-.268	-.232	-.251	1.000	
9	Change, income	.479	.426	.018	-.184	.173	-.229	.115	.041	1.000

regional stability. Similarly, concentration or specialisation of economic activity would be associated with greater fluctuations.[8] The concentration variable, the opposite of diversification, is used to capture regional specialisation. It is calculated as the sum of the absolute differences between the proportion of employment per industrial sector in the region (or state) and in the nation; the formula is given in the appendix.

Second, *changes* in the employment distribution are expected to be disruptive and induce fluctuations. In line with the hypothesised positive relationship between diversification and stability, a change that increases concentration should generate instability. On the other hand, structural change that diversifies the industry mix is also likely to destabilise the regional economy, at least in the short run. The *process* of altering the employment structure, rather than the *direction* of change, is seen as a destabilising influence regardless of whether the change diversifies or concentrates activity. Hence, the greater the degree of change over time in the regional employment structure, whether towards greater diversification or concentration, the greater should be instability.[9]

200

Third, aside from the concentration of employment in general, instability should depend on the types of productive activities that distinguish regions. Specialisation in inherently unstable activities would be expected to produce wider cyclical swings than concentration in activities that tend to follow national cycles. Farm production, and the income earned from it, depends to a large extent on exogenous factors such as government price supports and quotas, climate, and world demand and prices for food. Because demand can be postponed for consumer durables such as housing and cars, the output of these sectors is also especially volatile.

Output also fluctuates for industries, such as durables manufacturing, characterised by high income elasticities of demand. Particularly large swings in output typify the car industry, for example, with elasticities estimated at between 1.7 (Harberger, 1960), and 3 (Chow, 1957). The same would hold, however, for sectors with especially low demand elasticities. The demand elasticity for food, for example, has been estimated at 0.2 to 0.3 (Halvorson, 1953). Even if demand is relatively invariant to income, given macro-economic fluctuations, the economies of food-producing areas will be unstable, growing in comparison to total national output during slack periods and experiencing relative decline during prosperity. Thus, regional economies specialised in sectors with income elasticities at or near unity should be the most stable, and those farthest from unity, the most unstable.

Finally, high rates of economic expansion are likely to be associated with unstable growth. The demand for new products is characteristically unstable during their early phases following their introduction to the market. Technological change spreads unevenly, as Cappelin (1983) has shown for the regions of the European Economic Community, and generates uneven growth patterns. Investment of risk or venture capital in new enterprises with uncertain pay-offs may generate highly non-linear growth paths. Often growth, particularly at the local level, is short-lived. As the recent evidence demonstrates for the high-technology industries that have crowded into California's Silicon Valley, the first blush of success is frequently characterised by overestimates of market potential and underestimates of competition. On the other hand, economies that grow less dramatically have often locked themselves into structures that generate stability. Thus, rapid expansion, as proxied by the growth of income and employment, would be expected to have destabilising effects.

The results of the regressions on amplitude and volatility are shown in Table 11.6. The beta coefficients given in the last two columns weight the relative importance of each determinant. Only marginal differences distinguish the two measures of instability, a not surprising finding given their colinearity.

Table 11.6
Regressions on volatility and amplitude, US regions and states

Variable	Regression coefficients (t-values)		Beta coefficients	
	Amplitude	Volatility	Amplitude	Volatility
Intercept	-214.03	-10.65	–	–
Concentration	318.02 (5.11)***	13.64 (3.94)***	.482	.473
Change, concentration	-83.34 (-1.37)	0.366 (0.11)	-.121	.012
Agriculture, etc.	370.20 (2.76)***	14.48 (1.94)*	.304	.272
Manufacturing, durables	35.20 (0.28)	6.04 (0.86)	.031	.122
Manufacturing, non-durables	-171.29 (-1.34)	-9.98 (-1.41)	-.122	-.163
Change, income	205.51 (4.91)***	9.02 (3.88)***	.409	.411
Adjusted R^2	.70	.51	–	–

*Significant at .1
**Significant at .05
***Significant at .01

By far the most powerful underlying causes of instability are shown to be employment concentration and growth rate of income, with agricultural specialisation ranking next in importance. Except for the lack of statistical significance of the variables measuring manufacturing activity and change in concentration, the results accord with expectations.

Interpretation and conclusions for policy

The analysis of this chapter, based on fluctuations in per capita income, has examined the question of whether cycles have characterised US regional development and has attempted to identify the factors explaining variations over time and area.

First, as the graphed results indicate, the time path of US regional development has clearly been cyclical, fluctuating between periods of relative prosperity and recession. Moreover, cyclical behaviour differs substantially among states and regions.

Second, the more important determinants of regional instability are employment diversification, as measured by the resemblance of the regional to the national employment structure, and economic growth, as measured by the rate of increase in per capita income. These findings spring from the multiple regressions estimated to identify the significance and power of a set of hypothesised determinants. Except for concentration in agricultural activity, which was strongly correlated with fluctuations, other forms of employment specifically examined failed to significantly influence instability. This point, and another bearing on the impact of growth on stability, has important policy consequences.

According to the simple correlation coefficients listed in Table 11.5, employment in the three industry sectors examined — durables and non-durables manufacturing and agriculture — is significantly associated (at the 0.02 confidence level or better) with both volatility and amplitude. But when the three employment categories are held constant for concentration and for the other variables in the equations reported in Table 11.6, agricultural employment remains but manufacturing employment disappears as a significant determinant. From these outcomes it can be inferred, first, that diversification does far more to explain stability than does concentration in manufacturing activity even though it might be expected that output of that sector — and particularly of its durables component — is inherently unstable over time. The shifts in significance levels probably reflect the fact that the economies of states and regions dominated by manufacturing also host a broad variety of other activities whether directly or indirectly linked to the manufacturing sector via input—output relationships. Thus non-manufacturing activities help to insulate these state economies from the dominant industries' cycles. In this way, an economy such as Pennsylvania's, for example, can be highly dependent on durable goods production — as it is — yet rank as diversified and relatively stable.[10] The explanation of agriculture's more consistent positive relationship with instability is far less ambiguous. Because rural economies are much more specialised than areas that rely on secondary industry, they lack the alternative activities that cushion economic swings. Agriculture is significantly and positively correlated with concentration, and with volatility and amplitude. The policy conclusions that follow are that even for economies that depend on production that is highly cyclical, such as agricultural or durables production, the complexity that comes with diversification of the economic base moderates the impacts of sectoral swings. In sum, from this we conclude that employment diversification ranks as a key policy variable in stabilising regional economies.

The analysis leads to a second policy outcome that links the pace of economic progress with stability, two of the principal targets of economic policy. The analysis shows that at regional (and state) level, the two variables are correlated significantly, but negatively. That is, there is a trade-off between growth and stability. Policies that succeed in promoting rapid economic growth are apparently destined to generate economic instability — perhaps a small price to pay for the perceived advantages of high rates of expansion, but a cost nonetheless. Clearly, the rapidly growing states such as Hawaii, Alaska, Mississippi, and Georgia, have paid that price, for these are the state economies that also ranked among the most unstable during the 1950—80 period. This is one of the irksome trade-offs that must be faced by those who shape economic policy.

Regional income instability and regional income inequality share certain key features. Each is a distribution of income measured over a continuum. The latter refers to the evenness in the distribution of income over a set of regions at a particular time; stability connotes the evenness or 'equality' of income over time for a given area. Two additional similarities have greater practical importance. First, growth is apparently positively associated with both inequality and instability.[11] Second, public policy generally views the equalisation of income and stability as desirable social goals. Taken together, increased equality in the distribution of income over either regions or over time, requires sacrificing growth. What Johnson (1962, p. 153) has written about the growth-inequality parallel for nations — that 'there is likely to be a conflict between rapid growth and an equitable distribution of income, and a poor country anxious to develop would probably be well advised not to worry too much about the distribution of income' — may apply with equal force to regional growth policy.

Several trends that characterise contemporary US economic development are likely to have a moderating influence on the amplitude and volatility of regional cycles in the future. Among them are the declines in the relative importance of historically dominant industries such as manufacturing and agriculture, and parallel shifts to the less cyclically sensitive services sector. Regional economies are likely to become increasingly well rounded not only because of reduced dependence on resource-based production but due to the growth of footloose activities that, with falling transportation and communication costs, can locate and operate efficiently in increasingly diverse locales. Reductions in spatial concentration and increased economic diversification should moderate regional swings.

The trade-off between growth and stability presents the tougher question. In the past, economic growth ranked as a leading development goal explicitly and aggressively pursued by state and regional governments and it was the exception rather than the rule that a public agency discouraged the location within its jurisdiction of a new industry that promised employment and income generation. On the contrary, new industry was coveted and welcomed with tax benefits, subsidies, and bargain-rate loans. In the current era of slackened national economic growth rates and, with some areas pursuing no-growth (read: slow-growth) policies, the trade-off has become less awkward, and with it the possibility for increased regional stability.

Appendix   Formulas for calculating concentration, amplitude, and volatility

1   Concentration

$$\text{Concentration}_t = \sum_{i=1}^{n} \mid E_{is}^t \ / \sum_{i=1}^{n} E_{is}^t - \sum_{s=1}^{n} E_{is}^t \ / \sum_{i=1,\,s=1} E_{is}^t \mid$$

where E = employment
$\quad\quad\ t$ = 1950, 1960, 1970, 1980 (time)
$\quad\quad\ i$ = 1, 2, ... , n (industries)
$\quad\quad\ s$ = 1, 2, ... , s (states)

2   Amplitude

$$\text{Amplitude} = \sum_{t=1}^{T} \sqrt{(Y_t^s - Y_t)^2 + [(Y_t^s - Y_t) - (Y_{t-1}^s - Y_{t-1})]^2}$$

where t = time (1 = 1950–55, 2 = 1951–56, ... , T = 1975–80)
$\quad\quad Y^s$ = income growth rate of state s
$\quad\quad Y$ = income growth rate of US

3   Volatility

$$\text{Volatility} = \sqrt{\dfrac{\sum_{t=1}^{T} \left\{ \dfrac{Y_t^s - \hat{Y}_t^s}{\hat{Y}_t^s} \right\}^2 - [\sum_{t=1}^{T} \left\{ \dfrac{Y_t^s - \hat{Y}_t^s}{\hat{Y}_t^s} \right\}^2] \ / \ n}{n-1}}$$

where $\hat{Y}_t^s$ = expected income growth rate of state s

Notes

1   I am grateful to Leo H. Klaassen for helpful suggestions in the course of research for this chapter; to Marilou Uy and Sung Bae Kim for data processing and general research assistance; and to Eric Rose and Jin Ken Chun for the graphics.

2   According to Bretzfelder's (1973) research on the sensitivity of state and regional income to macro-economic cycles between 1948 and 1970, 'in nearly all cases, turning points (in quarterly personal income) coincide with or differ by only one quarter from the business cycle turning points established by the National Bureau of Economic Research; only one differs by as much as two quarters' (p. 22).

3   For a more detailed discussion of similarities and differences among US regions, see for example Garreau (1981), Jackson et al. (1981), and Congressional Quarterly, Inc. (1980).

4   Personal income consists of private and government wage and salary earnings, 'other' labour income, farm and non-farm proprietors' income, rental income, personal dividend and interest income, and transfer payments, less contributions to social insurance funds; it is income before the deduction of tax payments.

5   The use of the ratio, rather than of absolute income, filters out the influence of price changes which were substantial in some years, particularly during the late 1970s. If the unadjusted figures had been used, and fluctuations were calculated from a mean, the later years when nominal income rose rapidly due to inflation, would have unduly weighted the average; if deviations from a trend had been used, the trend line would have been determined to a large extent by the later observations. Regional price deflators have been estimated only in recent years; their use would have required significantly shortening the time series.

6   The parallel between size and diversification—stability can easily be overdrawn however. In preliminary runs of the regressions on instability reported later, population size was not a statistically significant correlate of stability.

7   The simple correlation between amplitude and income growth is 0.48, significant at the 0.01 confidence level (Table 11.5).

8   For an analysis of the relationship between regional economic growth and industrial structure during the 1959—83 period, see Friedenberg and Bretzfelder (1984); according to their research, industrial diversification accounted for the recent turnarounds experienced by New England and other areas.

9 Since any change is considered to be destabilising, the regressions are estimated to ignore the direction of change.

10 According to the rankings in Table 11.4, Pennsylvania stood sixth among states in the proportion of its labour force employed in producing durable goods, yet as eighth most diversified and near the bottom of the list (49th and 50th, respectively) in terms of volatility and amplitude.

11 A discussion of the reasons for the parallel, as intriguing as the topic is, goes beyond the scope of this chapter. However, on the parallel between growth and spatial inequalities, particularly at early stages of regional and national development, see, for example, Hirschman (1958) and Williamson (1965). The parallel between growth and instability has been pursued to some extent in the industrial organisation literature. For example, Sheshinski and Dreze (1976) present a theoretical proof that firms operating in markets with fluctuating demands produce less than do firms without. Yet, in their extension of that work, Mills and Schumann (1985) argue that demand fluctuations raise profits and increase the numbers of new entrants, and particularly of small firms that are able to compete successfully with larger firms through flexibility in their choice of production technology.

References

Bretzfelder, R.B. (1973), 'Sensitivity of State and Regional Income to National Business Cycles', *Survey of Current Business*, vol. 30, no. 4 (April), pp. 22–33.

Cappellin, R. (1983), 'Productivity Growth and Technological Change in a Regional Perspective', paper presented at the Eighth Pacific Regional Science Conference, Tokyo, Japan.

Chow, G.C. (1957), *Demand for Automobiles in the United States*, North-Holland Publishing Co., Amsterdam.

Congressional Quarterly, Inc. (1980), *American Regionalism*, Editorial Research Reports, Washington, D.C.

Friedenberg, H. and R. Bretzfelder (1984), 'Regional Shifts in Personal Income by Industrial Component, 1959–83', *Survey of Current Business*, vol. 61 (November), pp. 28–36.

Garreau, J. (1981), *The Nine Nations of North America*, Houghton Mifflin, Boston, Mass.

Halvorson, H.W. (1953), 'Long Range Domestic Demand Prospects for Food and Fiber', *Journal of Farm Economics*, vol. XXXVI (December).

Harberger, A.C. (1960), *The Demand for Durable Goods*, University of Chicago Press, Chicago, Ill.

Hirschman, A.O. (1958), *The Strategy of Economic Development*, Yale University Press, New Haven, Conn.

Jackson, G., G. Masnick, R. Bolton, S. Bartlett and J. Pitkin (1981), *Regional Diversity: Growth in the United States, 1960–1990*, Auburn House, Boston, Mass.

Johnson, H.G. (1962), *Money, Trade and Growth*, Allen and Unwin, London.

Mills, D.E. and L. Schumann (1985), 'Industry Structure with Fluctuating Demand', *American Economic Review*, vol. 75, no. 4 (September), pp. 758–67.

Sheshinski, E. and J.H. Dreze (1976), 'Demand Fluctuations, Capacity Utilization, and Costs', *American Economic Review*, vol. 66, no. 5 (December), pp. 731–42.

Williamson, J.G. (1965), 'Regional Inequality and the Process of National Development: A Description of the Patterns', *Economic Development and Cultural Change*, vol. 13, no. 4, Part 1 (July), pp. 3–45.

12 The fiscal costs of city decline: a case study of education

GORDON C. CAMERON AND STEPHEN BAILEY

The UK's major cities are in rapid decline. Every single city of over 175,000 inhabitants lost population in the latest census decade. Indeed, almost half of the 28 cities in this group have been losing population for between 20 and 30 years, some on a dramatic scale. Greater London, for example, had almost exactly eight million inhabitants in 1961 but 20 years later this number was down to 6.7 million. Liverpool's three-quarters of a million in 1961 had shrunk to almost exactly half a million by the second year of the 1980s.

This fall-off in population has been accompanied by a sharp decline in the level of city employment as well. Though boundary changes make comparisons difficult, nearly all these cities lost employment in the 1961—1971 decade and then again in the latest census decade.

In the postwar years there has been a general presumption in UK planning thought, and indeed in national policy making, that this decline of the largest cities was wholly healthy. Thus it was assumed that any process which allowed people to reside closer to work opportunities, in attractive physical surroundings and in smaller communities more susceptible to democratic control, was a pattern greatly to be preferred to one of dense, haphazardly planned and inhuman city environments. In a similar vein, private producers were thought to benefit directly and substantially from the improvements in communications technology which freed them from paying the high rentals and high rates inevitably found in high density cities. These technological improvements allowed them to shift to lower cost locations where they could exploit the advantages of extensive production lay-outs, and have scope for rapid unfettered expansion. Even the large cities themselves were alleged to benefit from this process of population and economic dispersal, since the loss of activity and population reduced the pressure on city land, permitted the provision of open space, lowered densities of new and existing housing and other buildings and made the task of comprehensive urban development without major dislocation to residents and other users that much easier.

Until the mid-1970s these kinds of arguments held complete sway. Public policy, in the form of infrastructure provision especially in new and expanded towns, industrial location certificates, financial incentives, green belts and planning permissions for private development, walked hand in hand with the private preferences of individuals, families and firms for development outside the major cities. Now, however, the consensus favouring decentralisation has been shattered and there are powerful voices arguing that this process of planned and voluntary *disurbanisation* is, at best, a gigantic zero sum game in which there are as many losers as gainers, and at worst a process which can only lead to the terminal social and economic decline of some of the UK's major cities. There are many dimensions to this portrayal of painful urban decline — persistent aggregate reductions in the demand for urban labour, persistent and heavy under-utilisation of the labour force, the withdrawal of private sector investment, the physical, social and economic decay of the inner city, and discrimination in housing and labour markets against the poor, and especially against ethnic minorities. These and many other symptoms of decline have been studied extensively and very often with considerable subtlety. Surprisingly, however, one aspect of the costs of decline which has received very little attention are the *fiscal effects* upon those local authorities which have to attempt to adjust their budgets to cope with the losses of economic activity and of population. This neglect is partly one of perception. Most commentators have focused on the more obvious symptoms of city decay; symptoms which have concrete physical forms such as crumbling buildings or derelict sites. Or they have sought human images — the black youth unemployed, or the aged homeless, or the harassed policeman attempting to control local crime without polarising local communities into pro- and anti-police factions. Even those who have analysed the issues more deeply have not seen financial problems as a central element in city decline. Unlike some cities in the US such as New York or Cleveland, no UK city in recent times has been on the verge of bankruptcy. Every major city has received heavy grant support from central governments of every political hue over many years. Indeed, despite their loss in population, the larger cities — the metropolitan areas and London — appear to have increased their per capita share of the most important central government grant (the rate support grant) relative to non-metropolitan areas (Table 12.1).

Furthermore, unlike the USA, much of the burden of alleviating the personal costs of economic change, such as job loss and income decline, is borne by the UK national social security system rather than by local governments. One can go further by pointing to the acceptance by every postwar UK government of a role in aiding specific regions and specific cities within them to improve their physical structures, their economic resilience and their job-creating capacities. The plethora of new urban schemes — enterprise zones, urban development grants, central government/local government partnerships, urban aid and urban development corporations — all these and more bear witness to a continuing governmental concern with the cities in their process of economic, physical and administrative adjustment.

Table 12.1
Shares of population and block grant per head by type of area,
England and Wales, 1974/75 and 1981/82

Area	Population %		1974/75[1]		1981/82[2]	
	1974	1975	Block grant per head	Area/England and Wales ratio	Block grant per head	Area/England and Wales ratio
Non-metropolitan areas	61.7	63.3	77.88	0.97	169.44	0.92
Metropolitan areas	23.7	23.0	90.08	1.13	220.96	1.19
London	14.6	13.7	72.66	0.91	196.76	1.06
England and Wales	100.0	100.0	80.02	1.00	185.05	1.00

Notes: Block grant for 1974/75 is the summation of the RSG Needs and Resources elements.

1 Initial entitlement before increase orders.
2 Initial entitlement with cash limits.

Sources: Office of Population Censuses and Surveys (series PP1 no. 1 and PP3 no. 3), Association of County Councils.

The nature of fiscal costs

The implication of all of this may seem to be that the negative *fiscal* effects of city decline upon local authorities are negligible and can safely be ignored. Such a conclusion would be premature since it ignores the real possibility of local *fiscal squeeze* as the per capita costs of service delivery rise whilst per capita revenue falls. Five causes of this fiscal squeeze are distinct possibilities, both theoretically and in practice. First, even if they wished to, local authorities cannot adjust their supply of services instantaneously and commensurately with the fall in their population and in the level of local economic activity. This arises from supply rigidities, notably indivisibilities in fixed capital and contractual commitments to staff which prevent speedy reductions of costly labour inputs. The consequence is that the cost of delivering services per unit of population must rise at least over some definable time period. Second, there may be genuine uncertainty as to whether and when the declines in population and/or in economic activity are likely to be replaced by stability or even growth. A policy of assuming continuous decline and a consequent withdrawal of capital and labour is likely to minimise the average costs of service delivery. The danger is that any overestimation of the rate of decline ultimately must lead to a higher than forecast level of demand, to shortages and a need to create new service capacity at a later date. By contrast, an underestimation of the rate of decline and an unnecessarily high preservation of capacity must lead ultimately to surpluses and to a higher average cost of delivery. To strike the right balance, especially when the life of capital assets is measured in decades rather than single years, is especially difficult. However, any failure to achieve this balance must increase the long-run average costs of delivery.

Third, the population loss may not be balanced but contain a high proportion of people who make less than average demands upon local services. The obvious outcome is that after a period of decline the population which remains in the city will contain proportionately more people who make above average demands upon local services. *Ceteris paribus* the per capita costs of delivery must rise in such circumstances. This proportionate increase in the service-dependent population may, over time, turn into an absolute increase as well. For example, if the economic decline of the city persists and more and more of the economically active resident population lose their jobs or have their relative incomes reduced, then the pressure upon the social and job-creating services of the local authority may grow.

The four possible causes of fiscal squeeze addressed above relate to the demand for services and the cost of supplying them. But another entirely possible effect of decline is upon the per capita revenues of local authorities. The revenue per capita from the local property tax (the rates) may decline if the population and economic activity losses result in a disproportionate migration or closure of domestic, industrial and commercial ratepayers who occupied highly rated properties. Simultaneously, or independently, the general relative reduction in prosperity associated with economic decline may reduce the local demand for services for which there is some form of user charge (e.g. swimming baths, transport) leading to a fall in per capita revenue.

The general deduction we can make from these points is that for local authorities to avoid fiscal difficulties from decline requires a set of very restrictive operating assumptions. Thus only if local authorities produce under conditions of constant returns to scale, have no contractual obligations, can forecast precisely future demands for their services, lose population in a balanced way and can avoid economic decline spilling over into poverty creation, then, and only then, can they avoid some adverse fiscal effects. Otherwise they are bound to face some increases in the cost of delivering existing services and/or some growth in the demand for their services and/or some decline in their per capita revenue. Of course, the immediate and obvious question is whether, to what degree and over what time period these costs are really unavoidable. A second crucial question is whether and to what extent the national taxpayer already bears the burden of these local costs of adjustment through such mechanisms as the rate support grant, specific grants for housing and urban aid.

In phrasing the questions in this way we make the assumption that all UK governments of every political complexion are likely to care about territorial justice. We assume that no UK government would adopt a policy stance which allowed city decline to spill over into high local tax rates for a given level and range of locally provided services. We cannot foresee any circumstances where a national government consciously would seek to encourage the process of population and economic decline. Thus they would not stand by in a situation where local budgets were so strained that critical public services could not be provided adequately or only financed in such a way that the burden of local rates and charges encouraged an even more rapid process of out-migration and decline. Accordingly, if it is shown that decline does result in fiscal pressure upon declining authorities, then we would anticipate action by government to reduce this pressure. This does not mean that we expect government to accept any level of relevant expenditure by declining city authorities as the level which automatically attracts government grants. There will always be disputes of principle and of detail between central government and local government over which types of anticipated expenditure and what level of anticipated expenditure deserve to be financed by central government allocations. In addition there will always be disputes about the precise way in which these grants should be determined and how they should be allocated to each local authority. Our concern is of a different order. Thus if we show that demographic and economic decline does impose fiscal costs upon local authorities, we would expect central government to take this into account as *one relevant factor* in determining the principles of grant allocation to individual local authorities.

Accordingly, given the policy relevance of this area of research, it becomes extremely important to clarify the general conditions in which government may be expected to act. The most elementary point is that the fiscal costs must be thought to be related to large population and large economic losses from central cities, that is the political jurisdictions at the centre of conurbations. It is the substantive net losses from these areas to other political jurisdictions which form the focus of our interest. Of course, if these losses in population and economic activity have been volatile in the past, unstable in the current period and subject to large uncertainties in the future, the need for governmental concern is diminished. This means that we are only concerned with those fiscal costs which are large and likely to persist in the future. Small fiscal costs of limited duration only necessitate small expenditure/revenue adjustments and need not trouble us.

We are also only concerned with costs which local authorities cannot avoid. For example, if their actions are entirely dictated by external forces over which they have no control, as for instance a legal obligation to supply services to certain clients, then this may generate unavoidable costs. If, at the other extreme, local authorities not only have complete freedom of action in relation to what they deliver, how and to whom, but take no steps to reduce fiscal costs by means used by other similarly placed authorities, then such costs cannot be described as unavoidable. Of course this last point oversimplifies a situation which is likely to be far more complex in reality. Essentially we are concerned not only with the interaction of demand for local services and the supply of services in conditions of change which affect population size, population mix and the level, structure and performance of local economic activity; but also with rates of inflation, changing national government preferences and the technology of service delivery. The political response to these changes is liable to be a complex mixture of decisions formulated in the light of previous commitments, local political ideology, national governmental pressures, the claims of national and local pressure groups, the actions of clients and ratepayers and the organisational strategies of affected

214

unions. Indeed, there is no simple continuum here where the costs of decline are identified and then the policies of local government are formulated after a discrete time interval. In reality the processes of decline, cost identification and policy response are likely to be inter-related and structured, not only by changing perceptions of the costs themselves but also by powerful factors other than decline which affect the revenues and expenditure of local authorities. This means that we have a difficult problem of *identifying* precisely what constitutes a fiscal cost of decline, what represents a policy response to this decline and what are the other factors having fiscal effects but not originating in decline itself. We turn to this problem of identification in the next section.

The objectives of the study and the methodology of measurement

The objective of this study is to delineate and to measure, wherever possible, the impact of population and economic decline upon the budgets of local authorities in seven major UK cities. Specifically the study seeks to establish whether, as population and economic decline occurs,

— per capita demands for key services increase, remain unchanged or decrease;
— per capita costs of supplying these services increase, remain constant or decline;
— local authority revenue per capita increases, remains constant or falls.

We use a time-series approach to scrutinise impact in terms of changes in the demand for services, in the supply of services and in the revenues of these local authorities.

The methodology rests upon the assumption that the expenditure and revenue consequences of decline can be distinguished by comparing how cities experiencing decline *differ* from non-declining cities in terms of per capita expenditure and per capita revenue, all other factors having been standardised. In simple terms, our model starts with decline leading to changes in the number and types of local clients to be served in given jurisdictions feeding into changes in demand, and over time, changes in supply. The latter are subject to revenue constraints which are partially determined by decisions on local taxation and user charges but also by national government financial objectives and national grant allocations.

All the subsequent budgetary effects are worked out in conditions where the local authority is subjected to influences from inside and outside its own jursidiction, but the critical element of the model is that particular authorities experiencing population and economic decline are subject to particular pressures not experienced by non-declining authorities (Figure 12.1).

On the *demand* side, population and economic decline changes the number and mix of clients who can claim consideration of their needs for, or rights to, public services. These changes lead, in turn, to changes in the derived demand for public service inputs and to changes in overall output. The way in which authorities consider responding to perceived changes in demand is likely to be shaped, not only by factors internal to the local area, but also by external pressures, political, economic, legal and so on. But the critical distinction is whether the demand change relates to the overall number of clients or changes in the mix of clients. The first type of change affects the volume of demand but is unlikely to alter the type of inputs required to satisfy this demand. The second is likely to affect the type of demand with changes being felt in the kinds of inputs required.

On the *supply* side, the way in which services can be adapted to changes in the level and mix of demand is a function of a number of service considerations of which the following are the most important. Thus we can ask whether the service is already operating at or beyond full capacity; what are the proportions of fixed costs in total costs; whether economies of scale in service provision are significant; what is the average age of capital assets and the proportion of assets due to be 'retired' in the short to medium run; if there is a high degree of substitutability of variable inputs for different tasks and what is the level of natural wastage of variable inputs? *A priori*, we can assume that the costs of decline are most likely to be greatest in those services which, before decline, were operating at or below full capacity; in those in which fixed costs formed a higher proportion of total costs and in which the possibilities of retiral of fixed assets in the short run is low. Moreover, where economies of scale are important, where there are limited opportunities for switching variable inputs to different tasks, and where there is low natural wastage of variable inputs, then once again we would anticipate major costs of adjustment.

These key service characteristics set the framework within which the local authority may attempt to alter its delivery of services as the level of demand and the type of clients to be served is altered. However, the extent to which a supply response is possible is conditioned by the revenue situation of the local authority. At one extreme is the position of an authority which receives full 'compensation' from the

216

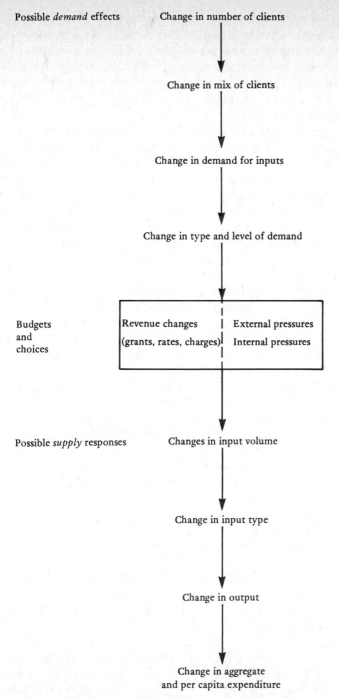

Figure 12.1   Effects of population and economic decline

central government for any costs necessitated by the decline in the number of clients and/or the change in their mix and/or a loss in local revenue. At the other extreme is the authority which receives no compensation from the government and is forced either to reduce its expenditure per capita, or else to tax and/or charge remaining residents and economic activities more heavily in order to cope with the per capita costs of decline.

In the larger study from which this chapter was drawn, three local authority services – primary and secondary education, social services and housing – were analysed in detail. Moreover, in all three services the costs of delivery, the client group and revenue sources were scrutinised. In this chapter we focus solely upon the major local authority service, that is, primary and secondary education provision, and we do not consider revenue consequences of decline. (Typically local education authorities spend 50 per cent of their budgets upon education.) All children of school age (ages 5–16) are obliged to attend school and since 95 per cent of British children attend state-funded institutions then we can hypothesise a clear relationship between population decline, the demand for state education and the costs of delivery. With regard to the selection of case study centres, seven UK cities (the analysis excluded Northern Ireland) from a list of 27 with over 175,000 population in 1951, were chosen for detailed study. Five of these cities had experienced population decline for three decades (1951–1981), one other had experienced population loss between 1961 and 1981 (Leeds) and one other had a static population throughout the period and was used as a 'control'. All the cities except Leicester had experienced absolute employment decline for at least the last decade. Thus the cities involved in the detailed case studies were in England – Birmingham, Leeds, Leicester, Liverpool, Manchester, Newcastle-upon-Tyne; and in Scotland – Glasgow.

Primary and secondary education scenarios

In terms of pupil numbers there are three possible scenarios as aggregate population falls in a given local authority area; first, falling population can be accompanied by falling pupil numbers; second, falling population may occur with constant pupil numbers; third, falling population may arise at the same time as pupil numbers are rising. If we assume the cost of educating each pupil remains constant, then *educational expenditure per head* of total population will tend to remain broadly unchanged if pupil numbers decline at the same rate as aggregate population declines. If pupil numbers decline more than population declines then educational expenditure per capita will be reduced. In all other circumstances, that is where the proportion of pupils in the total population rises (i.e. whether population is declining, constant or growing), then educational expenditure per head of population must rise. In fact all the cities experienced an increase in the proportion of school age children in the population before reorganisation (Table 12.2). Assuming a constant cost per pupil, a rise in educational expenditure per head of population must have occurred before 1973. Of course the same is true for England and Wales as a whole and also for Scotland as the data make clear. After reorganisation of the size, boundaries and service responsibilities of local authorities which occurred in 1973 (England and Wales) and in 1974 in Scotland, school population fell as a proportion of total population in Liverpool, Manchester, Newcastle, Glasgow and (marginally) Scotland, despite the raising of school-leaving age in 1973 (Table 12.3). In the other cities and nationally the proportion continued to rise. The key question here therefore is how these changes in pupil numbers relative to population changes within the case study cities compare with the relative changes in the nation as a whole; we return to this point in the next section.

All this analysis has assumed that the costs of educating each pupil have remained constant but it is precisely this assumption which needs to be evaluated not the least because rate support grant regimes in the UK have allowed for changes in client numbers (i.e. school rolls) but not typically for changes in the cost per client. In conditions where the number of pupils is falling very rapidly — a situation which has pertained for primary numbers in several of our case study cities — it is possible that costs per pupil may rise precisely because inputs are not easily shed at the margin. This may be because of indivisibilities of supply as for example with buildings and some internal equipment; it may also arise because the teaching input, though theoretically an input which can be easily varied with the level of demand, is subject to contractual conditions which affect both the speed and the cost of labour shedding. Moreover the teaching input is not homogeneous and educational priorities may dictate a minimum grouping of the variety of skills in each school and thus impose severe constraints on the scale of labour run down. Drawing upon these assumptions we can hypothesise that over any specified period:

1   if pupil numbers fall sharply, then unit costs (i.e. expenditure per pupil) will tend to rise;
2   if pupil numbers remain broadly unaltered, then unit costs will be unaffected;
3   if pupil numbers rise sharply then unit costs will tend to fall, initially, but then rise as pupil numbers continue to increase.

Table 12.2
School age population (5–15 years), seven local authorities, England and Wales, and Scotland, UK, 1951–71

Authority	School age population			Percentage change			Per cent of total population		
	1951	1961	1971	1951–61	1961–71	1951–71	1951	1961	1971
Birmingham	178,223	186,446	180,680	+4.6	−3.1	+1.4	16.0	16.8	17.8
Leeds	72,957	84,229	85,660	+15.5	+1.7	+17.4	14.4	16.5	17.3
Leicester	41,495	45,851	50,015	+10.5	+9.1	+20.5	14.6	16.8	17.6
Liverpool	137,424	136,674	113,215	−0.5	−17.2	−17.6	17.4	18.3	18.6
Manchester	104,832	113,555	95,815	+8.3	−15.6	−8.6	14.9	17.2	17.6
Newcastle	43,875	45,204	36,825	+3.0	−18.5	−16.1	15.0	16.8	16.6
England and Wales	6,524,870	7,635,832	8,341,390	+17.0	+9.2	+27.8	14.9	16.6	17.1
Glasgow	187,997	191,134	173,395	+1.7	−9.3	−7.8	17.3	18.1	19.3
Scotland	856,639	944,711	993,730	+10.3	+5.3	+16.0	16.8	18.2	19.0

Source: Census of Population 1951, 1961 and 1971.

Table 12.3
School age population (5—15 years), seven local authorities, England and Wales, and Scotland, UK, 1971—81

Authority	School age population		Percentage change	Per cent of Total population	
	1971	1981		1971	1981
Birmingham	196,260	185,041	−5.7	17.9	18.4
Leeds	126,645	126,958	+0.2	17.1	18.0
Leicester	50,015	50,183	+0.3	17.6	17.9
Liverpool	113,220	89,485	−21.0	18.6	17.5
Manchester	95,870	77,257	−19.4	17.6	17.2
Newcastle	53,185	44,781	−15.8	17.3	16.1
England and Wales	8,341,390	8,759,237	+5.0	17.1	17.8
Glasgow	190,130	136,209	−28.4	19.4	17.8
Scotland	993,730	963,353	−3.1	19.0	18.8

Note: Because school leaving age was raised from 15 to 16 years in 1973, 1971 data refer to 5—15 year-olds and 1981 data refer to 5—16 year-olds. Due to these changes, the data reported in this table are not precisely comparable to those in Table 12.2.

Sources: 1971 Census of Population, based on 1 April 1974 boundaries; 1981 Census of Population.

These hypotheses can be shown diagrammatically (Figure 12.2) which indicates our 'L'-shaped curve. Thus a given proportionate reduction in pupil numbers (B—A) leads to an increase in unit costs (OX to OY) since buildings and staff are under-utilised and, over time, labour shedding involves a cost. By contrast a similar increase in pupil numbers (C—B) results in costs falling OX to OZ) since the supply of teachers is elastic but buildings are not, so that the fixed costs of buildings are spread over larger numbers of pupils. In time, extensions to existing schools and the building of new schools results in a rise in unit costs which return to their former level (OX).

Before undertaking this analysis four notes of caution are in order. The first relates to the expenditure data we are obliged to use. Expenditure totals in any local authority service reflect the outcome of demand pressures, local political choices on the level and type of service to be supplied, the cost of inputs, the scale of production and the efficiency with which inputs are combined. It follows that it

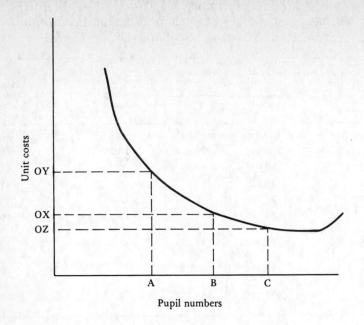

Figure 12.2   Unit costs and pupil numbers

is impossible, without detailed analysis within each area, to separate out the importance of these demand, output, cost, scale and efficiency components. Second, we have no nationally agreed standard of expenditure per pupil against which to judge how any local costs of decline should be measured. For this reason we are obliged to use the all-authority average as a benchmark. Third, the data analysed relate to local authority areas as a whole though we know that many of our LEAs experienced substantial *intra*-authority redistribution of school populations associated with slum clearance, the building of public housing estates, and the development of new private housing. Typically the cost of this kind of redistribution is felt in terms of the provision and maintenance of new school buildings and equipment, with additional proportional costs from under-utilisation of existing school buildings. We have not analysed such extra costs partly on the assumption that all local education authorities in large cities are likely to have faced such costs, though it is possible that the largest cities have experienced *proportionately* more population redistribution. It is true, in addition, that debt charges which are incurred on capital expenditures, principally school buildings, are a relatively small percentage of total current expenditure (Table 12.4). Therefore we have ignored this factor and assumed that any costs of population decline have come about as a result of *inter-authority* shifts in the residences of pupils and relatively low birth rates.

A final question remains. It is obvious that when decline in pupil numbers occurs, some authorities, with a stock of schools heavily weighted by old structures and with limited debt payments outstanding, may be in a better position than authorities with a large proportion of recently completed schools with many years of debt still to pay. Unless the second type of authority is able to sell off or lease redundant school buildings on favourable terms, then any reduction in the building stock is liable to leave the authority with long-lasting and heavy debt repayments and/or running costs. Because of the paucity of information on this point in the case study cities we have not been able to take full account of this factor though, once again, it is important to note the relatively small proportion of total costs accounted for by interest payments.

Assessing the fiscal costs of decline, 1950/51—1979/80

Educational expenditure per head of population can be expressed as the product of unit costs (expenditure per pupil) and the proportion of pupils in the population. If there are significant adjustment costs when pupil numbers fall, we would expect unit costs to rise. Whether this leads to an increase in per capita expenditure depends, as we have seen, on what happens to the proportion of pupils in the population as population declines. Table 12.5 shows how these two determinants of per capita expenditure have behaved in the case study cities. All the figures are given relative to England and Wales so that national trends in educational expenditure and pupil numbers are netted out thereby allowing us to concentrate on how the declining cities differed from national patterns. (Glasgow perforce is excluded from the analysis since it does not have educational expenditure figures produced separately for primary and secondary schools.)

In terms of *primary education* in 1950/51, all the cities except Newcastle and the control, Leicester, spent less per pupil than the national average. At the bottom of the league of spenders Birmingham laid out only three-quarters (76 per cent) of the England and Wales total and Liverpool also spent substantially less than average (83 per cent). Despite being relatively low spenders, all the cities except Newcastle had significantly higher proportions of school-age children in their population than the nation as a whole. The effect of this demographic factor was so large that it outweighed the relatively low unit costs in the cities and resulted in nearly all the cities spending

Table 12.4

Primary education revenue expenditure, seven local authorities and total, UK, 1950/51 to 1973/74

Authority/expenditure type	1950/51	1955/56	1960/61	1965/66	1970/71	1973/74
Birmingham						
Teaching salaries and wages	69.4	68.3	66.9	} 71.9	71.2	73.1
Non-teaching salaries and wages	2.3	2.1	2.2		18.7	16.8
Running expenses	} 28.3	} 29.6	30.9	18.7	9.9	10.0
Debt charges				9.0		
Other				0.3	0.2	0.1
Glasgow [1]						
Teaching salaries and wages	69.7	66.8	66.1	63.8	59.2	54.7
Non-teaching salaries and wages	9.2	10.3	10.8	11.2	13.7	14.2
Running expenses	} 21.1	} 22.9	} 23.1	25.0	27.1	31.1
Debt charges						
Other						
Leeds						
Teaching salaries and wages	63.6	67.3	} 72.5	73.7	71.1	72.1
Non-teaching salaries and wages	2.3	5.0		19.2	17.7	19.2
Running expenses	30.3	} 27.7	18.8	6.9	10.3	8.6
Debt charges	3.7		7.1			
Other	0.1		1.6	0.1	0.9	0.1
Leicester						
Teaching salaries and wages	62.5	60.8	59.7	60.9	59.8	59.1
Non-teaching salaries and wages	6.0	8.7	10.5	10.7	11.3	12.2
Running expenses	} 31.5	} 28.5	18.4	18.9	19.5	17.6
Debt charges			10.9	8.1	8.5	9.9
Other			0.5	1.4	0.9	1.2
Liverpool						
Teaching salaries and wages	72.1	70.2	69.9	64.5	63.6	61.6
Non-teaching salaries and wages	2.4	2.7	2.8	11.2	12.3	12.7
Running expenses	} 25.5	} 27.1	27.3	20.7	19.5	18.7
Debt charges				3.7	4.5	6.9
Other				0.4	0.1	0.1

Manchester						
Teaching salaries and wages	65.5	62.5	60.0	62.0	52.9	60.2
Non-teaching salaries and wages	4.6	4.6	10.7	11.0	11.0	13.2
Running expenses	} 29.9	} 32.9	23.8	20.5	17.8	20.3
Debt charges			5.1	4.9	16.1	6.8
Other			0.4	1.6	2.1	—
Newcastle						
Teaching salaries and wages	72.3	73.6	72.5	64.9	62.4	} 73.8
Non-teaching salaries and wages	4.7	2.6	2.3	7.3	8.9	
Running expenses	} 27.0	} 23.8	} 25.2	18.2	19.7	16.9
Debt charges				9.6	8.9	9.3
Other				—	—	—
All authorities						
Teaching salaries and wages	n.a.	n.a.	n.a.	n.a.	} 68.8	70.2
Non-teaching salaries and wages						19.2
Running expenses					20.4	9.8
Debt charges					9.4	0.8
Other					1.4	

Note:

1 Expenditure on *both* primary and secondary education.

Source: Annual Abstract of Accounts of Cities and Local Government Financial Statistics, HMSO.

Table 12.5
Per capita expenditure on primary education
relative to England and Wales, six local authorities,
UK, 1950/51 to 1979/80

Authority/expenditure	1950/51	1960/61	1970/71	1974/75	1979/80
Birmingham					
Unit cost	0.777	0.947	0.967	0.951	0.952
Pupils per capita	1.100	1.002	1.027	1.036	1.078
Per capita expenditure	0.836	1.017	0.925	0.966	1.029
Leeds					
Unit cost	0.913	0.927	0.920	n.a.	1.118
Pupils per capita	1.174	0.951	1.045	0.935	0.973
Per capita expenditure	1.054	0.928	0.900	1.013	1.093
Leicester					
Unit cost	1.063	1.091	0.986	n.a.	n.a.
Pupils per capita	1.043	1.045	1.137	n.a.	n.a.
Per capita expenditure	1.090	1.246	1.041	–	–
Liverpool					
Unit cost	0.807	0.836	1.018	0.919	1.091
Pupils per capita	1.311	1.197	1.031	1.053	1.064
Per capita expenditure	1.090	0.994	0.978	–	1.161
Manchester					
Unit cost	0.985	0.960	1.021	1.095	1.211
Pupils per capita	1.269	1.197	1.086	1.055	1.051
Per capita expenditure	1.230	1.077	1.033	1.132	1.282
Newcastle					
Unit cost	1.050	0.889	0.979	1.066	1.202
Pupils per capita	0.951	1.055	0.908	0.856	0.839
Per capita expenditure	0.982	0.880	0.829	0.895	1.011

Source: *Annual Abstract of Accounts of Cities, Local Government Financial Statistics,* HMSO.

more per capita on education. The two exceptions to this situation were Newcastle and most particularly Birmingham, which despite having a heavy 'weighting' of children, still only spent, per capita, at the level of 84 per cent of the nation.

The critical importance of the demographic factor is also evident if we examine trends over time. As already noted, only Liverpool, Manchester and Newcastle experienced a sharp fall in pupils per capita relative to the nation and in the case of Newcastle this really only occurred after 1960. In Liverpool and Manchester, two cities where pupil decline was continuous and local government reorganisation had negligible effects on boundaries, this demographic factor was of the utmost significance in affecting per capita expenditure. Thus if these cities had started the period under review with unit costs equal to the nation's and had experienced no adjustment costs, then their per capita expenditure would have fallen from 31 per cent above the national average in 1950/51 to 6 per cent above in 1979/ 80 (Liverpool) simply because of the fall in the proportion of the population accounted for by primary children. In the case of Manchester the fall would have been from 27 per cent above to only 5 per cent above.

If the demographic effect of population decline was to reduce per capita expenditure what was the apparent effect on costs per pupil? During the 1960s and relative to the nation, all the cities lost primary pupils with the exception of Newcastle, and there was a discernible and expected change in unit costs. Thus in Birmingham, Leeds, Leicester and Liverpool costs rose as hypothesised, but in Manchester, where the fall in numbers (both absolutely and relatively to the nation) was particularly large, unit costs fell. Similarly in Newcastle an increase in pupils was accompanied by a sharp fall in unit costs. (Newcastle experienced a fall in pupil numbers after 1955.) During the same period three cities lost pupils on a large scale, that is Liverpool, Manchester and Newcastle, and all of them experienced *modest* increases in relative unit costs. This appears to lend some support to the expected hypothesis of the costs of decline. By contrast in the three other cities, all of which experienced pupil increases, costs fell sharply relative to the nation in one (Leicester) and remained un-altered in another (Leeds) and showed a slight relative increase in the third (Birmingham). This supports, though not unequivocally, our notion that in the long run pupil increases do not increase unit costs.

After reorganisation all the cities lost pupils and all of them ex-perienced an increase in unit costs relative to England and Wales. In the case of Manchester and Newcastle these increases were especially large.

Overall this analysis seems to point to some connection between a fall in pupil numbers and an increase in unit costs. However the relationship was not consistent. Seemingly it did not apply uniformly and strongly in the 1950s but did thereafter in the 1960s and even more especially in the 1970s. There was no evidence that a rise in pupil numbers increased costs per capita; indeed in most instances of absolute (and relative) increases in numbers, unit costs fell. Put simply this suggests that there are some economies when scale in-creases but diseconomies in decline.

To examine this contention in detail we looked at the pattern of expenditure on primary education in the case study cities and nationally for each of the three main time segments 1950/51–1960/61, 1960/61–1973/74 and 1974/75–1979/80. In general the period between 1950 and 1960 was one in which local education authorities were purposively improving the quantity and quality of educational inputs/provision. At a national level real expenditure per primary pupil went up by a half (Table 12.6). The position in the individual cities varied. Real expenditures per pupil only rose less than the national average in Newcastle (and possibly Glasgow) but faster than the national average everywhere else. There is clear evidence that during this decade all the authorities with the exception of these two were catching up on the national average expenditure having spent relatively below average amounts in 1950/51. In contrast Newcastle was the only authority to spend more than in 1950/51. By 1960/61 all the authorities, with the exception of Newcastle, which went from an above average spending position to a below average position, had either overtaken the nation or narrowed the gap.

Table 12.6
Total real expenditure (1963) per pupil
on primary and secondary education, seven local authorities and total,
UK, 1950/51 to 1973/74

Authority/level		1950/51	1955/56	1960/61	1965/66	1970/71	1973/74
Birmingham	Primary	27.25	33.48	48.72	61.80	72.47	78.39
	Secondary	48.01	54.00	83.79	107.13	120.84	119.45
Glasgow[1]	Primary	} 49.38	56.84	70.34	85.34	108.79	120.92
	Secondary	}					
Leeds	Primary	32.22	35.80	53.03	57.27	54.93	57.79
	Secondary	55.89	58.04	84.06	110.18	105.18	92.76
Leicester	Primary	37.50	42.91	62.36	60.12	67.90	75.68
	Secondary	65.86	72.68	85.13	109.25	119.42	111.73
Liverpool	Primary	30.54	35.02	48.23	59.57	73.57	81.23
	Secondary	58.43	67.34	84.51	123.77	124.53	127.99
Manchester	Primary	33.00	39.16	53.44	65.71	72.66	91.49
	Secondary	67.59	78.34	92.55	127.44	142.40	145.73
Newcastle	Primary	38.23	32.32	45.03	56.10	66.89	75.88
	Secondary	39.54	71.55	81.03	116.79	131.64	129.00
All authorities	Primary	35.48	39.50	52.01	66.50	70.37	75.94
	Secondary	59.64	71.15	85.36	115.60	134.63	147.04

Note:

1 No separate data for primary and secondary expenditure.

Source: As Table 12.4.

228

Whilst the pattern of expenditure on individual inputs, for example, teachers' salaries, non-teaching salaries and wages, running expenses and debt charges varied city by city (Table 12.4), the most obvious reason for the relative increase in unit costs was that the ratio of pupils to teachers (PTRs), which had everywhere been higher than the nation in 1950/51 except in Leicester, was improved dramatically. By 1960/61, Birmingham and Liverpool had almost attained the national average and, of the cities experiencing pupil decline, only Manchester failed to narrow the gap (Table 12.7).

After 1960/61 the previous period of rapid increase in expenditure gave way at the national level to one of more modest growth. In Leeds and Leicester the slowdown was even greater than nationally though Leeds somehow managed a quite spectacular fall in its pupil—teacher ratio. Everywhere else the rate of per pupil expenditure growth was in excess of the nation's and the main explanation is the improvement in the pupil—teacher ratio (Table 12.7). Only Birmingham marginally

Table 12.7
Pupil—teacher ratios, seven local authorities and total,
UK, 1950/51 to 1973/74

Authority/level		1950/51	1955/56	1960/61	1965/66	1970/71	1973/74
Birmingham	Primary	37.0	36.0	30.0	28.7	29.0	25.5
	Secondary	26.0	25.0	21.5	18.7	17.7	17.3
Glasgow	Primary	n.a.	31.6	32.5	35.2	32.8	) 22.1
	Secondary	n.a.	18.2	17.7	12.9	15.5	)
Leeds	Primary	38.0	35.0	32.7	29.5	25.9	23.9
	Secondary	19.0	21.0	19.3	18.7	17.4	15.6
Leicester	Primary	29.8	30.4	27.3	28.0	25.9	23.9
	Secondary	20.4	20.0	21.7	19.0	17.9	17.9
Liverpool	Primary	34.0	33.0	31.0	31.2	25.7	23.7
	Secondary	21.0	21.0	20.0	18.1	18.2	18.1
Manchester	Primary	31.0	34.0	33.0	28.9	27.6	24.5
	Secondary	21.0	20.0	21.0	17.9	17.4	16.0
Newcastle	Primary	33.0	32.0	32.0	30.1	26.7	23.2
	Secondary	23.0	19.0	19.0	17.4	18.4	18.0
All authorities	Primary	30.5	31.1	29.0	28.5	27.4	24.9
	Secondary	21.6	20.7	20.7	18.3	17.8	17.3

Sources: IMTA, *Education Statistics*; IMTA, *Scottish Rating Review*; CIPFA, *Education Statistics*; Department of Education and Science; Strathclyde Regional Council; Leicestershire Education Department.

failed to do better than the national rate by 1973/74 and there is evidence from Table 12.4 that relatively heavy expenditure on school buildings is part of the explanation. Thus a clear picture emerges of cities which had consistently falling pupil numbers (Liverpool, Manchester, Newcastle) not reducing their primary teaching staff *pro rata* but either actually *increasing* their teacher numbers (Newcastle) or holding them fairly constant in absolute terms (Liverpool, Manchester). Similarly those cities where primary numbers increased saw a more than proportionate increase in teaching staffs.

After reorganisation with per pupil expenditure falling everywhere in real terms (Table 12.8) only Manchester and Newcastle had roughly the same level of real expenditure in 1979/80 as five years earlier and in Manchester's case this was only the result of a huge increase in spending in the one year between 1978/79 and 1979/80 (Table 12.9). Newcastle, however, despite its above national average drop in pupils, reduced its teaching force by a small proportion and its pupil—teacher ratio improved even further as a result (Table 12.9). Elsewhere the improvement in ratios very much mirrored that of the nation with the number of teachers falling in line with the fall-off in pupils.

Table 12.8
Total real expenditure (1963) per pupil
on primary and secondary education, five local authorities and total,
UK, 1974/75 to 1979/80

Authority/level		1974/75	1975/76	1976/77	1977/78	1978/79	1979/80
Birmingham	Primary	95.94	87.44	80.45	82.48	80.97	85.54
	Secondary	158.99	142.92	127.16	128.57	124.30	129.10
Leeds	Primary	98.39	89.78	82.87	84.58	83.45	90.18
	Secondary	153.99	142.74	126.34	127.25	124.29	127.34
Liverpool	Primary	107.61	101.79	93.76	93.80	92.21	97.18
	Secondary	161.23	150.53	138.43	134.56	134.50	142.80
Manchester	Primary	108.80	102.49	94.31	89.89	86.79	105.62
	Secondary	178.48	164.18	146.85	149.45	143.27	157.77
Newcastle	Primary	126.50	122.31	120.40	116.45	118.11	124.31
	Secondary	147.80	140.78	129.41	124.45	124.81	136.58
All authorities	Primary	95.44	87.63	80.60	80.83	82.97	83.55
	Secondary	150.57	138.38	131.03	130.85	140.50	142.02

Source: As Table 12.4.

Does any of this analysis support the notion that falling pupil numbers are associated with increased unit costs? The short answer is no. The 30-year period we have scrutinised shows unequivocally that unit costs rose because the city authorities perceived that their standard of educational provision was poor relative to the national average and in particular that their pupil–teacher ratios were inferior. In authorities experiencing overall pupil growth up to reorganisation their strategy was to employ proportionately more teachers than this pupil growth. In authorities facing persistent pupil decline the approach was either to employ absolutely more teachers or let their teaching force decline by less than pupil numbers. After reorganisation in a period of falling real expenditure occasioned by less generous rate support grant settlements, all the authorities, except Newcastle and Manchester, broadly followed the national pattern of expenditure per pupil.

None of this should be interpreted as a criticism of the strategies of the case study cities. That they should have wished to catch up on national standards of provision at a time when the whole service was being expanded dramatically in real terms is not surprising. And apart

Table 12.9

Pupil–teacher ratios, six local authorities and total,
UK, 1974/75 to 1979/80

Authority/level		1974/75	1975/76	1976/77	1977/78	1978/79	1979/80
Birmingham	Primary	25.6	25.3	24.4	24.2	23.8	23.3
	Secondary	16.8	16.7	16.6	16.6	16.5	16.2
Glasgow	Primary	–	26.6	25.4	25.1	24.6	–
	Secondary	–	16.3	15.6	15.3	15.5	–
Leeds	Primary	20.8	25.6	24.8	25.0	24.6	23.9
	Secondary	17.2	16.5	16.6	18.1	17.8	18.2
Liverpool	Primary	25.5	21.6	21.9	22.1	21.1	21.3
	Secondary	17.3	17.0	16.8	16.6	16.1	16.3
Manchester	Primary	23.7	23.8	23.1	23.6	21.2	21.7
	Secondary	15.7	16.3	16.2	15.6	14.9	14.6
Newcastle	Primary	20.9	21.0	19.5	18.7	18.6	18.6
	Secondary	16.4	15.9	15.1	15.0	14.7	14.7
All authorities	Primary	24.7	24.2	24.0	23.5	22.8	22.7
	Secondary	17.3	17.0	16.9	16.9	16.7	16.6

Source: As Table 12.7.

Table 12.10
Per capita expenditure on secondary education relative to England and Wales, six local authorities, UK, 1950/51 to 1979/80

Authority/expenditure	1950/51	1960/61	1970/71	1974/75	1979/80
Birmingham					
Unit cost	0.817	0.944	0.998	0.950	0.979
Pupils per capita	1.289	1.116	1.092	1.053	1.038
Per capita expenditure	1.036	1.211	0.925	0.998	1.020
Leeds					
Unit cost	0.935	0.991	0.943	n.a.	0.791
Pupils per capita	0.632	1.045	1.054	0.998	1.026
Per capita expenditure	0.581	1.142	0.844	0.876	0.817
Leicester					
Unit cost	1.097	0.930	0.910	n.a.	n.a.
Pupils per capita	1.282	1.195	1.148	n.a.	n.a.
Per capita expenditure	1.383	1.323	0.886	–	–
Liverpool					
Unit cost	0.944	0.956	0.994	0.908	1.114
Pupils per capita	1.076	1.020	1.129	1.144	1.058
Per capita expenditure	0.999	0.902	0.953	–	1.182
Manchester					
Unit cost	1.097	0.983	1.060	1.056	1.251
Pupils per capita	0.776	0.995	1.034	1.008	1.037
Per capita expenditure	0.837	0.905	0.931	1.058	1.019
Newcastle					
Unit cost	0.610	0.947	1.060	0.970	1.137
Pupils per capita	1.232	0.987	0.984	1.045	0.987
Per capita expenditure	0.739	0.865	0.869	1.007	1.126

Source: Annual Abstract of Accounts of Cities, Local Government Financial Statistics, HMSO.

from Newcastle their behaviour after reorganisation can be interpreted simply in terms of having attained national standards; there was no compelling pressure to continue to spend, per pupil, at levels which were markedly out of line with the nation.

But if the case study cities, and especially those with persistent pupil decline, did not suffer adjustment costs of the kind specified earlier but instead took advantage of falling numbers to improve the level of inputs per pupil, who actually bore the cost of these improvements? It seems reasonable to assume that the nation, through the rate support grant, should make financial provision for the costs associated with bringing the standard of provision into line with national average provision. There is however a related issue. Now that all the cities have achieved (or bettered) national average provision, there is no obvious case for special central governmental support for expenditure which improves upon this national average. Therefore in the future the critical question is whether primary school pupil numbers in the cities will decline faster than the national average and whether, as a result, such cities will face extra adjustment costs. A similar question relates to secondary pupils.

As we have noted already pupil decline did not affect the secondary schools in the case study cities until well into the 1970s so we cannot draw any conclusions for future costs of decline from past experience. Unit costs in the cities tended to be stable relative to the nation except in Newcastle where a markedly below average level of expenditure in 1950/51 was followed by a sharp rise in unit costs as that city improved upon its markedly above average pupil—teacher ratio (Tables 12.8 to 12.10).

Costing future decline: methodological and other problems

In 1979 the Conservative government specifically stated that no additional resources would be available in the future to support expansionist policies in education.[2] It argued that there was scope for redeploying available resources to bring about real improvements in the service. The main concerns now are the effective use of resources and the quality of output rather than volume of inputs per pupil. Hence the forecast fall in pupil numbers will lead to large potential surpluses of inputs.

The first objective is therefore to determine to what extent it is possible to reduce educational expenditures in aggregate. At one extreme, one course of action would be to reduce expenditure in line with falling pupil numbers. The other extreme course of action would be to do nothing, maintaining the same resource inputs in the face of falling pupil numbers, so increasing spending per pupil.

A fundamental problem is that projections of future pupil numbers are subject to an increasing degree of uncertainty the further ahead one looks. The number of primary pupils at between five and ten years into the future is influenced by estimates of the number of births in the next five years. But the prediction of future fertility rates is notoriously difficult, simply because the factors determining the birth rate at any one time are not susceptible to completely accurate forecasting. Projections of secondary pupils are less uncertain because infants born in 1980 will still be in secondary school in 1996, assuming no change in the school-leaving age. But pupils have a choice of whether to stay on at secondary school from age 16, so there is still potential for unanticipated changes. In planning educational provision, a substantial safety margin must be allowed to cope with these uncertainties. Education authorities may wish to hold on to surplus school accommodation since, if future pupil numbers are underestimated, the cost of new provision would be much greater than the cost of keeping available surplus pupil places for a few years until trends become clear. Nonetheless it is always possible that any future upturn in pupil numbers may not be precisely in those areas where surplus accommodation has been retained.

In addition to birth rate projection difficulties, the cities are also subject to uncertain rates of out-migration and the unpredictable effectiveness of measures presently being adopted to stem it. It would be only natural for them to tend towards an optimistic forecast of future population and pupils and hence retain more currently surplus accommodation.

As well as problems involved in forecasting future pupil numbers there is also a number of purely education obstacles preventing a *pro rata* reduction of educational inputs. Briefly these include the need to make adequate provision of specialist teachers for curricula purposes notwithstanding diminishing class size, the avoidance of excessive home to school travelling distances by maintaining underutilised school accommodation, the need to maintain adequate levels of denominational provision throughout each city, the continuing improvement of educational standards and maintenance of sixth-form provision. There are of course other critical factors affecting the issue such as inbuilt administrative time lags, departmentalism, pressure group resistance to school closures and so on.

However, notwithstanding these difficulties and constraints, given the scale of pupil decline there is obvious scope for reducing the volume of inputs. Over the long run fixed costs in education are very low, since labour costs constitute between two-thirds and three-quarters of current costs. Moreover, disposal of surplus fixed capital stock in the form of land and buildings may pose few problems, given relatively low demolition costs and potentially high resale values of sites for residential and other purposes. Furthermore, primary and secondary education is characterised by a highly replicative structure, in that educational output is provided by a multitude of individual schools.

Nonetheless, costs per pupil can be expected to rise due to a number of factors inherent in the rationalisation of provision. For example, and concentrating on the main item of expenditure, an authority can achieve a reduction in teaching staffs through one or more of the following methods. First, natural wastage (i.e. retirement and resignation) can be used to reduce the teaching force. Posts becoming vacant need not be automatically refilled, although it will be necessary to maintain a minimum level of recruitment to protect the curricula of individual schools. However, the difficulty here is that wastage rates can be expected to fall in the future as all local authorities are likely to be cutting down on recruitment thus reducing the opportunities for inter-authority mobility and therefore the volume of resignations. This reduction in wastage will be reinforced by a fall-off in recruitment of young teachers, many of whom normally have a high rate of resignation, as for example young women teachers who have high wastage rates caused by leaving to rear families. A second measure is the introduction of early retirement. However, the effectiveness of this policy is limited since the majority of both primary and secondary teachers fall within the younger age groups, with 30 years or more to retirement in all seven cities. Furthermore, since they have an exceptionally large number of technical subject staff in the older age groups, a policy of early retirement could deplete teacher resources in vocational subjects. Early retirement is also relatively expensive because the local authorities have to finance the extra cost of the early retirement scheme themselves. A third measure is that of planned (either compulsory or voluntary) redundancies. Redundancy payments would be substantial but teacher reduction could be more efficiently regulated in terms of subjects and schools than could be achieved by early retirement. Maximum savings over the long term (in the way of continuing teachers' salary obligations) could be achieved by redundancies amongst the youngest teachers at least compensatory cost. Under such a policy, however, grade drift would increase, for the proportion of promoted posts in total teaching posts would rise, as would incremental drift, in that the average age of teachers would increase.

It therefore seems inevitable that *teacher costs per pupil* will rise, whatever measures are adopted. The rise in costs per pupil will be greater if authorities do not react promptly to reduce teacher numbers. All authorities, urban and non-urban, will face these problems. The key question for this study however is whether the large case study city authorities will face significantly greater increases in teacher costs per pupil than the average. We return to the question shortly.

With regard to *accommodation costs per pupil* it is difficult to envisage how anything other than a rise is possible. Certainly given the density of urban schools as compared to rural schools it appears easier for urban authorities to dispense with these surpluses without greatly enlarging catchment areas, or causing denominational schools to amalgamate wholesale or force all schools into a limited number of geographical locations so as to ensure school viability both educationally and in terms of costs. However the Department of Education and Science does not think it practicable anywhere to expect a *pro rata* reduction in accommodation for fear of reducing educational standards, and infringing the rights of those wishing their children to attend denominational schools. For England and Wales as a whole the DES expects the maximum feasible closure rates to be three-quarters of total temporary accommodation and one-third and one-fifth of surplus primary and secondary places respectively. It follows from this that accommodation costs per pupil must rise, but once again the critical question for this study is whether the case study cities are likely to face larger costs per pupil than the average. We turn to this question next.

Costing future decline: the data

Comparing the forecast number of pupils (Table 12.11) with the existing number of places in the late 1970s (Table 12.12) reveals large potential surpluses of accommodation (Table 12.13). In proportionate terms the potential surpluses in primary school places are greater than the national average, in Liverpool, Manchester and Glasgow, but all cities except Birmingham can expect substantially above national average surpluses of secondary places.

Facing these surpluses some of the cities have relatively low proportions of temporary accommodation and much higher proportions of their primary schools have been built during the postwar period, no appreciable difference existing for secondary schools (Table 12.12). For primary schools then there is less scope in cities such as Manchester, Newcastle and Glasgow for adjustment to the emerging surplus of places by the closure of temporary accommodation or the phasing out of the oldest and least satisfactory accommodation.

The implications of the cities' projections of school rolls for their school buildings are dramatic (Table 12.14). In the 'do nothing' situation average primary school rolls would fall by at least a quarter up to the troughs in pupil numbers (with the exception of Leicester) and average secondary school rolls would fall by at least a third (again with the exception of Leicester and Leeds) with corresponding increases in the numbers of permanent places per pupil. Indeed if only one permanent place per pupil were allowed there would already have been surplus schools in 1978. These can be compared with the surpluses generated if 1978 average school rolls were maintained

Table 12.11

Peaks and troughs in pupil numbers, seven cities, England and Wales, and Scotland, UK

Area/city	Primary*						Secondary					
	Peak		Trough		Percentage fall		Peak		Trough		Percentage fall	
	Year	Number	Year	Number			Year	Number	Year	Number		
Birmingham	1971	113,362	1984	73,900	34.8		1976	94,310	1990	68,200	27.7	
Leeds	1975	75,769	1984	54,416	28.2		1979	72,645	1990	41,793	42.5	
Leicester	1974	29,848	1984	22,470	24.7		1977	26,196	1990	19,110	34.6	
Liverpool	1973	62,442	1985	36,756	41.1		1975	51,169	1990	30,164	41.1	
Manchester	1973	59,780	1986	32,695	45.3		1979	44,605	1990	24,750	44.5	
Newcastle**	1973	31,406	1986	20,440	34.9		1976	21,583	1989	14,396	33.3	
England and Wales	1973	4,900,000	1986	3,500,000	28.6		1979	4,100,000	1992	2,900,000	29.3	
Glasgow	1976	98,150	1985	55,365	43.6		1979	62,267	1991	30,058	51.8	
Scotland	1973	636,000	1985	445,000	30.1		1979	410,000	1991	288,000	29.8	

*Primary pupil data refer to areas as constituted after local government reorganisation.
**Newcastle primary numbers refer to pupils in primary, first and middle schools. Secondary numbers refer to comprehensive and high schools.

Sources: DES, SED and city education departments.

Table 12.12

Ages of schools and type of accommodation, six cities, England and Wales, and Scotland, UK, 1978*

Area/city	Age of main buildings (percentages)				Number of schools**	Total number of places	Number of temporary places	Temporary percentages in total	Number of pupils
	pre-1903	1903–18	1919–45	post-1945					
Primary									
Birmingham	31.7		21.2	47.1	361	115,000	n.a.	n.a.	109,601
Leeds	36.1	6.3	8.7	49.0	208	73,105	11,438	15.7	69,764
Leicester	22.3	1.9	26.2	49.5	103	36,162	6,655	18.4	26,720
Liverpool	23.4	11.0	22.9	42.7	218	73,800	n.a.	n.a.	50,760
Manchester	13.7	8.8	25.7	51.8	226	60,960	5,640	9.3	46,613
Newcastle	14.3	17.1	15.2	53.3	105	34,164	1,958	5.7	27,122
England and Wales***	36.0	8.0	10.0	46.0	23,280	5,881,000	624,000	10.6	4,876,000
Glasgow	24.8		13.6	61.6	258	139,224	8,295	6.0	81,075
Scotland	47.0		9.0	44.0	2,517	n.a.	n.a.	n.a.	569,000
Secondary									
Birmingham	26.6		13.7	59.7	110	94,875	n.a.	n.a.	92,199
Leeds	9.8	9.8	11.8	68.6	102	85,290	5,350	6.3	61,699
Leicester	10.0	–	30.0	60.0	30	29,265	4,630	15.8	25,642
Liverpool	10.4	6.3	26.0	57.3	96	56,470	n.a.	n.a.	46,586
Manchester	6.0	4.5	22.4	67.1	67	44,500	178	0.4	42,496
Newcastle		13.3	26.7	60.0	15	22,400	1,372	6.1	20,511
England and Wales***	13.0	8.0	18.0	61.0	5,030	4,010,000	299,000	7.5	4,093,000
Glasgow	8.8		19.3	71.9	57	81,556	1,138	3.8	63,543
Scotland	20.0		15.0	65.0	438	n.a.	n.a.	n.a.	410,000

*All data relate to 1978 except the national accommodation figures which relate to 1976. No later data are available from DES. No accommodation totals for Scotland are available from SED.

**Infant and junior primary schools and upper and lower secondary schools are treated as separate schools when housed in separate buildings except in the case of Glasgow.

***The England and Wales potential surpluses are based on the 40/70 space standards, whilst those of the cities are based on the standards adopted by the local authorities themselves. They are not necessarily coincident. However, the purpose of this chapter is to analyse the effects of decline in pupil numbers from a given level of service in each authority rather than to compare levels of service between authorities.

Sources: As for Table 12.11.

Table 12.13
Potentially surplus accommodation at pupil troughs, seven cities, England and Wales, and Scotland, UK*

Area/city	Primary		Secondary	
	Number of places	% of total	Number of places	% of total
Birmingham	41,100	35.7	26,675	28.1
Leeds	18,689	25.6	43,497	51.0
Leicester	13,692	37.9	10,155	34.7
Liverpool	37,035	50.2	26,306	46.6
Manchester	28,265	46.4	19,750	44.4
Newcastle	13,724	40.2	8,004	35.7
England and Wales	2,381,000	40.5	1,110,000	27.7
Glasgow	83,859	60.2	51,498	63.1
Scotland	n.a.	n.a.	n.a.	n.a.

*See Table 12.12 for dates of pupil troughs.

Source: Tables 12.11 and 12.12.

(Glasgow and Birmingham being notable for surplus primary schools) to give some idea of the realistic surpluses which will exist.

Assuming the maintenance of 1978 PTRs[3] and forecast pupil numbers we can calculate required teacher wastage rates (Table 12.15). Birmingham and Glasgow have notably high required wastage rates, but if we look in detail at one city, Liverpool, we see it has to lose an average of 174 teachers (primary and secondary) annually up to 1985. However retirals will constitute only a very small proportion of natural wastage with an average of only 27 teachers reaching the age of 65 each year up to 1985. If Liverpool reduced the retirement age to 60 then a maximum of 572 primary and secondary teachers could be (compulsorily) retired between 1978 and 1985 compared with the need to lose 1,218 teachers over the same period if PTRs were to be maintained at 1978 levels. Natural wastage caused by resignations would of course supplement this, although the future levels of resignations are likely to be low given the reasons noted earlier.

The councils of all the cities are against compulsory redundancies. Indeed, since most of these authorities have faced general teacher shortages in the past they may be unwilling to reduce teaching staff numbers sufficiently to maintain constant PTRs, especially since more teachers will be needed again if and when the upturn in pupil numbers occurs.

Consideration of changes in teacher and premises costs can now be

Table 12.14

Implications of projected rolls for school accommodations at pupil troughs, seven local authorities, UK

	Birmingham Primary		Birmingham Secondary		Glasgow Primary		Glasgow Secondary		Leeds Primary		Leeds Secondary		Leicester Primary		Leicester Secondary	
	1978	1984	1978	1990	1978	1985	1978	1991	1978	1984	1978	1990	1978	1984	1978	1990
Average roll per school if 1978 number of schools maintained	304	205	838	620	314	215	1115	527	335	262	551	373	225	218	855	637
Surplus schools if 1978 average school roll maintained	–	118	–	29	–	82	–	30	–	46	–	36	–	15	–	8
Average permanent places per school	n.a.	–	n.a.	–	507	–	1376	–	297	–	714	–	287	–	821	–
Permanent places per pupil if number of permanent places maintained as at 1978	n.a.	n.a.	n.a.	n.a.	1.61	2.36	1.23	2.60	0.88	1.13	1.30	1.91	1.1	1.31	0.96	1.29
Surplus schools if one permanent place per pupil allowed	n.a.	n.a.	n.a.	n.a.	98	149	11	35	NIL	28	33	102	10	32	NIL	9

	Liverpool Primary		Liverpool Secondary		Manchester Primary		Manchester Secondary		Newcastle Primary		Newcastle Secondary	
	1978	1985	1978	1990	1978	1986	1978	1990	1978	1986	1978	1989
Average roll per school if 1978 number of schools maintained	233	169	485	314	206	145	634	369	258	195	1367	960
Surplus schools if 1978 average school roll maintained	–	60	–	34	–	67	–	28	–	25	–	4
Average permanent places per school	n.a.	n.a.	n.a.	n.a.	244	–	662	–	307	–	1402	–
Permanent places per pupil if number of permanent places maintained as at 1978	n.a.	n.a.	n.a.	n.a.	1.19	1.69	1.04	1.79	1.19	1.58	1.03	1.46
Surplus schools if one permanent place per pupil allowed	n.a.	n.a.	n.a.	n.a.	36	93	1	30	16	38	–	4

Sources:
Tables 12.11, 12.12, 12.13 and city education departments.

Table 12.15
Implications of projected rolls for school teachers, seven local authorities, UK

	Birmingham Primary		Birmingham Secondary		Glasgow Primary		Glasgow Secondary		Leeds Primary		Leeds Secondary		Leicester Primary		Leicester Secondary	
	1978	1984	1978	1990	1978	1985	1978	1991	1978	1984	1978	1990	1978	1984	1978	1990
1978 PTRs	24.2	–	16.16	–	22.0	–	15.1	–	25.0	–	18.1	–	23.3	–	16.2	–
Teachers required to maintain 1978 PTRs	4,571	3,054	5,633	2,518	3,685	2,517	4,208	1,991	2,529	2,177	3,944	2,309	1,147	964	1,583	1,180
Annual teacher wastage rates required to maintain 1978 PTRs (%)	6.6		6.4		5.3		5.6		2.5		4.4		2.9		2.5	
Average annual teacher reduction required to maintain 1978 PTRs	253		260		167		171		59		136		31		34	

	Liverpool Primary		Liverpool Secondary		Manchester Primary		Manchester Secondary		Newcastle Primary		Newcastle Secondary	
	1978	1985	1978	1990	1978	1986	1978	1990	1978	1986	1978	1989
1978 PTRs	22.2	–	16.4	–	22.2	–	15.0	–	20.0	–	14.4	–
Teachers required to maintain 1978 PTRs	2,286	1,656	2,841	1,839	2,100	1,473	2,833	1,650	1,356	1,022	1,424	1,000
Annual teacher wastage rates required to maintain 1978 PTRs (%)	4.5		3.6		4.3		4.4		3.4		3.1	
Average annual teacher reduction required to maintain 1978 PTRs	90		84		78		99		42		39	

Source: Previous tables.

Table 12.16

Potential annual cost reduction in years of pupil troughs, seven local authorities, UK

Item	Birmingham		Glasgow		Leeds		Leicester	
	Primary	Secondary	Primary	Secondary	Primary	Secondary	Primary	Secondary
1 Employee cost per teacher p.a. (£)	6,912	6,877	4,918	6,174	8,128	6,450	6,877	6,687
2 Reduction in number of teachers by trough year	1,517	3,115	1,168	2,217	352	1,635	183	403
3 *Reduction in teacher costs p.a. by trough year (£)*	10.5 m	21.4 m	5.7 m	13.7 m	2.9 m	10.6 m	1.3 m	2.7 m
4 Premises and other employee costs per school p.a. (£)	28,627	102,062	65,158	305,482	29,979	63,467	66,770	292,945
5 Reduction in number of schools by trough year	n.a.	n.a.	n.a.	n.a.	n.a.	n.a.	n.a.	n.a.
6 *Reduction in premises costs p.a. by trough year (£)*	n.a.	n.a.	n.a.	n.a.	n.a.	n.a.	n.a.	n.a.
7 Supplies and services costs per pupil p.a. (£)	12	32	13	43	11	22	12	28
8 Reduction in number of pupils 1978 to trough	35,701	23,999	25,710	33,485	15,348	19,906	4,250	6,532
9 *Reduction in supplies and services costs p.a. by trough year (£)*	428,412	767,968	334,230	1,439,855	168,828	437,932	51,000	181,337
10 Total reduction of all costs p.a. (1978/79 values) (£)	n.a.	n.a.	n.a.	n.a.	n.a.	n.a.	n.a.	n.a.
11 Teacher cost savings as a percentage of total savings (lines 3 and 10)	n.a.	n.a.	n.a.	n.a.	n.a.	n.a.	n.a.	n.a.

Item	Liverpool		Manchester		Newcastle	
	Primary	Secondary	Primary	Secondary	Primary	Secondary
1 Employee cost per teacher p.a. (£)	6,475	6,449	6,627	6,145	6,164	6,199
2 Reduction in number of teachers by trough year	630	1,002	627	1,183	334	424
3 *Reduction in teacher costs p.a. by trough year (£)*	4.1 m	6.5 m	4.2 m	7.3 m	2.1 m	2.6 m
4 Premises and other employee costs per school p.a. (£)	29,469	74,702	27,895	106,443	29,206	195,513
5 Reduction in number of schools by trough year	n.a.	n.a.	33	11	14	2
6 *Reduction in premises costs p.a. by trough year (£)*	n.a.	n.a.	920,535	1.2 m	408,884	391,026
7 Supplies and services costs per pupil p.a. (£)	14	31	17	36	17	41
8 Reduction in number of pupils 1978 to trough	14,004	16,422	13,918	17,746	6,682	6,115
9 *Reduction in supplies and services costs p.a. by trough year (£)*	196,056	509,082	236,606	638,856	113,594	250,715
10 Total reduction of all costs p.a. (1978/79 values) (£)	n.a.	n.a.	5.4 m	9.1 m	2.6 m	3.2 m
11 Teacher cost savings as a percentage of total savings (lines 3 and 10)	n.a.	n.a.	77.8	80.2	80.8	81.3

Note: Unit costs are in 1978/79 prices.

Source: Previous tables.

undertaken using the results of the case studies and making certain simplifying assumptions. These are, first, that the 1978 PTRs are maintained throughout the period up to pupil troughs and that teacher costs fall in proportion with teacher numbers; second, that all other staff and premises costs fall in proportion to the number of schools; third, that supplies and services costs fall in proportion to the number of pupils, and fourth, that all other costs are constant. Most of these assumptions can be held to be *broadly* in accordance with real events, except for that of constant 1978 PTRs. The effect of relaxing the latter will be examined later.

If 1978 PTRs are maintained then the reduction in teacher costs will reach a maximum annual rate in the years of pupil troughs. The range of potential savings is great from £1.3 million for primary education in Leicester to £10.5 million in Birmingham and from £2.6 million per annum for secondary education in Newcastle to £21.4 million for secondary education in Birmingham (Table 12.16). Assuming premises and other employee costs are reduced *pro rata* to the reduced number of schools, and taking the numbers of schools that the cities have proposed to close (see Appendix) leads to a much smaller maximum annual saving in the trough year in comparison with savings in teacher costs. Similarly the cost reductions resulting if expenditure on supplies and services is reduced *pro rata* with pupil numbers produces even smaller savings. The overall result is that potential savings from teacher costs constitute approximately 80 per cent of total cost savings (Table 12.16). The resulting percentage reduction in gross expenditure in the trough year in each city is lower than the percentage reduction in pupils over the same period. Hence costs per pupil rise quite significantly by up to 20 per cent, although there is a wide variation between individual cities.

A clearer view of the degree to which individual authorities stabilise the standard of their education service is given by their cost reduction ratios. These ratios are the extent to which costs are actually reduced as a percentage of the reduction that would be achieved if all costs were reduced in the same proportion as pupil numbers. They are remarkably similar for the two cities for which data can be derived with a narrow range for primary and secondary education (Table 12.17). However, the assumption of constant 1978 PTRs is unrealistic. Hence the annual increased teacher costs brought about by a 10 per cent improvement in 1978 PTRs is given for illustration. This would lead both to lower cost reduction ratios and an increased disparity between the individual cities.

Decline of population has exacerbated decline of pupil numbers when Leicester and the national averages are compared with the other cities. However, Birmingham, Leeds and Newcastle themselves differ

Table 12.17
Potential annual cost reduction in years of pupil troughs, Manchester and Newcastle, UK

Item		Manchester		Newcastle	
		Primary	Secondary	Primary	Secondary
1	Total gross expenditure p.a. 1978/79	£22.9 million	£29.2 million	£13.1 million	£14.9 million
2	Reduction of gross expenditure p.a. from 1978/79	23.6%	31.2%	19.8%	21.5%
3	Reduction of pupils 1978 to trough year	29.9%	41.8%	24.6%	29.8%
4	Total cost per pupil 1978/79	£491.0	£686.0	£485.0	£729.0
5	Total cost per pupil in trough year	£535.0	£812.0	£514.0	£813.0
6	Increased cost per pupil 1978/79 to trough	9.0%	18.4%	6.0%	11.5%
7	Cost reduction ratio (from lines 1 to 3)	78.9%	74.6%	80.5%	72.1%
8	Increased teacher costs p.a. in trough year if 1978 PTRs improve by 10%	£1.1 million	£1.1 million	£0.7 million	£0.7 million
9	Revised cost reduction ratio if PTRs improve by 10%	62.9%	65.6%	58.9%	56.4%

Notes:

1 It has not proved possible to derive figures for the other cities due to their piecemeal rather than city wide approach to date.
2 Unit costs are in 1978/79 prices.

Source: Previous tables.

from Liverpool, Manchester and Glasgow in that the former group does conform with the national scenario in many respects whilst the latter group does not. These groupings exist throughout in terms of potentially surplus accommodation, surplus schools, required teacher wastage rates and associated costs. However, the sheer size of Birmingham and Leeds in terms of numbers of pupils causes the *absolute* magnitudes of surplus places and teachers and their associated costs to greatly overshadow Leicester and Newcastle.

Liverpool, Manchester and Glasgow have *both* high *absolute* and high *relative* magnitudes in all respects. Thus the increased cost per pupil is markedly greater for Manchester than Newcastle even with very similar cost reduction ratios (Table 12.17). Once it is accepted that constant PTRs cannot be maintained, Manchester can more fully achieve potential cost savings than can Newcastle for a given percentage reduction in PTRs, as shown by the revised cost reduction ratios. If these two cities are typical of their groups it implies that even if those cities with the greatest proportionate falls in pupil numbers are more successful than other cities at achieving potential cost savings they will nonetheless still suffer larger percentage increases in costs per pupil.

The relationship between future costs and form of rationalisation

The rises in per pupil costs in line 6 of Table 12.17 are 'unavoidable' since they are incurred even if 'surplus' resources are dispensed with in line with the above assumptions. If the differing options for rationalisation use the same resources as under the previous systems and impose no constraint upon the rest of the system then these increased costs per pupil will still be incurred. However, the crucial question is whether the form of rationalisation chosen affects an authority's ability to dispense with the surplus teachers, accommodation and other inputs as pupil numbers fall. This is a particularly relevant question for the rationalisation of sixth-form provision by the cities. A comparison of the relative costs of the differing systems proposed for Newcastle and being implemented in Manchester is possible under rather restrictive assumptions. There are four major problems in deriving cost comparisons. First, many of the costs will be incurred in the future and will in fact depend upon whether the forecast falls in pupil numbers are actually realised. Second, local authorities do not separate the costs of compulsory and post-16 secondary education in their annual accounts. However, for present purposes the proportionate breakdown adopted by the methodology used to derive Grant Related Expenditures (GRE) can be used. Third, the net cost of sixth-form rationalisation depends upon not only the actual costs incurred in providing the rationalised sixth-form system but also any costs (or savings) imposed upon the rest of the secondary sector. Fourth, actual costs incurred may not only be dependent upon maintaining given standards. Local authorities may take the opportunity to improve standards, e.g. by broadening the curriculum, introducing new types of examinations or encouraging increased staying-on rates. It is very difficult to separate out such cost influences.

Notwithstanding these problems it is possible to derive cost data which illustrate the broad magnitudes of relative costs for Manchester and Newcastle. Assume that Newcastle introduces its proposed cluster model. Manchester's new system is a combination of the sixth-form college model in cooperation with colleges of further education and with three 11—18 schools added on. The comparison will therefore be restricted to a study of the cooperative versus sixth-form college options.

Adopting the GRE methodology, 13.8 per cent of secondary education expenditures in Manchester and 15.4 per cent in Newcastle are attributable to sixth-form provision. If these percentages are applied to the 1978/9 costs then rough estimates for sixth-form expenditures in that year are £4 million for Manchester and £2.3 million for Newcastle. By way of comparison, the *maximum* potential *annual* cost reductions available to Manchester from the whole secondary sector are £9.1 million (Table 12.17: 31.2 per cent of £29.2 million) whilst for Newcastle the figure is £3.2 million. On average, therefore, potential cost savings clearly exceed the total cost of sixth-form provision each year. It should prove easier to dispose of surplus resources under the college option because it should be possible to close relatively more surplus accommodation as pupil numbers fall. It can be assumed that there will be less resistance to school closures where schools do not have sixth forms, as under the 11—16 schools plus colleges option in Manchester. Pupil catchment areas can be more easily amended when separated for compulsory and post-16 education. This is important since the fall in sixth-form numbers follows with a lag the fall in total secondary numbers. Hence separate provision of 11—16 and post-16 education will facilitate rationalisation of both accommodation and teachers.

As an example assume that Newcastle's cooperative option requires a fall in PTRs of 10 per cent over *all* the secondary sector. This would impose additional costs of £0.7 million in the year of lowest pupil numbers (Table 12.17) with higher costs in earlier years (which have larger pupil totals). If Manchester can take advantage of the college system's ability to use teachers more efficiently and pursues a policy of rationalising 11—16 school catchment areas to maintain constant PTRs then it will achieve a 'hidden saving' of £1.1 million in the year of lowest pupil numbers (Table 12.17) and larger annual savings before that. This is a saving since the college option avoids the 10 per cent reduction in PTRs. These figures are very large percentages of the costs of sixth-form provision, 27.5 per cent for Manchester and 30.4 per cent for Newcastle. Hence, there is clearly a significant relationship between the form of rationalisation and the burden of future costs. The relationship between demographic decline and change in costs both per pupil and per head of population is as indeterminate on an *ex ante* basis for the future as it was for the past. In both cases a knowledge of the educational policies adopted is required.

Conclusions

In general terms it can be said that there is no precise mathematical formula which states that if population declines by X per cent then educational expenditures per head of population will increase by Y per cent. This is simply because population decline may take place in a variety of ways affecting the constituent age groups differently. In attempting to assess what happens to costs per head of total population, therefore, changes in the demographic mix must be allowed for and this necessitates a consideration not only of changes in birth and death rates but also of age-specific migration rates.

The second component affecting expenditure per head of population is cost per pupil. Our historical analysis of primary education expenditures did not provide any evidence as to whether pupil decline actually had *caused* costs per pupil to rise. All we were able to show was that where pupils had declined persistently, local authorities employed more teachers per pupil so as to catch up with national pupil—teacher ratios. Thus rather than having had to face the costs of adjusting their inputs downwards they took advantage of the situation to improve their service. After reorganisation nearly all the authorities, having attained national standards of provision, tended to spend, per pupil, very much in line with the national level of expenditure. With secondary education none of the authorities has actually had to face a persistent long-run decline in pupil numbers. Thus taking primary and secondary education as a whole we cannot use the past to help us predict whether costs per pupil and costs per head of population in the future will rise under the expected conditions of a continuing fall in primary pupil numbers and the onset of a general and persistent decline in secondary numbers.

However, certain facts are clear. All the case study authorities are likely to experience a decline in secondary pupil numbers greater than that of the nation but the loss in *Leeds, Liverpool, Manchester and Glasgow* will be markedly above average. None of these authorities has a large 'cushion' of places in temporary accommodation and only Liverpool has a below national average percentage of older schools which might conceivably be closed with limited financial and educational cost. All the rest have an above average proportion of schools built since the Second World War. Three of the same authorities, *Liverpool, Manchester and Glasgow* are also likely to experience markedly above average reductions in primary pupil numbers. None of them has a buffer of temporary accommodation, though once again Liverpool may be able to take advantage of the situation by closing some of its relatively large stock of older primary schools.

In approaching possible economies, by far the most obvious cost item is teachers' salaries. Our calculations suggest this item is likely to represent 80 per cent of all potential savings. But the obstacles in the way of achieving a reduction of the teacher input *pro rata* with the decline in pupils, are formidable. The scale of pupil declines in these authorities is such that a combination of early retirement and natural wastage are most unlikely to be sufficient to permit a *pro rata* adjustment of the teaching input and since all the case study authorities have so far refused to countenance compulsory redundancies, the outcome is likely to be an increase in unit costs. Furthermore, we cannot say whether the authorities facing the severest drops in pupil numbers will face special costs not faced by authorities with national average reductions. Whilst there may be a threshold of decline beyond which it becomes more difficult to negotiate with teachers' unions over early retirement or even redundancies it seems inescapable that cities such as Liverpool, Manchester and Glasgow will face a situation of rising costs per pupil for both primary and secondary education and Leeds will experience the same for secondary education. We cannot predict for these cities precisely how much more than the national average unit costs will rise. Our illustrative examples in Manchester and Newcastle (see Appendix) have shown that costs are highly sensitive to the precise forms of reorganisation undertaken by each authority. What we can assert with confidence however is that unit costs will rise due to a political desire to retain surplus buildings in conditions of pupil number uncertainty, difficulties in shedding labour rapidly and community hostility to the loss of local schools. In this sense then the question which central government has to answer is whether each authority has taken adequate steps to minimise its costs of delivery consistent with a maintenance of educational standards and thereafter to decide what proportion of the rise in unit costs should be included in the rate support grant calculations.

Appendix: Manchester and Newcastle

Manchester

Secondary education in Manchester is currently characterised by a low staying-on rate into sixth form. (Over half of 'A' level groups in Manchester's secondary schools consists of five or fewer students. This will become worse as pupil numbers fall, *ceteris paribus*.) In order to maintain educationally viable sixth forms in an 11–18 system, Manchester would have to ensure intakes in excess of 12 forms of entry, necessitating closure of at least 12 schools in the state and Church of England sectors by 1988. On the other hand a viable alternative would be a uniform 11–16 system with six to eight forms of entry and with a system of three separate sixth-form colleges. This would necessitate closure of at least nine schools in the state and Church of England sectors by 1988 and at least five schools in the Roman Catholic sector. It would, however, facilitate the retention of a larger number of individual schools than under an 11–18 system and hence increase the future flexibility of school accommodation.

However, plans to introduce separate sixth-form colleges were rejected by the Secretary of State. He identified three schools as being of 'proven worth' which should not be reorganised on the lines proposed by the City Council. A modified proposal was subsequently approved for implementation in December 1982, which excluded the three schools previously identified, but which was in most other respects the same as that which was originally intended. Hence, a tertiary system of sixth-form colleges and further education colleges is now being implemented with full implementation by September 1985. Admission to the new sixth-form colleges does not depend on formal academic qualifications, high school attended or residence but will be open to pupils who wish to pursue approved courses of study provided at the colleges. Each sixth-form college will be linked to two further education colleges in consortia so as to widen the opportunities available to students.

The need to close 14 secondary schools in Manchester, as calculated by the local authority, constitutes only half the number of schools it would be necessary to close in order to maintain the average school roll at its 1978 level. The situation will most likely be similar for primary education in Manchester since the ongoing review so far recommends closure of an average of one primary school in each of the 33 primary sub-divisions of the city, this again constituting only half the number required in order to maintain the average school roll at its 1978 level.

Newcastle

Newcastle's reorganisation of its stock of school buildings is complicated by the non-uniform system of education comprising the three-tier system of first, middle and high schools (inherited from Northumberland) together with the two-tier system of primary and secondary schools (inherited from the former county borough). Mergers have been proposed where the combined enrolment for linked infant–junior departments or for 'twin' first schools are projected to fall to 300 pupils or thereabouts, being followed by closure of one of the buildings in each pair by 1984/5. On this basis 12 such schools would be closed. A similar approach for merger of middle schools (again projecting up to 1984/5) led to the proposed closure of two schools' buildings upon their merger with other schools. These closures would in total account for less than the surplus *already* existing in 1978 and little more than half the number of schools needing to be closed so as to maintain the average school roll at its 1978 level.

Reorganisation of secondary education in Newcastle has been considered under various options including 'no change', schools with and without sixth forms and a sixth-form college. The decline in the number of sixth-form pupils forecast by the authority will make inadequate the range of curricula at existing individual schools. The Education Department has concluded that an 11—18 system could be maintained in the *city* (i.e. the former county borough area) by closure of four out of the nine LEA comprehensive schools by 1989 but that uncertainty surrounding the future upturn is such that this would be dangerous as it would limit flexibility to meet varying circumstances. It is therefore considered sensible only to close two schools under this option. Decline in pupil numbers in the former county high schools will cause 1,600 of the 4,500 places to be nominally surplus by 1989. However, since there are only three high schools it is likely that no closure will take place, under-occupancy being necessitated by geographical considerations. A similar situation for the three voluntary comprehensive schools in the city is likely. This would again result in only half the number of closures required in order to maintain the average school roll at its 1978 level (Table 12.13).

The Education Committee decided in December 1980 *not* to establish a sixth-form college option. Four comprehensive schools are to be merged into two new schools in September 1983. Furthermore, the Committee agreed in principle in March 1983 to a 'cluster' model as a possible means of achieving a comprehensive tertiary approach to the needs of the 16—19 age group.

Notes

1 This chapter is drawn from a bigger study for the Department of the Environment. The authors of the larger study were the authors of this chapter and Diane Dawson, University of Cambridge; Professor Peter Jackson, Justin Meadows and Andy Taylor, University of Leicester; and Frank Mather, University of Glasgow.
2 'The government's primary objective is to reduce the burden of public expenditure which in recent years has inhibited economic

growth. No additional resources will be available in the foreseeable future to support expansionist policies in education.' Scottish Education Department, *16–18s in Scotland: The First Two Years in Post Compulsory Education*, HMSO, 1979.

3 This assumption holds only if average school rolls are maintained. Staffing standards are regulated in Scotland with the result that as school rolls fall both average class sizes and PTRs fall. Hence this assumption would not hold in Scotland and would be unlikely to hold in England (even though there are no staffing standards) if school rolls fell.

13 Urban growth and decline as a force in regional development: issues and a research agenda*

LELAND S. BURNS

About four out of 10 of the world population are counted as urban residents; the industrialised nations have a much higher ratio of 7 out of 10. Given the growth rates of a few years ago, forecasters would have predicted an ever-growing urban sphere limited only by the reservoir of rural population that cities could absorb. The powerful and consistent trends that characterised more than a century of history suggested that urbanisation was a well established process characterised by monotonic growth. In short, urbanisation was a trend phenomenon, not cyclical (Davis, 1972; Hoyt, 1962).

The decline of central city populations starting as early as the 1950s in some of the developed nations' largest metropoles served as a bellwether of things to come. However, the events were interpreted as shifts to the then-burgeoning suburbs and outlying new towns. When a decade or so later suburban population began to fall, there was a stronger hint that entire metropolitan regions *could* decline. The evidence of the 1970s showed accelerated growth of the rural sector and pointed at the possibility of a genuine turnaround.

Systematic patterns emerged both among and within the developed nations. Metropolitan population loss tended to appear earliest in those nations first visited by the Industrial Revolution. Within nations,

*I am indebted to John Friedmann, Leo Grebler, Robert G. Healy, Frank G. Mittelbach, and Donald C. Shoup for their comments on a draft of this chapter.

population loss began in the oldest, the most industrialised regions and the largest metropolitan units. At first decline was only relative — i.e. growth rates of the units slowed in comparison to the nation — then decline became absolute.

The evidence was greeted in several ways. First, the 'sharp-break' school maintained that the metropolitan sphere had shrunk and inferred that it would continue to do so (Beale, 1977; Leven, 1978; Vining and Strauss, 1977; Vining and Kontuly, 1978). Just as growth had characterised the past, decline would characterise the future. There was no hint of a subsequent turnaround. A second school of thought, refusing to take the data at face value, asserted that the clean break was, at least in large part, a statistical illusion with most of the apparent decline explained merely by further suburbanisation into areas officially designated as rural (Gordon, 1979). A third view held that just as decline could follow growth, growth could follow decline. In short, what appeared as trends were really segments of a long cycle related to development stages (van den Berg et al., 1982; Hall and Hay, 1980).

Running through these arguments is the notion, however implicit, that the dynamics of change are fully captured by changing population size as its single indicator. There are of course many other dimensions of territorial growth and decline that reach deeply into the economic, social and political realms as well. No less, there are other aspects of demography, as listed in the next section, that serve as cause and consequence.

With the evidence of changing urban and rural population balance as backdrop, this chapter considers the problems and forces linked to spatial growth and decline. The emphasis is on the latter dynamic if only because of its comparative currency and the under-emphasis accorded it in the literature. Many problem areas could be identified but, given the limited scope of this chapter, only a few are chosen as illustrative of a broader range of phenomena amenable to analysis, policy, and research.

Demographic shifts

Changing demographics, coupled with the social revolution starting in the 1960s, have left their mark on national settlement patterns, and on the dynamics of urban and regional growth. Four of particular importance concern age, women, families, and internationalisation.

The ageing of the population

The age-cohort comprising the postwar baby boom is moving towards middle age. The decline of the fertility rate to below replacement level in most industrialised nations foreshadows an era of zero population growth. Mortality rates have dropped and people are living longer. Retired people are increasing in number and will comprise growing shares of future populations. Proportions of persons in the work-force entry age will correspondingly decline.

The changing size and composition of households

As a legacy of the social revolution, the conjugal family, though still the dominant family type in most nations, is declining in importance. There has been a parallel growth in atypical living arrangements such as single-person (and never-married) households, and families headed by single persons whether female or male. Reinforcing these trends is the rapid surge in divorce, a rate that has doubled in the US and West Germany in 20 years. The net effect of these changes has been to reduce average household size.

The changing role of women

This has been marked by their growing economic independence, changed family roles, and increasing work force participation, especially during their child-bearing age. Running in tandem is the emergence of the multiple earner household where both partners are employed in paid work (Gerson, 1983).

The internationalisation of the metropolis

The influx of guest workers into Northern Europe and of foreign immigrants into North America have introduced the third world into the cities of the first world and, in many cases, imported to the core the problems of the periphery. Many cities, as the spatial articulation of a global economy, have moved into world class status interconnected by decision making, finance, and production, with a new set of dependencies. The powerful decisions of transnational capital, partially influenced by the world economy and partly autonomous, can powerfully shape and restructure the future of many metropolitan economies, and threaten to widen core—periphery differences (Portes and Walton, 1981; Friedmann and Wolff, 1982).

Fuchs (1983) has ingeniously woven together demographic and other trends and teased out their economic and social implications but, in his analysis, stopped short of making the spatial translation. Others have dealt with some of the factors. For example, Haddon (1981) shows that, by altering commuting patterns and the residential site choice, the emergence of dual-earner households will reshape urban form. Hayden (1984) shows how housing consumption must shift to accommodate women's large-scale advance on the workplace. Rosen (1980) demonstrates how changes in the population's age composition will affect the structure of future housing demand. And so on. But the full implications of these shifts — some of them of dramatic magnitude — on urban/regional dynamics remains as a challenge for research. If the challenge is taken up, the research could be most productively undertaken in an internationally comparative framework.

Migration

With a drop in fertility to below replacement level, future population growth of the industrialised nations' regions and metropolitan areas will be fed by shifts of both inter-regional and international scope. Thus, understanding and predicting the migration of labour has taken on new importance.

The neo-classical migration model that so accurately accounted for population and labour flows (Shaw, 1975) lost much of its explanatory power, coincidentally, at about the same time as rural growth rates began to exceed metropolitan rates. The new evidence showed that, indeed, labour continues to move in response to perceived opportunities, but the nature of those opportunities has shifted from near-exclusive reliance on better jobs and higher wages (e.g. Lowry, 1966; Klaassen and Drewe, 1973) to the more elusive determinants of life quality such as climate and other amenities (Burns and Van Ness, 1981; Liu, 1975; Cebula and Vedder, 1973; Graves, 1979). In the wake of the information explosion, new data are continually becoming available to facilitate measuring such intangibles and warrant testing in new, more descriptive models. To identify the underlying dynamics of structural change, the analyses should be carried out in terms of gross flows as well as net migration streams.

Central cities

There are signs of a turnaround in the secular decline of central cities. Old industrial and commercial buildings, many of historical worth, are being recycled. Parks and other public facilities have been developed on land cleared by urban renewal. New hotels and convention centres have sprouted up. New rapid transit systems have helped revive some central districts.

But these factors apparently spurring a renewal in Europe's, North America's, and Japan's central business districts are minor compared to the construction, on a vast scale, of high-rise office buildings — most house financial institutions. The office building boom that characterises the major cities of the industrialised world, whether Chicago, Frankfurt or Tokyo, and many in the third world as well, has not only breathed a new and different life into sagging centres, but one that may be risky. By replacing housing and related land-using activities that are utilised more or less around-the-clock, office buildings have reduced the activity life of central cities to one limited to working hours.

The longer-run consequences of this boom pose an even greater threat to sustained CBD growth. Rapid advances in office technology could have two devastating future effects. One involves *re*placement of labour; the other involves its spatial *dis*placement. First, it seems inevitable that microcomputers and large-scale data processing equipment threaten to replace many office workers, particularly those who perform routine chores. Second, given the ubiquity of work done by computers, and the very real possibility that telecommunications will free workers from their traditional worksites, clerical jobs could be decentralised to outlying business parks, and even to residences where employees are connected by cable to their workplaces. If the prediction is borne out, then the result is also ironic: the high-rise office building could become the awkward steel and concrete monument that recalls the renaissance that it stimulated. Moreover, the monuments could remain as hollow reminders of the past, for office structures rank among the most specialised of all architectural designs, with highly limited possibilities for alternative use.

If the staged cyclical model of urban growth works (van den Berg et al., 1982), and if central cities experience sustained growth, then there is the promise of renewed metropolitan expansion as the system starts to move into a new development cycle. The verification of the long cycle theory alone merits continued study of central city growth. There are more reasons as well. Research could continue to study the strength of agglomeration economies as centripetal forces in physically shaping urban systems. Other research might concern itself with the long-term viability of centrally sited investments in sustaining robust labour markets, particularly in the light of the threats of technological advance.

Suburbs and new towns

Three decades ago, suburbia and new towns defined the urban frontier. When they were built in the aftermath of the Second World War, both provided an alternative to, and in many respects refuge from, deteriorating conditions in central cities. In the years since then, peripheral suburbs and outlying new towns have aged, their residents have outgrown them, and today, many are beginning to share the characteristics of the cores they were designed to replace.

At least three distinct dimensions — physical, functional, and economic — can be identified as separate manifestations of decline. In most cases, each housing tract, whether in a suburban or new town neighbourhood, was built and occupied simultaneously. The possibilities of physical decline on such a large scale prompted futurists in the 1950s and 1960s to predict that, by the turn of the century, time would have taken its toll and the once fresh neighbourhoods would have been transformed into massive slums.

The second dimension, functional obsolescence, or the increasing mismatch between housing and the characteristics and activities of its occupants, also threatens the future. With the children's departure, the parents are left behind with a dwelling originally built to serve the stereotype two-parent and two-child family and public spaces designed to accommodate the social and recreational needs of a 'typical' family go unused. Yet inertia keeps families in houses built for earlier stages in their life cycle even when their homes are too big and poorly equipped. They prefer to age in place.

Both physical and functional decline are, to a large extent, endogenous to communities. If optimistic about the future of their neighbourhoods and themselves, residents confront depreciation through staged maintenance and continued upgrading of their housing and communities. Expectations are the key. The response to functional obsolescence is renovation to restore the match between the inventory of occupied units and the character of their occupants, and the retooling of social enterprises to keep them in step with current tastes and preferences.

A third type of decline, economic obsolescence, is exogenous, at least from the community's vantage point. The future of even a well maintained suburban community or new town can be jeopardised by a plant closing, by persistent and severe air pollution, or increased aeroplane flight paths.

Research activity on new towns and suburbs has tended to run in tandem with policy interest in these forms of urban development. It peaked in the 1960s and early 1970s when they were much in the public eye, and waned thereafter. The time is opportune to return to their study particularly since enough years have elapsed to provide sufficient evidence for longitudinal investigation. The potentials for decline, just outlined, give the subject added urgency.

Fiscal impacts

Population change is the yardstick commonly used for measuring metropolitan growth and decline, but social, fiscal, and economic consequences tend often to run in parallel with demographic changes. Sustained growth must be supported by an ever-expanding network of public infrastructure: schools, health and medical facilities, roads, etc. Expansion usually requires capital transfers and a corresponding drain on the local economy to cover debt-service costs. Oddly, the demand for credit to finance capital improvements is asymmetrical with respect to growth and decline — for many services, high under both conditions (Muller, 1976, 1981).

During out-migration, an area's tax base shrinks in both aggregate and per capita terms. Population losses reduce the total base and if the migratory outflows are biased towards the young, skilled, and well paid, then per capita revenues fall as well (Hoover and Vernon, 1959). The departure of higher income groups leaves in its wake a diminished capacity to sustain public services for those left behind. Moreover, lower-income populations frequently require more costly services.

The complexities of the revenue—cost squeeze are compounded by three other factors. There is an increasing need in declining communities to replace outdated public infrastructures. Because of the scarcity of public revenues, their public facilities frequently are run down, as casualties of deferred maintenance, yet there remains the necessity for rebuilding and modernising them if the areas are to attract new enterprises and restructure their economies. Second, local financing for rebuilding infrastructures is scarce for, in the older cities, both per capita taxes and current operating expenses per capita are higher (Stamm and Howell, 1980). Third, public services cannot be scaled down to match a population of reduced size since so many services are provided in indivisible units (Eversley, 1973).

While the cost effects probably apply across the board, the revenue consequences of decline are more serious in countries like the US and the UK where local economies are largely dependent on locally generated revenues. Even in nations whose central governments supply local government with revenues through massive transfers, however, metropolitan finance is seriously jeopardised by the public expenditures limitation movement ('Proposition 13' and 'Thatcherism') that has spread throughout the industrialised world. The effects are dual.

Capital investment projects

Within the field of local public finance, capital budgeting ranks as one of the most understudied areas. Capital budgets are particularly vulnerable in times of duress. It was perhaps no coincidence that New York City's dire financial straits surfaced in the controversy surrounding the management of its capital budget (US Congress, 1975).

Constructing, maintaining, and preserving the public realty raise serious questions, made more difficult by differential pressures that growth and decline place on the public purse. Growth brings with it demands for capital expansion during periods when a wide variety of other activities also compete for funding. Economic stress that accompanies decline encourages deferring maintenance and even sacrificing irreplaceable assets. Three aspects of capital budgeting are central to the issue: environmental projects, historic preservation, and maintenance of public infrastructures.

Maintaining the infrastructure

The state of a region's physical infrastructure serves as a reasonable proxy for its growth stage. The capital stock is fully utilised during expansion and there are strong pressures for additions to the stock. Decline brings with it overcapacity and pressures for retiring functionally obsolete assets. During periods of fiscal stress, the infrastructure runs down as maintenance is postponed.

In many countries there is serious concern over the rapid deterioration of urban infrastructures. Overexpansion of facilities during the heyday of metropolitan growth is partly to blame for current deficiencies. Roads, schools and parks may have been optimally sited when they were built but today are in the wrong places. Or they may have been built in response to over-optimistic forecasts of need and ability to pay for their upkeep, or in response to needs evidenced by age structures that change cyclically. Often, because of the incentive provided by national subsidies, cities commit capital for constructing expensive projects, such as rapid transit, while failing to budget adequately for the high costs of maintenance that can represent the lion's share of total outlays. Or the demand for facilities may shift leaving redundancies in its wake. At present unused roads recall the days when trucks freighted the output of heavy industry, long since closed down or relocated. It is estimated that one US school building in five is currently not needed (Hulten and Peterson, 1984). And the UK is worrying about what to do with empty churches, as tastes have apparently changed from things ecclesiastical.

Expenditures for upkeep are particularly vulnerable to the vicissitudes of public revenues since maintenance can be deferred for many years before the adverse consequences become noticeable. Indeed, research that traces the decline in public maintenance expenditures during the past decade locates the most severely neglected infrastructures, not surprisingly, in fiscally troubled cities and regions (Peterson, Miller, Godwin and Shapiro, 1984). Yet the need to maintain and replace public assets is greatest in these areas to set the stage for their revival. Moreover, maintenance cannot be indefinitely postponed. Most assets, whether bridges, highways, water and sewer systems, or mass transit vehicles, have normal maintenance cycles for maximum cost-effectiveness. Interrupted maintenance generates short-term savings, but requires higher expenditures over the long period when replacement is required.

Preserving historical monuments

The difference in time preferences between politicians and the rest of us is well known. Economists tend towards the long view, measuring the social attractiveness of public investments with the aid of social discount rates. Thus public investments that pay off only in future years may rank as attractively as those paying off quickly. Politicians who make the decisions, however, prefer investments generating quick returns that can be pointed to as accomplishments made during their comparatively brief terms in office. For example, rent control, though leading often to large private and social costs through disinvestment over the long haul, has popular appeal because it generates substantial benefits in the short run. Capital costs of underground rapid transit, another example, are a fairly small part of the total costs of building and operating such systems. For this reason, there is usually much truth in the politician's standard claim that they have inherited their predecessor's problems (read: deficits).

The time preference disjunction is a particularly dangerous one in cities facing decline and the urgency of re-tooling the urban fabric to more 'profitable' uses. This often means large-scale bulldozing and jeopardises the architectural monuments of past ages. Many of Europe's greatest monuments survived periods of economic distress simply because town councils, too impoverished to modernise them, left them alone. They were saved by benign neglect. In an age of sophisticated investment strategies and urgent needs to stabilise faltering economies, the apparent indifference that was the salvation of Renaissance town halls, Baroque city gates, even Gothic cathedrals,

261

can no longer be counted on to save priceless historical treasures for future generations. The fault lies in the technical nature of the discounting process and the difficulties of bringing to the present the returns (if they can be estimated), at anything but a miniscule discount rate, that accrue many decades or generations in the future.

Protecting the environment

Once seen as the privilege of wealthy countries, the quest for maintaining and upgrading environmental quality has spread through the industrialised nations and into the Third World. Partly this is due to greater appreciation of the economic consequences of environmental quality (such as health); partly it is due to widespread recognition of the importance of quality of life factors in personal consumption. The environmental movement has had many, and important, impacts at urban and regional level and has contributed to the reshaping of settlement patterns. Business and industry have been driven from the city not only because of the higher relative private costs of doing business there but also due to social costs such as congestion, noise and air pollution. Labour also appears to be moving strongly towards areas, such as rural places, offering environmental amenities.

The influence of explicit environmental policy is, however, less clear. Environmental regulation, despite efforts to make it locationally neutral, may be favouring already developed areas by making it relatively more difficult to build on 'greenfield' sites (Duerksen, 1983).

Commitments to maintaining environmental quality, as with most economic activities, may be cyclical: powerful in times of expansion, weak during contraction. The environmental movement has made great strides in its relatively brief history but times of slowed or negative economic growth could threaten past accomplishments. Stressed budgets tend to be reallocated in favour of investment producing real (monetary) gains and short-term benefits. As with architectural treasures, many, if not most, returns to environmental projects are neither of these. Benefits are elusive and often measured in terms incompatible with costs; for example, rivers dammed to produce cheap hydroelectric power may sacrifice recreational areas. Moreover, short-term returns from a variety of environmental investments, such as soil erosion programmes, are low relative to the total stream of benefits generated. Some types of environmental projects are characterised by high intergenerational transfers, with irreversible effects if they are not made; projects that protect endangered species are of that sort. The nature of familiar measurement techniques, e.g. cost—benefit analysis, fail to work well as devices for ranking investments of this type. The fragility of benefits from preservation, the difficulty of accurate measurement, and the fact that they are scattered over generations rather than years offers a challenge for policy analysis to discover new tools of assessment.

Summary: a research agenda

The forces at work shaping and reshaping settlement patterns in the industrialised nations offer many challenges for research. The issues set out in this chapter are intended to suggest but a few.

The consequences of the complex set of demographic, economic, social and technological changes characterising recent decades deserve to be integrated and interpreted for their bearing on changing urban and regional dynamics. The major forces at work concern the ageing of the population, changing household composition and size, the altered social and economic roles of women, the internationalisation of the metropolis, and the emergence of a post-industrial society characterised by rapid technological advance and occupational shifts favouring information-intensive services. The neo-classical model of labour migration has lost much of its explanatory power. New factors, particularly those describing amenities, need to be identified and assessed to better explain the locational preferences of both labour and firms. The nature of agglomeration economies that give vitality to central cities has weakened with declining transport and communication costs, but the technological revolution further threatens the centre's new viability. The pivotal role played by suburbia in metropolitan change deserves to be re-examined with emphasis on the several dimensions of potential obsolescence. Research addressed to the spatial impacts of technological change could reveal much about the futures of central cities and suburbs and the balance of activities between them. The fiscal consequences associated with decline deserve investigation given the 'snowballing' effects of population loss and tax base erosion. Decline can also jeopardise fragile capital projects that preserve environmental features, conserve historical treasures, and maintain physical infrastructures.

There is a sizeable gap, as noted, in both our knowledge of capital budgeting at the urban and regional levels, and its use as a device for planning orderly development. As a partial remedy, I propose the consideration of an 'urban capital agenda' as an alternative to the often uncoordinated, poorly specified, short-run capital development programmes that now serve as the basis for many areas' efforts to plan for the renewal and expansion of their public real estate. The 'agenda' would require drawing up a list of projects for implementation at non-specified dates during a long planning period. When structural employment rises to a specified level, high-priority projects with factor inputs matching unemployed factors would be activated. US experience has shown that public work projects, chiefly because of their long delays in implementation, fare badly as economic stabilisation instruments (Maisel, 1949; Burns and Grebler, 1985). Modern technology and improved public and private management practices, however, could contribute much towards shortening lead-times and accelerating the pace of construction. Research could make a major contribution to the formulation of the urban capital agenda by assisting public administrators in setting goals, ordering priorities, specifying the composition of required factor inputs, and monitoring local economies.

Finally, returning full circle to the beginning, there is considerable merit in research that continues to assess changing settlement patterns, and their causes and consequences. While there is no shortage of good work on metropolitan growth, and its causes and consequences, equivalent work on decline consists only of first approximations. Understanding decline is far more complicated than simply multiplying the equations of growth models through by minus one, assuming that a sort of Palladian symmetry governs dynamics regardless of direction.

If the cyclical theory comes to dominate the linear stage theory as an explanation of metropolitan development, forecasting the future becomes a far more intriguing intellectual and practical exercise. The questions then are: what size units in the urban system can be expected to decline (or grow) next; are there limits to decline (as to growth); can turning points, amplitudes, and periodicity be predicted accurately? It is worth returning once again to studies of the optimal size of cities but in a dynamic framework that measures consequences, as the dependent variable, against positive and negative population change, as a determinant.

References

Beale, C.L. (1977), 'The Recent shift of United States Population to Nonmetropolitan Areas, 1970—75', *International Regional Science Review*, vol. 2, no. 2, pp. 112—22.

van den Berg, L., R. Drewett, L.H. Klaassen, A. Rossi and C.H.T. Vijverberg (1982), *Urban Europe: A Study of Growth and Decline*, Pergamon, Oxford.

Burns, L.S. and L. Grebler (1985), 'Is Public Construction Countercyclical?', *Land Economics*, vol. 60, no. 4, pp. 367—77.

Burns, L.S. and K. Van Ness (1981), 'The Decline of the Metropolitan Economy', *Urban Studies*, vol. 18, pp. 169–80.

Cameron, G.C. (ed.) (1980), *The Future of the British Conurbations: Policies and Prescriptions for Change*, Longman, London.

Cebula, R.J. and R.K. Vedder (1973), 'A Note on Migration, Economic Opportunity and the Quality of Life', *Journal of Regional Science*, vol. 13, pp. 205–11.

Davies, K. (1972), *World Urbanization 1950–1970*, vol. II, *Analysis of Trends, Relationships and Developments*, Population Monograph Series no. 9, University of California, Berkeley, Ca.

Duerksen, C.J. (1983), *Environmental Regulation of Industrial Plant Siting: How to Make it Work Better*, The Conservation Foundation, Washington, D.C.

Eversley, D.E.C. (1973), 'Rising Costs and Static Incomes: Some Economic Consequences of Regional Planning in London', *Cities, Regions, and Public Policy* (G.C. Cameron and L. Wingo, eds), Oliver & Boyd, Edinburgh, pp. 249–70.

Friedmann, J. and G. Wolff (1982), 'World City Formation: An Agenda for Research and Action', *International Journal of Urban and Regional Research*, vol. 6, no. 3, pp. 309–44.

Fuchs, V.I. (1983), *How We Live*, Harvard University Press, Cambridge, Mass.

Gerson, K. (1983), 'Changing Family Structure and the Position of Women: A Review of the Trends', *Journal of the American Planning Association*, vol. 49, no. 2 (Spring), pp. 138–48.

Gordon, P. (1979), 'Deconcentration Without a "Clean Break"', *Environment and Planning A*, vol. 11, pp. 281–90.

Graves, P.E. (1979), 'A Life-Cycle Empirical Analysis of Migration and Climate, by Race', *Journal of Urban Economics*, vol. VI, pp. 135–47.

Haddon, J. (1981), 'Why Women Work Closer to Home', *Urban Studies*, vol. 18, pp. 181–94.

Hall, P. and D. Hay (1980), *Growth Centers in the European Urban System*, University of California Press, Berkeley, Ca.

Hayden, D. (1984), *Redesigning the American Dream: The Future of Housing, Work, and Family Life*, W.W. Norton, New York.

Hoover, E.M. and R. Vernon (1959), *Anatomy of a Metropolis*, Harvard University Press, Cambridge, Mass.

Hoyt, H. (1962), *World Urbanization*, Technical Bulletin 43, Urban Land Institute, Washington, D.C.

Hulten, Charles R. and G.E. Peterson (1984), 'The Public Capital Stock: Needs, Trends, and Performance', *American Economic Review*, vol. 74, no. 2 (May), pp. 166–73.

Klaassen, L.H. and P. Drewe (1973), *Migration Policy in Europe*, Saxon, Farnborough.

Leven, C.L. (ed.) (1978), *The Mature Metropolis*, D.C. Heath, Lexington, Mass.

Liu, B.-C. (1975), 'Differential Net Migration Rates and the Quality of Life', *Review of Economics and Statistics*, vol. 52, pp. 329–37.

Lowry, I.S. (1966), *Migration and Metropolitan Growth: Two Analytical Models*, University of California Press, Los Angeles, Ca.

Maisel, S.J. (1949), 'Timing and Flexibility of a Public Works Program', *Review of Economics and Statistics*, vol. XXXI (August), pp. 147–52.

Muller, T. (1976), *Growing and Declining Urban Areas: A Fiscal Comparison*, The Urban Institute, Washington, D.C.

Muller, T. (1981), *Changing Expenditures and Service Demand Patterns of Stressed Cities*, The Urban Institute, Washington, D.C.

Peterson, G.E., M.J. Miller, S. Godwin and C. Shapiro (1984), *Benchmarks of Urban Capital Conditions*, The Urban Institute, Washington, D.C.

Portes, A. and J. Walton (1981), *Labor, Class, and the International System*, Academic Press, New York, N.Y.

Rosen, K.T. (1980), 'The Demand for Housing in the 1980s', Working Paper 80-14, University of California, Berkeley, Ca (mimeographed).

Shaw, R.P. (1975), *Migration Theory and Fact: A Review and Bibliography of Current Literature*, Regional Science Research Institute, Philadelphia, Pa.

Stamm, C.F. and J.M. Howell (1980), 'Urban Fiscal Problems; A Comparative Analysis of 66 U.S. Cities', *Taxing & Spending*, vol. III, no. 4, pp. 41–58.

US Congress, Congressional Budget Office (1975), *New York City's Fiscal Problem: Its Origins, Potential Repercussions, and Some Alternative Policy Responses*, Background Paper no. 1, US Government Printing Office, Washington, D.C.

Vining, D.R. and A. Strauss (1977), 'A Demonstration that the Current Deconcentration of Population in the United States is a Clean Break with the Past', *Environment and Planning A*, vol. 9, pp. 751–8.

Vining, D.R. and T. Kantuly (1978), 'Population Dispersal from Major Metropolitan Regions: An International Comparison', *International Regional Science Review*, vol. 3, no. 1 (Fall), pp. 49–74.

Index

accelerator—multiplier effects, 13, 74, 96, 160
actively growing FUCs, 113, 120
actively growing SMSAs, 106, 109, 110
activity nodes, 24—5, 28—9, 35
administrative process, 70, 72—4, 78—80
age
  composition (population), 254—5, 256
  school-leaving, 219, 221, 234
  -specific migration, 6, 248
ageing population, 13, 21, 32—3, 254—5
agglomerations, 74, 76, 80
  core-ring, 60—63, 85—8, 98
  decentralisation, 5, 6, 8
  development model, 13, 84—91, 97
  functional bonds, 4—5, 160
  future trends, 15, 91—6, 98
agglomerations (Netherlands)
  development (1950—74), 129—32
  development since 1970, 132—42, 145
  future, 17, 142—4

integrative approach, 19, 158—74
agriculture, 5, 20, 180, 198—204
Alden, J., 124
Allen, P.M., 54, 58
Alonso, W., 24, 26
amplitude (regional cycles), 19, 196—200, 201—5 *passim*, 207
Andersson, A., 48
Arminger, G., 52
assets (subsystem), 13, 69, 71—3, 75, 80
automation, 6, 31

Baerwald, T.J., 25, 28
Batten, D.F., 58
Beale, C., 124, 254
Beaumont, J.R., 59
Berg, van den, L., 60, 84, 127
  on development stages, 168, 254, 257
  urban change, 24, 25, 34, 124, 129
Berry, B.J.L., 25, 28, 32, 124
Biehl, D., 48
Birch, D.L., 27
Birmingham, 45, 53, 218, 220—24, 226—32, 236—42, 244—5

birth rate, 13, 233, 234, 248
Blommestein, H.J., 46
Blum, U.C.H., 69, 71, 72
Blumenfeld, H., 34
Boeckhout, S., 97, 127
bottlenecks, 12, 13, 47, 54—5
Bourne, L.S., 24, 25, 26
Bradbury, K.L., 28
breeding place principle, 53—4
Bretzfelder, R.B., 206 *bis*
Brinkman, G.L., 25, 27
Brown, P.W., 26
building technology, 31—2
Burns, L.S., 25, 256, 264
business cycles, 18, 180, 181, 184, 206

capital, 4, 48—9
  agenda, urban, 22, 263—4
  assets, 13, 69, 71—3, 75, 80
  budgeting, 21—2, 260, 263
  investment projects, 22, 259, 260—63
  see also investment
Cappellin, R., 201
car ownership, 10, 24, 68, 128
catchment area (school), 235, 247
categorisation matrix, 105—6, 108
causality, 46, 50, 52, 53, 72
CBD growth, 28, 257
Cebula, R.J., 256
centralisation, 10, 11, 25, 32, 88
centrifugal trends, 10, 18, 24, 25, 28, 35
centripetal trends, 10, 24, 25, 28, 35
challenge and response principle, 13, 54—6, 60
change (and non-change), 9—11
  episodes/events as, 12, 43—4
  urban structure, 23—37
'change generators', 46
Cheshire, P., 91
Chow, G.C., 201
Church of England schools, 249—50
Cigno, A., 58
cities, 1—2, 7—8, 10, 55
  Randstad (big), 146—7, 149—50, 152—3, 155—7

Randstad (remaining), *see* towns
  urban structure, 23—30, 34—7
cities (central), 18, 27—30, 68, 253, 256—7
  Japan, 112, 114—20
  Netherlands, 127—9, 133, 135, 137—8, 143
  USA, 15, 101—6, 110—11, 124—5
city decline (fiscal costs), 20—21, 209—11
  assessment (1950—80), 223—33
  future decline, 233—49
  nature of, 212—15
  objectives/methodology, 215—18
  scenarios, 218—23
  see also individual UK cities
Clark, W.A.V., 49
Clay, P.L., 25, 29
cluster model (education), 246, 251
Cobb-Douglas production function, 74
Coleman, J.S., 44, 50
commodity flows, 73
communications, 48—9, 204
  technology, 30, 31, 36, 209—10, 263
  see also telecommunications
commuting, 6, 72, 73, 74, 77—8, 86—7, 128, 255
'compact city', 143
competition, 53, 56—7, 62—3
comprehensive education, 251
computers, 6, 7, 31, 257
concentration
  instability and, 198—205 *passim*
  spatial (urban system), 159—62, 166
Congressional Quarterly, 206
constancy, urban, 33—4, 35
  see also stability
constraints (urban events), 47
consumer demand, 18, 74—5, 201
containment policies, 18
contextual issues, 30—33
cooperative model (education), 247, 250
coordination, policy (lack), 55—6
core-periphery, 13, 62—3, 255

core-ring, 60–63, 85–8, 93–4, 98, 255
  Netherlands, 133–7, 144, 162–4, 166–71
cost reduction ratios, 244–6
counterurbanisation, 2
crime, 128
cross-cultural studies, 24
cultural process (subsystem), 70, 72–4, 77–8, 80
CURB Project, 84–91, 94, 98
cycle components, 194–7, 202–5
cycle hypothesis, 1–3
  income development, see regional economic development
  income growth, 184–94
  regional cycles, 19, 151–3
  spatial cycles, 87, 100–124
  staged development, 18–19, 148–51, 153–4, 166–7, 181
  urban–rural dichotomy, 4–8
  urban development, 13, 75, 78–9, 81
cyclical patterns, see regional development (USA)

Dahmann, D.C., 25
Dantzig, G.B., 25
Davies, S., 47
Davis, K., 253
Day, R., 58
decentralisation, 5–7, 10, 18, 24–5, 88, 161, 162, 210
decline, see city decline (fiscal costs); urban decline
degenerating FUCs, 113, 120
degenerating SMSAs, 106, 109, 111
deLeon, P., 30
demand elasticities, 201
demographic shifts, 6, 9–10, 21, 26, 132–5, 145, 254–6
Dendrinos, D.S., 58
denominational schools, 235–6, 249–50
densification, 143
depression, 19, 153, 166–71, 181–4
  see also recession
DES, 236

development
  areas, 19, 148–51, 166–7
  areas (potential), 18, 148–51, 153–4, 166–7
  stages, 19, 153, 166–71, 181–4
discrete choice models, 55
discrete spatial models, 49
disinvestment, 29, 30
disurbanisation, 8, 86–8, 100
  Europe, 14, 16, 84, 89–91, 94, 96
  Japan, 15, 16, 101, 112–24, 125
  Netherlands, 17, 97, 127–30, 132, 140–42, 144, 166, 168–9, 172
  UK (fiscal costs), 20–21, 209–10
  USA, 15–16, 101–11, 124–5
diversification, 20, 200, 203–4, 206
'domino effect', 10
Dortmund region, 45
Downs, A., 28
Drewe, P., 256
Drewett, R., 127, 129
Dreze, J.H., 207
'driving to maturity', 54–5
Duerksen, C.J., 262
Dunphy, R.T., 25
dynamic structure (analysis), 46

economic
  decline, see city decline (fiscal costs)
  development, 15, 16, 37, 100–101
  development (spatial), 19, 159–62
  growth, instability and, 20, 197–205
  obsolescence, 258
  process (subsystems), 70, 72–6, 80
  trends, 7–8, 9–10, 67, 68
economies of scale, 24, 27
Edelstein, R.G., 32
education (case study), 248–52
  costing future decline, 233–46
  fiscal costs (decline), 20, 218–19, 223, 226–33

education (cont.)
   future costs, 246–7
   scenarios, 218–25
   see also pupil(s); school; school
      buildings; teacher(s)
EEC, 91, 201
Elster, S., 28, 32
emanation areas, 19, 87, 130, 139,
      142, 146–7, 148–53, 155–7
   incomes by, 162, 164, 166, 167–
      73
'emergent realities', 24
employment, 127–8, 143, 209, 255,
      264
   concentration, 159–62, 198–
      202, 203
   footloose, 5, 6, 11, 15, 91–4, 96,
      204
   home-based, 11, 31, 257
   location, 18, 27–8
   regional, 146, 150–54, 157
   structure, instability and, 198–
      203
   technology and, 21, 30–31, 257
   see also labour; unemployment
energy industry, 12, 128, 143, 176
Enns, J., 30
environmental protection, 22, 262–3
episodes (in urban history), 12–13,
      17
   industrial, 45, 48–9, 53–8
   infrastructural, 53–8
   interaction, 53–8
   simple model, 58–62
   space–time, core–periphery
      model, 62–3
   in statistical analysis, 50–52
   in urban dynamics, 43–5
Europe, Eastern, 14, 16, 84, 85, 91
Europe, Western
   agglomerations (future trends),
      84–98
   disurbanisation, 14, 16, 84, 89–
      91, 94, 96
   EEC, 91, 201
   urbanisation, 14, 84, 89–91, 94
Evans, A., 28
event histories, urban, 12, 17

spatial analysis, 53–8
statistical analysis of, 49–53
in urban dynamics, 43–5
urban dynamics as, 45–9
Eversley, D., 28, 259
evolution, urban, 43–9
exclusion, competitive, 53, 56–7
expansionist policies, 233, 251–2
expectations, investment and, 10–
      11, 29–30
expulsion areas/process, 5
'exurbs', 27, 29

family, 21, 26, 255, 256, 258
fertility rates, 26, 233, 255, 256
fiscal costs, *see* city decline (fiscal
      costs)
fiscal squeeze, 20–21, 212–13, 259
Foley, D.L., 24
Folmer, H., 53
'friction of distance', 10
Friedenberg, H., 206
Friedmann, J., 255
frostbelt (USA), 26, 28
Funck, R., 69, 71
functional obsolescence, 258
functional structure, 46
Functional Urban Cores (Japan), 15,
      16, 101, 105, 112–23, 125
functional urban regions, 5, 160

Garreau, J., 206
Gastarbeiter, 4, 13
Germany, West, 13, 67–8, 79
Gerson, K., 255
Gertler, L.O., 25
Glasgow, 218–24, 227–32, 236–42,
      245, 248–9
Godwin, S., 261
Goetze, R., 29
Goldberg, M.A., 29, 30, 34, 36
Gordon, P., 124, 254
Gothenburg region, 45
government
   investment, 29–30, 78–9, 260–
      63
   policies, *see* policy
   rate support grants, 210–11,

213–14, 216, 218–19, 231–2, 249

see also local authorities

Grant Related Expenditures, 246, 247

graph-theoretic approach, 46

Graves, P.E., 256

Grebler, L., 264

greenfield sites, 262

Griffith, D.A., 44

growth, 37, 97
  economic, 20, 197–205
  poles, 4, 5, 96, 98, 132, 159–60
  rates, regional, 148–51

Guttenberg, A.E., 24

Haag, G., 46

Haddon, J., 255

Hägerstrand, T., 49

Haining, R., 46

Hall, P.A., 25, 34, 124, 254

Halvorson, H.W., 201

Hannan, M.T., 50, 51, 53

Hansen, N.M., 25

Harberger, A.C., 201

Harkness, R.C., 31

Hay, D., 25, 34, 91, 124, 254

Hayden, D., 256

hazard function, 51

Hee, B. van der, 46

Hirschman, A.O., 47, 48, 207

historical monuments, 22, 261–2

Hoch, I., 24

home working, 11, 31, 257

Hooper, D., 25

Hoover, E., 27, 259

household (formation), 21, 26, 255–6

housing, 11–12, 18, 68, 128, 256, 258

Howell, J.M., 259

Hoyt, H., 24, 253

Hughes, J.W., 25, 28

Hulten, C.R., 260

income
  development, 168, 169
  growth rate, instability and, 197–

202, 204–5, 207

growth rate (USA), 177–84, 196–7

growth ratio, 194–5, 206

integrative approach, 19, 158–74

per capita personal, 177–80, 206

per capita regional, 184–94

regional, 146–9, 152–4, 156, 172–3

urban, *see* urban income

incubator hypothesis, 27

industrial
  dynamics (event history), 47–8
  episodes, 45, 48–9, 53–8
  growth poles, 4, 5, 96, 98, 132, 159–60
  location, 18, 27–8
  technology, 30–32

information
  quarternary sector, 5, 6, 7, 11, 91
  technology, 30, 69

infrastructure, 13
  industrial episodes and, 48–9, 53–8
  investment, 22, 68–9, 259, 260–61

innovations, 45, 53, 54

input potentials, 73, 74

instability (determinants), 19, 197–205 *passim*, 207
  see also amplitude; volatility

integration approach (urban/regional income), 19, 158–74

inter-metropolitan
  contraction, 159–60, 161–2
  deconcentration, 94
  dispersal, 161

interest rate (public debt), 78, 79

intra-metropolitan dispersal, 160–61

investment, 10–11, 54, 201
  behaviour, 29–30, 36
  capital projects, 22, 259, 260–63
  government, 29–30, 78–9, 260–63
  urban development model, 74–5, 78–9
  urban episode models, 58–9, 60, 63

Jackson, G., 206
Jacobs, J., 25, 45
James, F.L., 27
Japan, 15, 16, 101, 112–24, 125
Johansson, B., 43, 48
Johnson, H.G., 204

Kawashima, T., 101, 124, 125
Kellas, H., 28
Kendig, H., 34
key factors (urban dynamics), 46
Klaassen, L.H., 124, 127, 129, 173, 256
Kontuly, T., 254
Korcelli, P., 24, 25, 124
Kowalski, J.S., 69

labour
   imported, 4, 5, 13, 67–8, 255, 256
   migrant, 14–15, 21, 158, 160, 255–6
   reserve, regional, 150–51, 152, 157
   urban development model, 74, 75, 77–8, 80
   urban episode model, 59, 60, 61
land use, 10–11, 26–33, 36–7, 257
Laska, S.B., 25
Lea, A.C., 44
Leeds, 218, 220–22, 224, 226–32, 236–42, 244–5, 248–9
Leicester, 218, 220–24, 226–32, 236–42, 244–5
Leonardi, G., 49
Leven, C.L., 25, 124, 254
Li, T., 59
Lierop, W.F.J. van, 49
life cycle analogy, 2
Lisrel V models, 53
Liu, B.-C., 256
Liverpool, 218–24, 226–32, 236–41, 243, 245, 248–9
loans (urban budget), 78
local authorities
   capital investment projects, 22, 259, 260–63

client mix, 216, 218
education services, see education
expenditure, 213–15, 218
policies, 209–11, 213–14
rates, 213, 215
revenue, 210–16 passim, 218
services, 212–16, 259
see also rate support grant
location behaviour, 28–9, 36, 49
   residential, 26–7, 32–3, 86–7, 91–4, 127–9, 143, 255–6
logistic growth process, 58–60
longitudinal analysis, 44, 49–50, 53
Lowry, I.S., 256

McKeever, J.R., 28
Maisel, S.J., 264
Manchester, 45, 218–22, 225–32, 236–41, 243, 245–8, 249–50
manufacturing activity, instability and, 197–202, 203, 204, 207
Mark, J.H., 29, 30, 34
Markov models, 50
mathematical analysis, 46
May, R.M., 59
Meadows, P., 24
Meer, J. van der, 97, 127, 168
Meier, R.L., 31
Mercer, J., 34
metasystem, 13, 69–74, 76, 80
metropolitan areas, 8, 14, 94, 264
   development phases, 17–18
   FUCs, 15, 16, 101, 105, 112–23, 125
   internationalisation of, 21, 255–6
   population, 18, 100–101, 124, 253–4
   SMSAs, 15–16, 101–11, 122–5
migration, 4–6, 26–7, 67–8, 73, 77–8, 87, 93–4
   labour, 14–15, 21, 158, 160, 255, 256
   Netherlands, 135–8, 142, 143
Miller, M.J., 261
Mills, D.E., 207
Mixed Use Developments, 28
mixed use zoning, 11, 33

Miyao, T., 55
mobility, 24–5, 27–8, 36, 67
Molle, W.T.M., 173
Moomaw, R., 27
Morrill, R.L., 24
Morris, R.S., 25
mortality rates, 6, 248, 255
Muller, T., 259
multi-episodes, 58–60
multiplier–accelerator effect, 13, 74, 96, 160
Mumford, L., 25

National Bureau of Economic Research, 206
natural resources, 13, 71, 72, 73
Nelson, H.J., 24
neo-classical models, 21, 256
Netherlands
    disurbanisation, 17, 127–30, 132, 140–42, 144, 166, 168–9, 172
    income development, 19, 158–74
    regional development, 18–19, 146–57, 181, 182
    reurbanisation, 17–18, 127–9, 142–4
    urbanisation, 17, 129–30, 140–42, 144, 169, 172
    see also agglomerations (Netherlands)
new towns, 258–9
Newcastle, 218–23, 225–33, 236–41, 243–7, 250–51
Nijkamp, P., 44, 46, 47, 49, 54, 58, 59
nodes of activity, 24–5, 28–9, 35
Noguchi, T., 25, 28
Noord-Holland, 97
Norton, R.D., 25

office sector, 21, 31, 257
oil industry, 18, 128, 176
old people, 6, 26
    see also ageing population
optimal control theory, 49

Paelinck, J.H.P., 124

panel studies, 44, 49–50, 53
Passoneau, J.R., 24
peripheral areas, 19, 130, 139, 142, 146–7, 148–53, 155–7
    incomes by, 162, 164, 166, 167–73
Peterson, G.E., 260, 261
policy
    coordination (lack), 55–6
    local, 209–11, 213–14
    regional, 153–4, 205
    urban structure, 23, 32–3, 36–7
political process, 70, 72–4, 78–80
politics (of local government), 214–15
population
    age composition, 254–5, 256
    ageing, 13, 21, 32–3, 254–5
    centralisation, 10, 11, 25, 32, 88
    decentralisation, 5–7, 10, 18, 24–5, 88, 161–2, 210
    decline, see city decline (fiscal costs)
    migrant, see migration
    natural increase, 135–7
    regional, 155–7
    stages, see disurbanisation; reurbanisation; suburbanisation; urbanisation
    structural change, 67–8
    as subsystem, 13, 71–3, 77, 80, 81
    urban development theory, 85–91
population growth rate
    Japan, 112, 113, 118–21, 123
    USA, 102–3, 105–6, 109–11
Porell, F.W., 25
Portes, A., 255
pre-disurbanisation SMSAs, 109, 125
primary education, 20, 218, 223–33, 236–45, 248–51
'prisoner's dilemma', 29
probabilities (of events), 51–2
production
    capacities, 58–60, 63
    factors, 70, 71, 72–3, 74, 75
    infrastructure and, 48–9, 54–8

productivity, 12, 45, 47—8
profit maximisation, 74
prosperity, 19, 153, 166—71, 181—4
prosperous area, 18, 19, 148—51, 166—7
prosperous area (potentially), 19, 148—51, 153, 166—7
public expenditure, 213—15, 218, 259
   see also education (case study)
pupil(s)
   numbers, 20, 218—23, 226—7, 229—31, 233—4, 248
   numbers (forecast), 236—7, 239—41, 244—6, 249, 252
   school-leaving age, 219, 221, 234
   -teacher ratios, 20, 229—31, 233, 239, 241, 244—8, 252
   unit costs, 20, 219, 221—3, 226—7, 229, 231—2, 235—6, 242—9
push factors, 18, 128

quality factors, 70, 71—2, 73, 77
quality of life, 14, 18, 96—7, 180
quarternary industries, 5, 6, 7, 11, 91
quasi-growing FUCs, 113, 120
quasi-growing SMSAs, 106, 110—11

Randstad, 19, 130, 139, 142
   big cities, 146—50, 152—3, 155—7
   incomes by, 162, 164, 166, 167—73
   remaining towns, 146—50, 152—3, 155—7
Ratcliff, R.U., 31
rate support grant, 210—11, 213—14, 216, 218—19, 231—2, 249
rates, 213, 215
rationalisation policies, 246—7
recentralisation, 25
recession, 18, 153, 166—71, 181—4
   see also depression
recovery, 19, 153, 166—71, 181—4
redundancies, teacher, 235, 239, 249
refugees (in West Germany), 67

regional
   cycles, 19, 151—3
   divisions (Netherlands), 129, 131, 138—42
   income dynamics, 172—3
   level spatial dynamics, 18—22
   policy, 153—4, 205
   'town centres', 28
regional development, 1—6, 68
   cyclical nature, 19, 151—3
   policy issues, 153—4
   problem issues, 21—2, 253—63
   research agenda, 21—2, 263—4
   stages, 18—19, 148—51, 153—4, 166—7, 181
   types, 18—19, 146—51
regional development (USA)
   analytical framework, 181—4
   cycle components, 194—7, 202—5
   data and regions, 177—81
   empirical testing, 184—94
   instability (determinants), 197—205
regional dynamics, 18—19, 155—7
   quadripartition of regions, 146—51
   regional cycles, 19, 151—3
regional economic development
   cyclical patterns (USA), 19—20, 175—205
   spatial, 19, 158, 159—62
   urban income and, 162—73
regressions (amplitude/volatility), 201
regulation, governmental, 32—3, 37, 262
'relative income', 180
research agenda, 23, 34—6, 263—4
research and development, 13, 54—5
residential location, 26—7, 32—3, 86—7, 91—4, 127—9, 143, 255—6
   see also housing
resources
   financial, *see* capital
   human, *see* labour
   natural, 13, 71, 72, 73

retail commercial location, 28–9
retirement, 6
    teacher (early), 235, 239, 249
reurbanisation, 7, 14, 25, 86, 87–8, 89–91, 98, 100–101, 107, 161–2
    development and, 129–42
    Netherlands, 17–18, 127–9, 142–4
Rimcity, 149–50, 155–7
ring
    municipalities, 135, 137, 144, 145
    see also core-ring
Robins, P., 50
robotics, 6, 7, 30
Roman Catholic schools, 250
Rosen, K.T., 256
Rossi, A., 127, 129
ROXY index, 101, 121–4, 125
rural development, 4–8
rural emanation area, 146–50, 152–3, 155–7
rural income, 166–8
rural periphery, 146–50, 152, 155–7
rural Randstad, 146–50, 152–3, 155–7

Saaty, T.L., 25
Sandefur, G.D., 50
Sanglier, M., 54, 58
savings, 74, 75
Schnore, L.F., 24
school
    leaving age (ROSLA), 219, 221, 234
    rolls, *see* pupil(s)
school buildings, 219
    accommodation costs, 221–3, 230, 239, 242–4
    age and type, 235–6, 248
    surplus, 234, 236, 238–43, 245–7, 249, 260
Schubert, U., 58, 59
Schumann, L., 207
Scott, W.J., 50
Scottish Education Department, 252

secondary education, 20, 218, 228–34, 236–45, 247, 248–51
services, 212–13, 214, 215, 259
    client mix, 216, 218
    see also education (case study)
settlement systems, 7–8, 10, 263, 264
    incomes and, 158, 159
    national, 25, 254
Shapiro, C., 261
Shapiro, P., 55
Shaw, R.P., 256
Sheshinski, E., 207
Silicon Valley, 45, 53, 201
Simmons, J.W., 25
sixth form education, 246–7, 249–51
size class, 129–30, 133–5, 139–42, 145
    agglomerations by, 17, 162, 164–6
Small, K.A., 28
social benefits, 159, 160, 174, 206, 211
social process (subsystem), 70, 72–4, 77–8, 80
Solomon, A.P., 25
Sonis, M., 53
space–time relationship, 2–3, 21, 45–6, 49, 62–3, 261–3
Spain, D., 25
spatial
    allocation effects, 80
    concentration, 159–62, 166
    cycles, 87, 100–124
    dynamics (regional level), 18–22
    dynamics (urban level), 9–18, 96–7
    economic development, 19, 158, 159–62
    structuring, 13, 60–63, 85–6
spatiotemporal data, 50, 53
specialisation, 48, 53–4, 56
    instability and, 197, 200–202
Spreiregen, P.D., 34
stability, regional, 185, 206
    see also constancy; instability

Stamm, C.F., 259
Standard Metropolitan Statistical Areas (USA), 15—16, 101—11, 122—5
statistical analysis
  event histories, 49—53
  urban decline (Europe), 89—91
Sternlieb, G., 25, 28
Strauss, A., 254
structures, see historical monuments; housing; infrastructure; school buildings
Struyk, R., 27
subnational economies, 2—3, 7
subsidies, 30, 201, 205
subsystems
  dynamic model, 72—80
  indicators, 13, 69—72
  interactions, 13, 56—8
suburbanisation, 8, 15, 86—8, 97, 100—101, 254
  Europe, Western, 14, 84, 89—90, 93—4
  Netherlands, 17, 128—30, 132—4, 137, 140—42, 144, 166, 168—9, 172
suburbs, 5, 28, 29
  decline, 21, 258—9
sunbelt (USA), 26, 27
survivor function (events), 51
synergistic phenomenon, 13, 47, 57—8

taxation, 29—30, 72, 74, 78, 79, 174, 213
teacher(s)
  costs, 219, 221, 234—5, 239, 242—5
  —pupil ratios, 20, 229—31, 233, 239, 241, 244—8, 252
  salaries, 224—5, 229, 234, 249
  wastage, 235, 239, 241, 245, 249
technology, 8, 28, 69, 201
  communications, 30, 31, 36, 209—10, 263
  computer, 6, 7, 31, 257
  core-ring configuration, 60—63

employment and, 21, 30—31, 257
information, 30, 69
quarternary industries, 5, 6, 7, 11, 91
urban structure and, 30—32
telecommunications, 31, 36, 257
tertiary education, 250, 251
tertiary sector, 91, 92
Third World, 5, 8, 23, 257, 262
Thomas, B., 54
Thomlinson, R., 24
threshold phenomenon, 47, 54
time
  hierarchical relation, 52, 53
  lags, 7, 8, 48—9, 73—4
  preference disjunction, 261—2
  series approach, 19, 181, 184, 202—3, 215
  —space relationship, 2—3, 21, 45—6, 49, 62—3, 261—3
towns
  new, 258—9
  Randstad (remaining), 146—50, 152—3, 155—7
Toynbee, A., 54
traffic capacity, 7, 86—7, 129
  see also car ownership; transportation
transfer payments, 159, 160, 174, 206, 211
transition process, 50, 52—3, 54
transportation, 31, 33, 86—7
  commuter, see commuting
  costs, 18, 74, 76, 204, 263
  infrastructure system, 48—9
  land use and, 36, 37
  Netherlands, 127, 128, 142—3
  see also car ownership; traffic
Tuma, N.B., 50, 51, 53
Turner, J., 46
Tweeten, L., 25, 27

UK (city decline), 20—21, 209—52
  see also individual cities
unemployment, 67, 68, 175—6, 264
  benefit, 159, 160
unit costs (per pupil), 20, 219, 221—2, 223, 226—7, 229,

231—2, 235—6, 242—9
urban
  budget, 72, 78, 80—81, 83
  capital agenda, 22, 263—4
  change, 67—83
  concentration, 100, 121, 123, 129, 140—43
  deconcentration, 121, 127, 129, 140—43
  dispersal, 160—61
  dynamics, 9—18, 43—9, 96—8
  emanation areas, 146—8, 150—53, 155—7, 164—8
  episodes, 12—13, 43—5, 53—63
  growth/decline (regional), 253—64
  periphery, 146—52, 155—7, 167—8
  product, 73, 76
  quality factors, 70, 71—2, 73
  —rural dichotomy, 4—8
  space, 72, 73, 80
  structure, 13, 23—37
  system, 69—70, 96—7, 159—62
  see also event histories, urban
urban decline, 84
  costs, see city decline (fiscal costs)
  development theory, 85—8
  future, 14—15, 96—7, 98
  problem issues, 253—63
  research agenda, 263—4
  statistics (Europe), 89—91, 98
urban development, 32—3, 70—71, 168—9
  dynamic model, 13, 72—80
  future, 91—5, 142—4
  Netherlands, 127—42
  staged, 14—15, 85—91, 100—101, 257
urban income
  changes (1950—78), 162—6
  development model, 74—5, 79, 80, 82
  regional economic development and, 166—73
  spatial economic development and, 159—62

Urban Land Institute, 32
urbanisation, 86—8, 97
  Europe, Western, 14, 84, 89—91, 94
  Netherlands, 17, 129—30, 140—42, 144, 169, 172
  stages, see disurbanisation; re-urbanisation; suburbanisation
  trends, 1—4, 253
  USA, 15—16, 101
USA, 85, 260
  disurbanisation, 15—16, 101—11, 122—5
  urban structure, 33—4
  see also regional development (USA)

Van Ness, K., 256
Vancouver Economic Advisory Commission, 37
Vancouver Planning Commission, 37
Vedder, R.K., 256
Vernon, R., 259
Vijverberg, C.H.T., 127, 129
Vining, D.R., 254
volatility (regional cycles), 19, 194—5, 197—205 passim, 207
votes and voters, 72, 78, 79

wages, 6, 74, 75, 159, 160—62, 206
  education, 224—5, 229, 234, 249
waiting-time distribution function, 51
Walton, J., 255
Webber, M.M., 24, 25
Weidlich, W., 46
Weller, R.H., 24
Wibe, S., 48
Williamson, J.G., 207
Wilson, A.G., 59
Witherspoon, R.E., 28
Wolff, G., 255
women (role), 21, 255, 256
work, see employment; labour
Wurster, C.B., 24

Yorke, J.A., 59

Zuid-Holland, 97